URUGUAY
the politics of failure

Martin Weinstein

URUGUAY
the politics of failure

GREENWOOD PRESS

Westport, Connecticut   London, England

Library of Congress Cataloging in Publication Data

Weinstein, Martin.
    Uruguay: the politics of failure.

    Bibliography: p.
    Includes index.
    1. Uruguay—Politics and government—1904-
2. Uruguay—Social conditions. 3. Uruguay—
Economic conditions—1918-
F2728.W44   309.1'895'06   74-19809
ISBN 0-8371-7845-2

Library of Congress Catalog Card Number: 74-19809
ISBN: 0-8371-7845-2

First published in 1975

Greenwood Press, a division of Williamhouse-Regency Inc.
51 Riverside Avenue, Westport, Connecticut 06880

Manufactured in the United States of America

To Ruth

and the *Tupamaros*

. . . Two Forms of Love

CONTENTS

TABLES

ACKNOWLEDGMENTS

This study bears my name, but it was fortunately undertaken in an intellectual climate that made it a social endeavor. I had the support and encouragement of many friends and associates. Two in particular deserve special mention: Kalman Silvert, who combines the all too rare talents of friend, colleague, and mentor, and Morris Blachman, who proves that Kal's gift is not limited to a single generation.

In addition, I should like to thank the Center for International Studies at New York University for support during my graduate work and the Fulbright Commission for a grant which enabled me to conduct field research in Uruguay during 1969 and 1970.

INTRODUCTION

The "Switzerland of South America" was the title Uruguay enjoyed for much of this century. The reference was not topographical; rather it was meant to describe a small nation-state (almost a city-state) whose citizens enjoyed a standard of living, levels of literacy and health care, and, most importantly, a degree of political democracy and public decency which set the country apart from its sister South American republics. Uruguay was considered an idyllic pastoral land with two traditional and highly competitive political parties, a flourishing academic and cultural life, and two and one-half million people, almost half of whom lived in the sophisticated urban sprawl of the capital city of Montevideo. As the Uruguayans themselves put it, "Como el Uruguay no hay," "There is no place like Uruguay."

The image, like all stereotypes, was exaggerated, but it did reflect reality, at least until recent years. Today, Uruguay is a de facto military dictatorship. The country is economically and politically bankrupt. Congress is closed, unions and most political parties are outlawed, press censorship is strictly enforced, an externally controlled university barely functions, and thousands of political prisoners languish in cells while tens of thousands of their fellow countrymen emigrate.

The question that begs for the social scientist's attention is obvious: How and why did a nation that was regarded as so different from and superior to its neighbors so quickly "fall" and come to resemble them? To answer the question, this work focuses on the relationship between nationalism and development. Specifically, a theoretical framework is introduced in Chapter 1 which combines the concepts of ideology as symbol-system, nationalism as a social value, and corporatism as a model of political life in a multidimensional construct to be employed in the analysis of political development in Uruguay.

The literature on political development has, in recent years, paid

xiii

particular attention to the performance of systems. This performance has most often been measured in terms of the overcoming of crises of development, the performance of the functional requisites of government, or the striking of a balance between institutionalization and social mobilization. While these approaches have their uses and have made a contribution to the study of developing areas, they have neglected the individual as a component in the process of political development.

I conceive of political development as human development, and agree, as many have argued, that man is a self-actualizing animal. Thus, for me the values, symbol systems, and institutions which promote the most open and liberating process of human interaction, permit the development of potential abilities, and increase the range of human choice may consequently be seen as the most conducive to development. Thus, ideology becomes the symbol system through which men comprehend their world. Nationalism becomes a social value which nurtures community by establishing a reciprocal relationship between the state and its citizens and among fellow citizens. Corporatist politics is seen as a particular way of structuring society with inimical results for many individuals and, eventually, for society as a whole.

Essentially, then, the symbols available in a social system define the parameters in which (at least until such time as new symbols emerge or old ones are transformed), the nation will be explicitly conceived (ideology) and implicitly held (values). In turn, the dominant symbols with which the nation is so conceived will be reflected in its structural and institutional development. The structures and institutions found in corporatist political systems, reflecting a basic judgment about human nature and human inequality, are essentially class-bound and seek to freeze existing class and social relationships—the existing distribution of power. Such a system cannot conceive of and therefore cannot implement a politics of political development which is a politics of human development.

One further consideration: this work frequently refers to Uruguay as a city-state or a city-nation-state. The denomination of Uruguay as a city-state is not uncommon in the literature and has considerable merit. Demographically and institutionally, Montevideo is the heart of Uruguay. The capital contains almost one-half of the population of the country, all of the principal television and radio stations, all of the major printed media, and is the site of the only university. It is the political capital of a highly centralized national government. But, perhaps more importantly, the overconcentration of resources and population in one city is an important clue to the nature of power and social relationships. Political style, as might be expected, is intensely personalistic. Individuals are in contact with each other in a manner which, while it is conducive to a kind of familiarity and civility, also impedes the growth of impersonal loyalties and relationships. The effect of this personalism and subsequent clientelistic politics is crucial to the understanding of politics in Uruguay.

In this work I will argue that the symbol system (ideology) predominantly employed in Uruguayan society, while paying obeisance to the program and style of José Batlle y Ordóñez (the political doctrine known as *Batllismo*), has lacked the ability and reflects the inability to create the values, political language, and political institutions conducive to nationalism as defined here. The result is the creation and maintenance of a corporate political structure which both nurtures and is sustained by a strong personalistic politics.

Thus, despite the record of the five decades of this century that could justify the description of Uruguay as a "welfare state," "utopia," or the "Switzerland of South America," the system and the values underlying it have remained subnational. The fruits of this situation are the economic decline, urban guerrilla struggle, and destruction of civil liberties, which are the facts of the 1960s and 1970s.

After the theoretical framework has been presented, Chapter 2 deals with ideology in twentieth century Uruguay and posits the existence of a clash between two essentially antithetical belief systems. *Batllismo*, rooted in the politics and promise of the city, is seen as an integrating, nationalist ideology promoting the concepts of development, citizenship, and social change. However, it was confronted from the very beginning by a powerful counter-ideology, espoused by rural interests and promoting the values of tradition, hierarchy, and order. The *Batllista* vision dominated Uruguayan politics in the first three decades of this century and built the institutions and structures which would ostensibly color the society for decades thereafter. But the counter-ideology slowly became dominant and ultimately circumvented the very institutions created by its ideological rival.

Chapter 3 is concerned with the dynamics of institutional development. It is argued that Uruguay developed a mechanism for containing conflict that was more successful and, at least on the surface, more open, plural, and democratic than the mechanisms employed by most other Latin American political systems. The mechanism was coparticipation, whose meaning extended beyond the formal connotations of a sharing of positions in government and state-run enterprises between the principal political factions. Rather, it was reflective of a profound underlying vision of politics as a zero-sum game. Thus, a coparticipation which served well the turn-of-the-century need for a stable civil politics became a particularistic mechanism supportive of a powerful clientelist politics and incapable of a valid response to the need for change and reform. Since the national enterprise was not seen as a common endeavor, and government was seen as responsive only to those who held power, the institutions which helped give Uruguay its reputation as a modern and integrated society were not really fulfilling the functions attributed to them.

Chapter 4 relates the discussions of ideology and institutions to the power relationships and class structure of Uruguayan society. An examination of urban-rural differences, the performance of educational structures, and social mobility patterns points up the increasing failure to promote or sustain an integrated society in which citizenship is concomitant with reasonably equal life chances, and accidents of geography and birth do not preclude participation in and benefit from the national enterprise. As the contradictions grew, choices became more obvious, if not more ominous.

In the final chapter, events in the 1960s and 1970s are analyzed with a view toward demonstrating the explanatory and predictive value of the theoretical framework. Uruguay's economic decline, the growth of an urban guerrilla movement (the *Tupamaros*), and the destruction of constitutional government are discussed in terms of the relationship between nationalism, capitalism, and corporatist politics. The emergence of a corporatist authoritarian regime under military tutelage—the opting for dictatorship over democracy—is seen not merely as an isolated phenomenon, peculiar to that country. Rather, it is argued that the events of recent years make it painfully obvious that the choice confronted by Uruguay is faced equally by the modern and developing nations of this world.

Restating briefly, I suggest that in Uruguay there exists a system with a high order of institutionalization but a low order of synthesis of institutions, a situation which results in a secular polity which is not national, a polity which lacks any real center of power. Subnational values and institutional structures give us a particular kind of political man and a particular kind of polity: a free man who does not partake of full citizenship and a sovereign nation without the power to guide its own destiny.

ABOUT THE AUTHOR

Martin Weinstein is an instructor in political science at the William Paterson College of New Jersey. He received his B.A. at Columbia College and his M.A. and Ph.D. at New York University. His special interests are Latin American politics, comparative politics, comparative theory on development and modernization, and the role of ideology in shaping political systems. He has written numerous articles for scholarly journals here and in Uruguay.

URUGUAY
the politics of failure

1
THE THEORETICAL FRAMEWORK

The theoretical framework employed in this study encompasses the concepts of ideology, nationalism, and corporatism. Although the heart of the framework lies in the concept of nationalism, discussion begins with the question of ideology as symbol system, for the development of a nation requires a particular set of values which can be sustained only within particular kinds of ideological matrices. In addition, the most exciting and useful interpretations of nationalism come out of a framework which accepts a symbol-creating foundation of human activity and a "shared conceptual perception" bias toward the concept of nationalism.

Since Marx, the concept of ideology has more and more taken on a pejorative coloration, most often associated with the term "false consciousness," implying either the special pleading of a group to maintain itself in power, or the needed construction of a society to live with the tension inherent in the chasm separating the ideal from the real.[1] In *Ideology and Utopia,* Mannheim argued the ideological basis of all thought, even asserting the ideological basis of scientific evaluation of thought (the so-called Mannheim Paradox), thus raising epistemological difficulties. More recently, the debate in the literature has concerned the "end of ideology" and has progressed to an "end to the end of ideology" series of articles.[2]

Clifford Geertz, in his essay entitled "Ideology as a Cultural System," attempts to clarify the confused situation.[3] Taking his cue from the philosophy of symbols and symbolic form, which finds its most powerful modern expression in the work of Ernst Cassirer and Suzanne Langer,[4] Geertz calls for a nonevaluative conception of ideology. Briefly, Cassirer espouses a conception of man based on symbolic formulation. The social life of man has meaning because of man's ability to create the symbols which convey meaning. Indeed, for these authors, the essence of being

3

human is the impulse and ability and even need of man to create, transform, and transmit symbols. Man is the *animal symbolicum.*[5] Picking up on this theme, Geertz argues the importance of the philosophy of symbolic form for an understanding of the concept of ideology.

The reason for this weakness [inability to operationalize the concept of ideology through functional analysis] is the virtual absence . . . of anything more than the most rudimentary conception of the process of symbolic formulation. There is a good deal of talk about emotion "finding a symbolic outlet" or "becoming attached to appropriate symbols"—but very little idea how the trick is really accomplished. The link between the cause of ideology and its effects seems adventitious because the connecting element—the autonomous process of symbolic formulation—is passed over in virtual silence.[6]

The study of symbolic formulation is for Geertz the study of human consciousness, for perception is an act of recognition. In this judgment, Geertz is in agreement with Walker Percy.

It is not enough to say that one is conscious of something; one is also conscious of something being something. There is a difference between the apprehension of a Gestalt (a chicken perceived the Jastrow effect as well as a human) and the grasping of it under its symbolic vehicle. As I gaze about the room, I am aware of a series of almost effortless acts of *matching*: seeing an object and knowing what it is. If my eye falls upon an unfamiliar something, I am immediately aware that one term of the match is missing, I ask what the object is, an exceedingly mysterious question.[7]

Once this concept is fully understood, it becomes obvious that "culture patterns—religious, philosophical, esthetic, scientific, ideological—are 'programs'; they provide the template or blueprint for the organization of social and psychological processes, much as genetic systems provide such a template for the organization of organic processes."[8] Man, as Cassirer and Langer have forcefully argued, is the one animal that has escaped the bonds of the genetic template and made his own history through the creation of symbols. As Geertz sums it up:

The agent of his own realization, he [man] creates out of his general capacity for the construction of symbolic models the specific capabilities that define him. Or—to return at last to our subject—it is through the construction of the ideologies, schematic images of social order that man makes himself for better or worse, a political animal. ... The function of ideology is to make an autonomous politics possible by providing the authoritative concepts that render it meaningful, the suasive images by means of which it can be sensibly grasped.[9]

Geertz's perceptive contribution has slowly filtered into the literature on ideology. However, the trend toward the development of a non-evaluational conception of the subject had begun long before Geertz' essay and is perhaps most evident in the attempt to separate the concept of value from that of ideology.

We consider this attempt to distinguish between "value" and "ideology" to be methodologically and empirically necessary. The literature, when it makes the distinction, usually does so on the basis of the more overtly explicit and systemic nature of ideologies (belief systems) as compared with values. Values are generally seen as the basic world view, *Weltanschauung,* which colors the individual's perception, and hence definition, of his world. There is, however, much remaining conceptual and semantic confusion here. Typical of this is Mannheim's definition of ideology as the "whole outlook of a social group" or "its total Weltanschauung," definitions that cloud the use of the terms value and ideology.[10]

One of the more interesting attempts to formulate the distinction between ideology and value is found in Clyde Kluckhohn's essay, "Values and Value Orientation in the Theory of Action."[11] Although somewhat confused and ultimately unsatisfactory in its distinction between ideology and value, Kluckhohn's contribution nevertheless provides a useful definition of value: "A value is a conception, explicit or implicit, distinctive of an individual or characteristic of a group, of the desirable which influences the selection from available modes, means and ends of action."[12]

The conception of a value as influencing selection is a helpful methodological tool. We can assume that the choice an individual makes is influenced by his values, although we would not argue that a particular value held by two individuals need necessarily lead to similar activity. Robert Lane has discussed this seeming contradiction.

> For example, Mannheim reports how the idea of 'freedom' in the nineteenth century meant to the German aristocrat 'the right of each estate to live according to its privileges,' while to the liberal intellectual, it meant the abolition of these privileges and the idea that 'all men have the same fundamental rights at their disposal.' This conflict followed in part from the fact that the social position of each posed certain restraints that to the other, were, in fact, conditions of freedom. It also followed from the 'true' perceptions of the nature of man and society afforded by the particular angle of vision the aristocrat and the intellectual each enjoyed.[13]

Thus, the same nominally verbalized value can be comfortably adhered to within quite different ideological frameworks, although "it might legitimately be argued that ideologies determine the choice between existing paths of action, which are equally compatible with the underlying values."[14] Again, basic value stance can indeed imbue the same symbols with different meaning, but the general belief system adhered to will usually reflect an attempt at congruence between underlying values and political activity.

It must be granted that this issue has opened strong debate, perhaps best exemplified in the observations by Philip Converse in "The Nature of Belief Systems in Mass Publics," in which belief systems (including ideologies) are seen as being much more constrained, i.e., the elements of the system are more closely linked and broader in range among articulate, educated elites than among the public in general.[15] We are thus faced with two distinct methodological and theoretical problems: first, whether the political symbols that are created and transmitted by active and articulate elites permeate to the public at large; second, whether one can assume that these symbol systems reflect implicit values. The particular stance taken in this work assumes that basic values can be inferred only from the ideological positions and the particular institutional and class structures found in a society and that there will ultimately be a congruence between structure, institution, and underlying values in a society that has been successful in containing conflict, without resort to overt coercion, at levels which permit the continued existence of the basic institutions and structures of the society.[16]

The study of nationalism, like that of ideology, has a much maligned history in the literature. The early development of the concept, coming as it did with the emergence of the nation-state, held a very positive connotation. The experience of World War I and the even more depressing circumstances of World War II with the rise of totalitarianism and racism saw the term take on a pejorative connotation. Nationalism became synonymous with fascism and totalitarianism for many, and a major writer on the subject decried, at least in early works, the religious or ideological side of the phenomenon. For Hans Kohn, nationalism "has become a powerful political threat, not only to international peace but also to human freedom, perhaps the most powerful threat because nationalism in our time far excels other appeals to human emotions—social or religious appeals—by the impact on masses and individuals alike."[17]

Carlton Hayes, in a 1926 work, condemns nationalism as a belief, "for its fruit has been intolerance, militarism and war."[18] Five years later, Hayes had developed an analysis of the ideological strands of nationalism through history, arguing that the early "humanitarian, liberal, Jacobin and traditional" strands had been "supplemented by economic protectionist nationalism . . . and finally by integral totalitarianism (Maurras, etc.), the forerunner of fascism."[19]

There were, however, other attempts to deal with the concept of nationalism, and several of them took symbolic formulation as their starting point. Thus, Graham Wallas argued that "the modern state must exist . . . *as an entity of the mind, a symbol.*"[20] Quincy Wright argued that "nationalism differs from . . . other opinions supporting the solidarity of a group only in respect to the symbols toward which it is directed . . . in fact, during the modern period . . . populations have become more intensely homogeneously and continuously favorable to the symbol of some nation-state than to other symbols."[21]

The point here is that there was an early attempt in the literature to conceptualize the idea of nation or nationalism in a symbolic mode. This attempt was carried forward in the seminal work by Karl Deutsch, *Nationalism and Social Communication.* In this volume, Deutsch argues for a theory of nation in which one may consider, "a people as a community of social communication habits,"[22] while membership in a people essentially consists in a wide complementarity of social communication.[23] Nationality or nationalism becomes the sharing of a symbol system and functions through channels of communication which allow the necessary flow of and obedience to the decisions taken in the political arena. This leads to the establishment of legitimate political institutions.

> Perhaps we may suspect, accordingly, that it is rather in the more or less far-reaching coincidence between legitimacy beliefs and social communication channels that political power can be found. Thus, when we speak loosely of the "manipulation of political symbols" we might do well to distinguish sharply between their manipulation in a speech or book, and the manipulation of those human and institutional chains of communication that must carry and disseminate these symbols and all other information and that are crucial for the functioning of political power.[24]

Building upon and enriching Deutsch's contribution, Kalman Silvert has argued for a conception of nationalism that has the greatest explanatory power. His approach has apparently taken an important clue from Max Weber.

> If the concept of nation can in any way be defined unambiguously, it certainly cannot be stated in terms of empirical qualities common to those who count as members of the nation. In the sense of those using the term at a given time, the concept undoubtedly means, above all, that one may exact from certain groups of men a specific sentiment of solidarity in the face of other groups. Thus, the concept belongs to the sphere of values. Yet, there is no agreement on how these groups should be delimited or about what concerted action should result from such solidarity.[25]

In his review of the literature on nationalism, Silvert sees the subject divided into four basic categories:

1. Nationalism in the formal juridical sense.
2. Nationalism as a symbolic concept referring to the particular symbols of nation, such as flag, anthem, etc.
3. Nationalism as explicit ideology "concerning what the nation is, was and ought to be."
4. Nationalism as a social value, "that norm defining loyalty due to fellow citizens and to the mandates of the state."[26]

Silvert's emphasis is on the final two categories, and it is basically within these categories that he develops a core definition of nationalism as "the acceptance of the state as the impersonal and ultimate arbiter of human affairs."[27] Because the definition is open to much interpretation and misinterpretation, let us allow its author to explain it in his own words.

As bald as this definition may at first appear, then, its implications are fullsome. The statement describes a function—the settlement of dispute. It names the state as the institutionalized means of bringing power to bear to satisfy that function. The necessity for the loyal participation of a citizenry within an explicit community which creates the consensual power necessary to the primary function of the state is indicated in the word "acceptance." And the definition states that the function must be exercised "impersonally"—over an appreciable territorial extension and across broad class lines, in ultimate cases overriding primary loyalties to intermediate family, religious, or other competing areas of identification.[28]

Two observations should be made here: first, Silvert's definition appears to be a step forward in interpreting the concept of legitimacy as it applies to the acts of the state. Second, the key term in the definition is *impersonal*. This position seems correct for several reasons, but the most important concerns the debate over whether truly fascist or totalitarian systems can be national within the above definition. Despite the fascist society's ability to produce an overriding state, a state that would conceivably be considered the ultimate arbiter of human affairs within that society, it has been incapable of functioning in an impersonal manner. A true fascism can produce a society which finds its ultimate institutional referent in the state, but the definition of the national community within that society would assume either systematic exclusion or unequal treatment of some of its members. We recognize the obvious fact that no society truly acts in a totally impersonal manner toward all of its members. What is essential here, however, is a question of whether the very ideology of the system precludes, excludes, or overtly hinders the ability of a particular state to act impersonally. In general, fascist systems are built on an ideological foundation that makes difficult, if not impossible, the expectation of an impersonal political marketplace.

Nowhere is the question of impersonal state action more pertinent than in the area of class and class relationships. As Silvert puts it:

> If class is the first large sub-category analytically and actually carved out of a people as a whole, then it follows that a society which pretends to wholeness over a fairly broad range of human activities must invoke and enforce supraclass identifications at the level of the entire society itself. The invention of nationalism ascribes this enforcement function to the state in the name of the nation.[29]

Silvert, as well as most development theorists, argues that the increased complexity of a society demands certain mechanisms for the adjudication of disputes and the regulation and integration of individuals within the society. The legacy of Western civilization in this particular area has been "the rule of law." It is the rule of law that has permitted the creation of a secular and relativistic political marketplace.[30]

The rule of law, as practiced ideally, increases the size of the "We" group at the societal level. Much the same point has been made, in a different framework, at the individual level by Daniel Lerner in *The Passing of Traditional Society.* The basic mental trait of the modern individual is his empathic capacity, i.e., "the capacity to see oneself in the other fellow's situation."[31] This capacity becomes the cement which helps bind individuals together in the modern nation-state.

> It is a major hypothesis of this study that high empathic capacity is the predominant personal style only in modern society, which is distinctively industrial, urban, literate and *participant.* Traditional society is non-participant—it deploys people by kinship into communities isolated from each other and from a center; without an urban rural division of labor, it develops few needs requiring economic inter-dependence; lacking the bonds of inter-dependence, peoples' horizons are limited by locale and their decisions involve only other *known* people in *known* situations. Hence there is no need for a trans-personal common doctrine formulated in terms of shared secondary symbols—a national "ideology" which enables persons unknown to each other to engage in political controversy or achieve "consensus" by comparing their opinions.[32]

Empathy and the rule of law are individual and societal mechanisms which permit the notion of citizenship to be extended to more and more individuals within the society. The notion of citizenship, however, is in constant tension with that of class. The theme has perhaps been most profoundly handled by T. H. Marshall and E. H. Carr. With great insight, Marshall weaves a tapestry of citizenship, class, and national development. As S. M. Lipset remarked:

> For Marshall, the concept of citizenship has three components: civil, political and social. The civil aspect of citizenship arose with the emergence of the bourgeoisie in the eighteenth century and involves a set of individual rights—liberty, freedom of speech, equality before the law, and the right to own property. Political rights, the access to decision-making process through participation in the choice of parliament by universal manhood suffrage, emerged in the nineteenth century and reflects in part the demands of the working classes for citizenship. Social rights—welfare, security, and education—have become a major component in the definition of citizenship in the twentieth century.[33]

Marshall sees the modern question in development as the notion of equality which creates a constant tension between citizenship and class. Much the same schema is found in E. H. Carr's *Nationalism and After.* Carr sees three basic stages in the development of the nation. The first stage involves the rise of the nation-state with the concomitant identification of the "nation with the person of the sovereign."[34] The second stage involves the rise of the bourgeois state in the nineteenth century, which Carr calls the "democratization of nationalism," with property "a condition of political rights."[35] The third stage, an essentially twentieth century phenomenon, involves "the rise of social strata into full membership in the nation," the "socialization of the nation."[36] Again, it is the tension of citizenship and class that becomes the dominant problem within society.

At this point, a society must decide if it will move further out of the constrictions of traditionalism and continue the momentum of its developmental path. A society can opt for the creation of symbols, both valorative and ideological, that are conducive to pluralism and the development of nationalism. It can, on the other hand, choose to pursue "ideologies of nationalism that prevent a full acceptance of the values of national identification, and that tend to block the continued path of development and modernization."[37]

The path often attempted in Latin America—and we argue that Uruguay is no exception—has tended to reinforce a vision of polity and society which, while it created a framework of institutional differentiation and allowed for a good deal of modernization, did not break out of the class-bound and hence nonegalitarian (Marshall) and nonsocialized (Carr) condition of national being. The system that has frequently developed in Latin America has alternatively been called corporatism, falangism, or Mediterranean syndicalism. These terms are used to describe what for some observers is one of the principal competing models of polity and society in the Iberic-Latin world. They comprehend the general political system of Spain, Italy, Portugal, and most of Latin America. A corporatist model or view of society is not new, having found its medieval expression in Aquinas (reinterpreting Plato within a Christian ethic) and in the great theorists of sixteenth century Spain, Vitoria and Suarez. At the heart of the Spanish heritage to the New World, this view of society has been the operative mode in Latin America despite the fact that the area achieved its independence from Spain over 150 years ago. Indeed, the overt rebirth of corporatist and falangist ideology in the interwar period in Spain, Italy, and Portugal certainly was not lost on Latin America.

It was not until the 1950s that the literature on Latin America took cognizance of the issue of the nature of Latin corporatist society. In 1954 Richard M. Morse argued for an approach to Spanish American government based on the importance of the corporate medieval heritage from Spain. In discussing the *Siete Partidas* as exemplary of the Spanish vision of society, Morse states:

> The Partidas assumed the nuclear element of society to be not Lockean atomistic man, but religious, societal man; man with a salvable soul (i.e., in relationship with God) and man in a station of life (i.e., having mutual obligations with fellow humans determinable by principles of Christian justice). The ruler, though not procedurally responsible to the people or the estates, was bound, through his conscience, to be the instrument of God's immutable, publicly ascertainable law. The Partidas in fact excoriated the tyrant who strove to keep his people poor, ignorant and timorous and to forbid their fellowship and assemblies.[38]

In a more recent work, Morse describes the foundation of the system as a "Thomistic-Aristotelian notion of functional social hierarchy."[39] Little was done with the insight he suggested until quite recently, although one Latin Americanist has long argued the importance of understanding the nature of corporatist society in Latin America in order truly to understand its politics. Kalman Silvert dubbed the phenomenon "Mediterranean syndicalism" and described it as follows:

> The theory of Mediterranean syndicalism is essentially a complication of the hierarchical order of medieval society. The Doctrine of the Two Swords is amended to become the doctrine of six or seven or eight swords, depending upon the number of institutional pillars created to become the fasces, so to speak, of quasi-modern traditionalism. . . .
>
> The good society pictured by the syndicalist would have the individual firmly rooted in his institutional place. His representation in government would not be a result of his individuality or his mere citizenship, but rather a function of his place in the institutional order of events.[40]

This view has recently been echoed by many, among them, Irving Louis Horowitz, who, in an essay on the process of politics in Latin America, makes the following observation: "What evolves are neo-Falangist systems. There is no elite in Latin America which legitimizes itself simply by legal secession of its power. Rather, there are class columns of particularistic power, each a pillar supporting a weak public government, and each cancelling the other classes' or sectors' potential for total power."[41] What is important and exciting is the recent spate of work picking up on the concept of corporatism as it has been expressed in the above general statements. These works have attempted to interpret the specific ideological, legal, and institutional manifestations of the phenomenon subsumed under the general label of corporatism.

A principal representative of this new generation is Howard J. Wiarda of the University of Massachusetts. In such essays as "Toward a Framework for the Study of Political Change in the Iberic-Latin Tradition: The Corporative Model," Wiarda has attempted to synthesize the literature on the subject and present certain crucial themes for further investigation.

Wiarda, like Silvert, sees the corporate model being adapted by Latin American *Pensadores* and their society to enable the system to meet the stresses and demands of modernization without paying a subsequent price in terms of the reordering and restructuring of power and class within them.

The Iberic-Latin writers built upon the newer and reformist currents emanating from the church and also drew upon their own considerable historical tradition. Still within the corporate-organic mold, they thought to fashion a framework for thought and action which blended the traditional regard for order and hierarchy with the newer imperative of change and modernization. They attempted, for instance, to deal with the new phenomenon of mass man through the erection of corporate structures that would provide for class harmony rather than conflict, togetherness and structured participation rather than rootlessness and alienation. Representation was generally to be determined by functions (labor, business, agriculture, religion, etc.) rather than through divisive interest groups and political parties. The state was to regulate, oversee, and harmonize the entire process.[42]

As I have previously argued,[43] corporative politics supports a particular kind of pluralism and creates or acknowledges the existence of a particular form of group structure in the society. As one writer has observed, "In this tradition [Hispanic-Romano legal system] the State does not take cognizance of a group: it creates the group by endowing it with juridical personality. Therefore in systems like those of Spanish America, in which the State's recognition and patronage are all-important for privilege, places, and institutional legitimacy, the unrecognized group drifts in an uncomfortable, harried limbo."[44] The State's recognition, however, is not a one-sided affair. The State endows a group with juridical existence, but the *interés creado* has a powerful protection in law and custom.

> The polarity of these opposing concepts is most often made manifest in the acrimonious negotiations over the concession or revision of the *estatuto básico* or *ley orgánica*. It is a struggle that generates much affect, and it is notable that this affect is thence often transferred to the objective symbol of corporate legitimacy, the *ley* or *estatuto* itself. . . . For the historian, the sense of familiarity is strong, for the *ley* or *estatuto,* taken together with the heterogeny of custom-derived informal immunities and prerogatives, constitutes a special and differential juridical status very strongly reminiscent of the corporate *fuero* of the ancien regime.[45]

One of the most significant dimensions of corporate identity is the vertical nature of solidarity patterns and the concomitant lack of horizontal (cross-cutting) solidarity, with a consequent societal inability to achieve a synthesizing consensus based on a commitment to basic equality and effective participation in the national community. Two key aspects of corporatively organized societies are the class-striated, hierarchically ordered relationships within each corporate pillar and the relative lack of interaction between the individuals in each pillar, except at the elite level. Man in a corporative world can look up and down but not across. Vertical solidarity based on hierarchy and the patron-client relationship exists, but the growth of horizontal solidarity and shared consensual perceptions does not ensue—despite the complication of an increased number of corporate pillars and the finer gradation of socio-economic differentiation within them. Again, effective national community implies an ability to see beyond the loyalty to family, class, or region, and this requires the creation or availability of a symbol system that nurtures and reinforces the requisite values, structures, and power relationships.

A helpful conceptual tool for an understanding of the dichotomy between the modern value stance concomitant with nationalism as we define it and the closed antidevelopmental stance of traditional subnational societies may be found in Talcott Parsons' pattern variables. Of the five dichotomies established by Parsons, three are particularly useful for our purposes:

1. Universalism—Particularism
2. Ascription—Achievement
3. Specificity—Diffuseness

As Parsons and Edward A. Shils have stated, "the pattern variables are most important as characteristics of value standards. . . ."[46] They may not be so for any specific choice, "but as soon as certain consistency of choosing can be inferred from a series of concrete acts, then we can begin to make statements about the value standards involved and the formulation of these standards in terms of the variables of the pattern-variable scheme."[47]

For our purposes, the aspect of the variables as they affect the social system seems most pertinent. In this regard, the universal-particular dichotomy refers to the expectation that, in the universalistic mode, in deciding "qualifications for memberships and decisions for differential treatment, priorities will be given to standards defined in completely generalized terms, independent of the particular relationship of the actor's own statuses," while, in a particularistic mode, priorities "assert the primacy of values attached to objects by their particular relations to the actor's properties."[48] Closely allied to the above variable is the ascriptive-achievement dichotomy. Briefly, this concerns whether recognition and status are conferred by the given attributes of an object or individual (ascription), or by objective achievements and expected performance.

It is clear that an ascription-particularistic axis creates a different set of power relationships and expectations than does a universalistic-achievement axis. It is the latter that is conducive to the operation of an impersonal state and the relationships between fellow citizens, and the state and its citizens, necessary to that operation.

Corporatist theory and practice produce a legal system based on a particular view of the foundation and source of law. Little research has been done on the Latin American legal system from this perspective, but some insights can be extracted from the literature. From the legal-constitutional perspective, the ideology of corporatism has been recently analyzed by Glen Dealy. Carefully reviewing the constitutions and major civil liberty legislation of several Latin American countries, Dealy concludes that the political ethos of the region was never biased in favor of democracy. "It is possible," he concludes, "that the failure of Spanish American government in 1810 as in 1966 is really not a failure to achieve democracy, but a triumph for the ideals and aspirations which were theirs since colonial days."[49]

Similarly, Francisco Moreno makes a useful distinction between *ley* (*lex*) and *derecho* (*ius* or justice). Moreno argues that *ley* in Latin America refers to positive legislation which may be nullified or ignored in the name of *derecho*, which he sees as the society's abstract conception of justice, including its psychological and philosophical aspects. The king as dispenser of justice reflects the authoritarian strain of Hispanic culture—a strain that remains predominant up to the present.[50]

This conception of law is a far cry from the Anglo-Saxon counterpart. In the latter system, positive legislation (law) becomes the yardstick and restraint on the abuse of authority and power. As Charles H. McIlwain has argued:

In brief for the ancients, the state makes the law: for moderns, the law makes the state. The first known extension of the latter idea was in the Hellenistic period by the Stoics, but the fullest surviving expression of it was by the Romans and the *locus classicus* is in the writings of Cicero. "What is the state," he asks, "except a society (or sharing) in law" (*juris societas*)? "Law is the bond of civil society" (*civilis societatis vinculum*).[51]

Paraphrasing McIlwain, I would argue that for the good corporatist, the state makes the law, while for the libertarian, the law makes the state. The Latin corporate state, reified (or perhaps deified) by religious sanction, is the giver of law.

Discussion of corporatist political philosophy often overlooks the importance of the historical contribution of Catholic social thought to the doctrine. There are important examples of the revival of medieval corporative thought in the papal encyclicals of the last eighty years. The stimulus to the study of Thomist doctrine, encouraged by Pope Leo XIII, had much to do with this rebirth, as did the tension of the industrial revolution and the challenge of radical social doctrine. While Leo's *Rerum Novarum* (1891) is correctly seen as a landmark in the development of the social conscience of the church, it presents a profoundly hierarchical conception of society.

Let it, then, be taken as granted, in the first place, that the condition of things human must be endured, for it is impossible to reduce civil society to one dead level. Socialists may in that intent do their utmost, but all striving against nature is in vain. There naturally exist among mankind manifold differences of the most important kind; people differ in capacity, skill, health, strength; and unequal fortune is a necessary result of unequal condition.[52]

The reconciliation of labor and capital could be accomplished within the framework of the above view. Thus, in addressing himself to this problem, Leo remains perfectly consistent.

The great mistake in regard to the matter now under consideration is to take up with the notion that class is naturally hostile to class, and that the wealthy and the working men are intended by nature to live in mutual conflict. So irrational and so false is this view, that the direct contrary is the truth. Just as the symmetry of the human frame is the resultant of the disposition of the bodily members, so in a State is it ordained by nature that these two classes should dwell in harmony and agreement, and should, as it were, groove into one another, so as to maintain the balance of the body politic. Each needs the other; Capital cannot do without Labor, nor Labor without Capital. Mutual agreement results in pleasantness of life and the beauty of good order; while perpetual conflict necessarily produces confusion and savage barbarity. Now in preventing such strife as this, and in uprooting it, the efficacy of Christian institutions is marvellous and manifold.[53]

The view of society propounded in *Rerum Novarum* was not lost on Pius XI. On the fortieth anniversary of its proclamation, Pius restated its philosophy and made it applicable to the current world situation. Thus his *Quadrogessimo Anno* [*On Reconstructing the Social Order,* 1931] accepts the earlier notions of functional social hierarchy, but proceeds beyond it to a more overtly corporatist solution.

Everyone understands that this grave evil [class conflict] which is plunging all human society to destruction must be remedied as soon as possible. But complete cure will not come until this opposition has been abolished and well-ordered members of the social body— industries and professions—are constituted in which men may have their place, not according to the position each has in the labor market but according to the respective social functions which each performs.[54]

Pius XI stayed with this theme throughout his Papacy. In a 1937 encyclical, he restated his position.

We have indicated how a sound prosperity is to be restored according to the true principles of a sane corporative system which respects the proper hierarchic structure of society; and how the occupational groups should be fused into a harmonious unity inspired by the principle of the common good.[55]

His successor, Pius XII, remained faithful to this conception of society. In a work on German corporatism, Ralph Bowen cites a 1946 letter by Pius favoring the corporate organization of society to meet the pressure of communist and socialist ideas:

> Corporative enthusiasts among German Catholics, in particular, may well derive considerable encouragement from declarations of Papal approval of "corporative associations" of the means of carrying out "just social reforms." A dispatch to the New York Times, July 21, 1946, p. 1, reported that Pope Pius XII, in a letter to the professor Charles Flory, president of the *Semaines Sociales de France,* had called for the institution of such bodies 'in every branch of the national economy' in preference to nationalization. The Pope had concluded by affirming that, "under present circumstances," there was no doubt that "a corporate form of social life, and especially of economic life, in practice favors Christian doctrine concerning the individual, community, labor, and private property."[56]

It is evident from the above citations that corporatist political ideas have a prominent place in the recent social doctrine of the Church. More importantly, the view of man implicit in corporatist ideology and the structures it offers to civil society have continued to influence the politics of the Iberian Peninsula and Latin America.[57]

2
BATLLISMO AND ITS OPPONENTS: IDEOLOGY IN TWENTIETH-CENTURY URUGUAY

Bold social and political innovation is not considered the norm in Latin America. Traditionally semifeudal, oligarchic, static regimes are more often than not the picture drawn by journalists, travelers, and social scientists. It is true that the last fifteen years have brought Castro, Allende, and the nationalist military in Peru, but these are exceptions, or, depending on one's political focus, aberrations. Certainly one does not expect to find bold innovation forty to sixty years ago, especially in a peripheral buffer state with a population of approximately one million and with a political history torn by civil war. Yet, Uruguay in the first three decades of the twentieth century is, with the possible exception of Argentina, the most interesting socio-political laboratory in Latin America.

La República Oriental del Uruguay, created by an Argentine-Brazilian agreement mediated by the British, had a tumultuous first eighty years.[1] Civil war, assassination, militarism, and foreign intrigue were the constant themes. Nevertheless, the population grew from some 200,000 in 1860 to over 1,000,000 by 1904, due to a heavy immigration of Latin Europeans.[2] The 1904 civil war saw the victory of the *Colorado* president, José Batlle y Ordóñez. This chapter will present and interpret Batlle's ideology *(Batllismo)*—an ideology that would transform and dominate Uruguayan politics and political institutions for thirty years, color it until the present, but ultimately fail.

Given the huge influx of immigrants in the last decades of the nineteenth century and the first two decades of the twentieth, the challenge for Batlle and his lieutenants within the *Colorado* party was to integrate this new and overwhelmingly urban mass into society at large and the *Colorado* party in particular. The route chosen for such an integration was above all a prolabor government policy. As pragmatic as this might appear, it nevertheless had strong roots in an ideological framework

that accepted state intervention as a means to control conflict within
the society.

Batlle's pronouncements on labor preceded by many years his
ascension to the presidency. From 1890 on, the influx of Spaniards and
Italians saw an increasing labor militancy which borrowed much of its
ideological strength from syndicalist and anarcho-syndicalist theories
imported from Europe. So-called *sociedades de resistencia* were formed
during this period. In 1905 the first nationwide syndicate (FORU-
Workers Federation of the Republic of Uruguay) had been established.
As early as 1896, Batlle's newspaper, *El Día,* had come out strongly in
support of labor's demands, recognizing that the labor movement could
form the basis of a new urban strength for the *Colorado* party. Typical
is this editorial from *El Día:*

> Among us the labor movement should be considered as the arrival
> of working people into public life, and seen in this light the movement
> acquires a national importance. In effect, this enormous mass of men
> that until now believed that their interest and their duty consisted in
> working in silence, far from all popular agitation, in the narrow sphere
> of action in which they exercised their position, are going to enter
> public life. Here we have a numerous and therefore powerful social
> class that until now has vegetated among us without being collectively
> concerned with its interests or showing signs of life, that suddenly
> was awakened by the murmur of the struggle that sustains this same
> class in almost all the nations of the civilized world and is disposed
> to make its aspirations and rights count in an intelligent and able
> manner. We salute them.[3]

Throughout his lifetime, Batlle remained faithful to the cause of
labor and workers' rights. During his first administration, he began to
propose the legislation on hours, safety, and retirement that slowly but
surely became the backbone of labor legislation in Uruguay over the
next fifteen years. In his message to Parliament on the *cuestión obrera,*
Batlle argued that the young and relatively underdeveloped nature of
Uruguay afforded the possibility for bold social legislation that might
avoid future problems and conflict.

> Our Republic should take the advantage currently available to it of
> this period of formation, in which it is as easy to correct vices and

incipient defects as it is to implant new institutions . . . our condition
as a new people enables us to realize ideals of government and social
organization that older countries cannot effectively implement without
overcoming enormous and tenacious resistance.[4]

Batlle steadfastly refused to use his power as president to tilt the
worker-owner struggle in favor of the owner. When the opposition and
even some of his own party brought up charges of extremism and "outside agitators" in the labor movement, Batlle responded that "as a
general rule, all new ideas, the great ideas of all times were launched into
existence and propagated by agitators."[5]

There emerges out of Batlle's defense of labor and the workers' movement a tint of socialism that carries through the entire early period of the
Batllista phenomenon. In a discussion of the just wage in 1896, one finds
an argument that reads like a section of *Das Kapital:*

Strikes are a protest and struggle against this invariably precarious
general situation of the worker, against modern slavery which converts
the owner into a master. They say: "We want the salary of a working
man to be measured not by what is absolutely indispensable for his
subsistence, but by the value of his labor; we desire that if he produces
at the rate of fifty pesos a month, he earns fifty pesos a month, which
is what he produced and not thirty, which is what he needs to survive;
we wish to take this difference of twenty pesos out of the hands of
the owner in order to return it to the hands of the worker to whom
it rightfully belongs. This is the goal of the organization of strikes
and its demands.[6]

It was statements like this that the opposition constantly seized upon
to demonstrate the radical intention of the *Batllista* program. Yet, at
the start of his second term in 1911, Batlle would still speak of the "ease
with which the capitalist regime imposes impossible hours on tender
children."[7] It was only after the setback over the *colegiado* and the subsequent split with trusted and loyal members of his own party that Batlle
began to tone down both the style and content of his approach and program. In its formative years, however, the socialist, Marxist, and anarcho-
syndicalist currents brought to the Plata region by the waves of immigrants were an excellent prod to the *Batllista* philosophy. The democratic

socialism which emerged as the dominant *Batllista* theme took early exception to the conflict-laden approach of the Marxist school. Batlle was always careful, especially under opposition political attack, to differentiate his approach from that of the more radical movements in which his enemies attempted to place him. Thus, the following caveat:

> What we have denied is that inequality is deliberate and the work of the immoral will of those that have more. We have attributed it to the difficulty of making a just distribution.
>
> At the same time we have denied that the manner of correcting this distribution constitutes the animosity in the class struggle. This will not destroy injustice. It will further it! The victorious class will be left with that which belonged to the vanquished.
>
> What we have affirmed and demonstrated is that societies are not divided into two hostile classes, perfectly defined and separated, and between which there can be no sentiment aside from hate since one is only interested in exploiting the other.[8]

While accepting the enormous disequilibrium between men, Batlle rejects the Marxist interpretation. The imbalance does not have to result in or inspire a struggle between classes. No master class has brought about the unequal distribution of goods in society. This maldistribution is merely the result of the difficulty of achieving a mechanism for equitable distribution of resources. The solution for Batlle is not the destruction of the state, but rather the construction of an interventionist state whose principal function would be the regulation and more just distribution of the goods and services of the society. This approach is possible for Batlle since he rejects the economic determinism of Marx and believes that the higher motives and aspirations of man can take precedence over the conflicts created by personal interest or personal gain.[9]

Batlle's conception of social justice required an activist, interventionist state, for only such an overriding institution could insure the protection of the collective interest. The state could act indirectly through regulatory legislation (e.g., labor laws and retirement provisions) or directly as the provider of essential services and owner-operator of key commercial and industrial activities. It was especially in this second area that *Batllismo* was to create a whole new set of institutions for Uruguay.

The creation of the industrial state units (*entes autónomos*) that were
to carry out the necessary economic activities of the state was justified
principally on three grounds: (1) the modern state was seen as an economic
organization, (2) only the state could insure the collective economic and
social justice of the society, and (3) the activity of the state was the most
effective way of countering foreign influence and exploitation. Each of
these points merits separate discussion.

In his message calling for a state monopoly on insurance, Batlle clearly
presented his conception of the modern state. In his campaign to muster
support for this and other proposals, Batlle always laid emphasis on the
sound fiscal benefits they embodied. In a discussion in *El Día* two weeks
after the formal proposal of the insurance monopoly, it was pointed out
that there were basically two traditional sources of revenue: the foreign
loan (Batlle used the term *empréstito* for this type of financing) and
taxes. However, there was a third way to raise capital—the exploitation
of certain industries by the state.

The release from the dependence on the foreign loan was an early
indication of what was to become a sophisticated conception of economic
nationalism. This theme continued throughout the nationalization program. For instance, in a 1913 message requesting the complete integration
of the financial resources of the national bank, Batlle argued:

> If such were not the fundamental moral base that authorizes the
> State's invasion into the domain of activities associated with private
> industry, one would be doing nothing more than substituting the
> evil inherent in the egoism of private interest, for an analogous evil
> cast in an official mold. . . . If it did not take the foresight of assuring
> the automatic increase in capital, the State would find itself in the
> overbearing necessity of again relying on loans, which always imply a
> considerable sacrifice.[10]

The duty of the modern state is to control those services that are in the
national interest. The state could control through its power of regulation
and, where necessary, by establishing a public monopoly. The test of the
merit of competition versus monopoly does not reside in an outdated
conception of these terms, but in a careful evaluation of the national need
and the public interest.

The state public utility and industrial corporations would be serving many social and political functions. They would be providing cheap services while paying higher salaries to the workers, for profit in the private sense would not be their goal. Additionally, as one important Batlle lieutenant saw it, these public corporations would counteract the detrimental aspects of private expropriation.[11]

These activities of the state would gradually free the economy from the dependence on foreign capital and foreign management. The *Batllista* vision held that Uruguay was fully capable of taking on a true national responsibility for both the management and the generation of capital for these corporations. Thus Batlle's position on public works:

> The times have already passed in which because of our internal upheavals, the lack of honesty on the part of our governments or the lack of capital and technical resources, we had to surrender the administration and utilities [of public works] to foreign companies. . . . In order to diminish the cost and to maintain ownership of utilities and national pride . . . we should, except for exceptional cases, be forced to execute our own public works under our immediate supervision and direction.[12]

The state enterprises were set up as individual corporations. Some would see in this the old *intereses* or *fueros* of medieval Spanish political life. Admittedly, as will be discussed later, one could argue that these corporations take on the function and particularistic character indicative of institutions in a corporatist society.[13] However true this may be in the future, the *Batllista* conception of the nature of these corporations was based on the feeling that the very independence of each of them would be conducive to a more independent, resourceful, and imaginative management. As it has been put by the principal theorist on the subject:

> The problem was to make each public corporation a distinct personality, jealous of its interests and its earnings, and to establish among the personnel an *esprit de suite,* an enthusiasm for the economic struggle, and the mentality of the individual trader or individualist. This commercial mentality, the subordination of all other interests to the success of the institution, was the principal cause of the success of the public corporation, and it originated in independence.[14]

The state enterprises were to be an important consideration in the constitutional debates of 1917, with decentralization the major point of contention. The final outcome of this conflict was a vaguely worded article that merely indicated that "the diverse services that constitute the industrial dominion of the state, higher, secondary, and primary instruction, and public assistance and hygiene will be administered by autonomous councils. Except where the laws of these councils declare the positions elective, the members will be designated by the National Council."[15]

There is no question, as many observers are quick to point out, that the creation of these *entes* on paper does not describe accurately their activity in practice. Legislation and operative reality are never a one-to-one fit, but we do have the evaluation of a perceptive English economist, Simon Hanson, who came to Uruguay in the 1930s with a skeptic's eye on the "socialist" experiment of Batlle. Surprisingly, Hanson's conclusions were very positive. The *entes* had operated efficiently. The cost of services, especially electricity, had been reduced. Indeed, Hanson's major criticism was directed at the conservative fiscal practices of the directors, i.e., "their adoption of profits—the common gauge of private industry's success—as the measure of their effectiveness."[16]

One objective measure of the performance of the *entes* can be found in the energy output of the country. In 1896 total electrical output was estimated at 584,000 kilowatts. In 1911, when the production of electricity was nationalized, the figure was over 16 million kilowatts. By 1923-1924, the total had reached 72 million kilowatts.[17]

The effective operation of the modern state implied, for Batlle, a politically active and aware citizenry. Frequent elections and mechanisms for active citizen participation in legislation and public policy formation were seen as the cornerstone of the entire political process. The time and energy expended by the individual was seen not so much as a duty but as a responsibility—a responsibility that brings with it "the satisfaction of the advantages that a political society derives from being able to guide its own destiny and fully live its own life."[18] In this vein, Batlle argued that the referendum was an essential tool for insuring effective citizen participation, given the limits to direct participation imposed by the size and complexity of modern society.[19]

The end result of this constant dialectic between a modern, active, interventionist state seeking justice and a participant, aware citizenry is the creation of those bonds of solidarity which would truly tie the individual to his nation in a manner which goes far beyond merely formal citizenship. The consequence is that synthetic combination of individual and nation which finds its highest expression in the empathic vision of its citizens.

> From these considerations, one can deduce that it is not exactly true that a man does not have any greater relation to his country than the fact that he was born there and that emigration is almost natural to him. On the contrary, it could be said that the great and ancient nations, like France, Italy, England, Germany, etc. reveal, in reality, the character of large families, whose members are all related to each other. One can also affirm that the modern nations of America, composed of immigrant populations, increasingly present the same character. Very well, from this concept of the true fatherland, which we consider correct, the concept cannot follow of a citizen who looks with cold indifference at the misfortune of his fellow citizens and when seeing them attacked, brushes the sand from his sandals and with a smile on his lips moves to any other territory to put up his shop in whatever other country.[20]

The creation of social solidarity based on an underlying search and commitment to social justice is the constant leitmotiv of Batlle's nationalism. As expressed by one of his chief political lieutenants, Dr. Juan J. Amézaga, the search is based on a most profound conception of justice. He argued both the necessity of and the beneficent results afforded by the commitment to public welfare and public assistance, a commitment that strengthened the bonds of society and the solidarity of its members.[21]

As the debate over Batlle's proposal for a collegial form of government (the *colegiado*) intensified, the opposition used the opportunity to attack the entire *Batllista* program. In the midst of doing so, they offered a different, more static, and less optimistic image of society.

> In reality our country is nothing more than a prairie with a large village for its capital. Outside of Montevideo (the village) there is nothing except one or two hamlets (miserable little villages) where, according to the phrase of a writer, gossip gives way to slander. Here the exponents of culture are the politicaster, and, in the country, the

horse thief, the smuggler, and the shyster. We even lack national unity, for the coastal region is subordinated to Argentina, and the border to Brazil. They don't even speak Spanish there!

So, let us leave the workers, the humble sons of labor, alone to eat in peace the bread they honorably earn. Where are we going with eight hour laws, weekly day of rest legislation, etc. if there are no great masses of workers among us, nor anyone to admire us? Let us wait until Montevideo is as large as Paris and the Republic has forty million inhabitants.[22]

Batlle rejected this view of Uruguay and of his social program, and held out a more noble if chiding vision.

In effect, the government will not limit itself to countenance the eight hour day; it also desires to see the project which establishes a day of rest for each five days of work sanctioned, and the legislation which grants a pension to all those over 60 who do not have a livelihood, without excluding those who fight in the ranks of the *Nacionalista* party, projects that will be under consideration by the Assembly as soon as they are reported out of their respective commissions. We may be a poor and obscure mini-republic; but we will have advanced mini-laws.[23]

The challenge from the conservatives sharpened the debate and heightened the *Batllista* sense of economic nationalism and the language used in its defense. Thus, "the modern state unhesitatingly accepts its status as an economic organization. It will enter industry when competition is not practicable, when control by private interests vests in them authority inconsistent with the welfare of the state, when a fiscal monopoly may serve as a great source of income to meet urgent tax problems, when the continued export of national wealth is considered undesirable. State socialism makes it possible to use for the general good that portion of the results of labor which is not paid to labor."[24]

At the 1919 party convention, Batlle began the work which was carried on in committee and led to the formal adoption of a party program during the 1922 convention. This program remained the official platform of the party into the 1930s and is an important ideological document.[25] The first part of the program is a statement of accomplishments, a list of thirty-seven *obras realizadas,* which includes the nationalizations, separation of church and state, and the development of free secular education. The second section of the program covers future goals, and consists of forty articles divided into chapters on government and party institutions, welfare and labor, education, taxes, and public lands.

The most important proposal from the point of view of government institutions was a call for the adoption of a totally collegial executive by eliminating the office of the president completely. In addition, there was a call for the establishment of a plebiscite and referendum on legislation. In the area of party reform, the platform called for the revocation of the mandate of elected officials when they have failed to fulfill the commitments made to the electorate. Such individuals would be judged by their fellow party members. This provision was an obvious attempt by Batlle to create the kind of party discipline he knew was necessary to complete and preserve his program

The platform commitment on work and welfare was basically an extension of several pieces of labor legislation concerning minimum wages and protection for minors. Two very innovative and, indeed, radical proposals, however, were presented in this section. Article 62 called for a profit-share plan for workers and employees in state enterprises.[26] Article 66 called for inexpensive medical service to be available in each judicial section, to be accomplished by the appointment of a practitioner to the position of a public service doctor for a one-year period.

It was the last four articles of the party program that undoubtedly represented the most explosive issue for society. These articles concerned taxes on and the use and accumulation of public land. In essence the proposal sought to reduce taxation on products of labor (*trabajo nacional*) by substituting land taxes, increasing the state's percentage of inheritance and gift taxes, and increasing the state's taxation on foreign investment and certain imports. All real property was to have an appraised valuation submitted by the owner. The state could then expropriate such property by paying 40 percent above the said valuation. To blunt the obvious resistance to this proposal, the owner was given the right to demand a new appraisal of his property if he felt special conditions had caused an extraordinary increase in its value. It is important to note that the proposal had actually been passed by one legislature but was repealed by the subsequent legislature before it had actually been implemented.

The final article concerning public land called for a government policy directed towards conserving and adding to the amount of land held by the state. This land would be rented out to those willing to work it, and the funds derived from this policy would be used for the acquisition of new land.

The 1921 party program on land reform was but one chapter in the long history of the politics of rural versus urban interests. The conflict did not end with the *Colorado* civil war victory in 1904; indeed, the issue remained a delicate one throughout Batlle's lifetime (and, one could add, until the present). In 1910, faced with a possible *Blanco* insurrection over his second presidential term, Batlle attempted to assuage his opponents by declaring:

> I do not recognize the existence of an agrarian problem in this country that urgently demands the attention of the public powers. I understand that the rational division of the land has operated and continues operating through the unfolding of our rural wealth. There is no reason to pay tribute to noble but dangerous impatience.[27]

Despite this disclaimer, Batlle was to propose an absentee land tax in 1912 which became law in 1916. Controversial legislation, especially when it might affect future power relationships, led to heated debate over the entire *Batllista* program. Legislation on rural wages, colonization, and similar issues never was at the heart of the threat perceived by the landed interest. They could live with this kind of legislation, often delaying its implementation for years. The fiscal policy gradually evolved by Batlle was, however, the real bone of contention. The proposals in the 1921 party program became the basis of the *Batllista* agrarian policy for the next decade.

Batlle stuck with these policy objectives but carefully avoided a direct conflict with the *estancieros* by not painting them as the single conspiratorial cause of the land tenure situation. Instead, he argued that society as a whole was responsible for the situation through a general consensus that had permitted the accumulation of vast tracts of land by a few individuals.[28] The opposition could take little comfort from this kind of statement, for, in explaining his agrarian policy to the 1925 party convention, Batlle argued for a profoundly social conception of real property.

Property in reality should not belong to anybody, or better said, should belong to everybody, and the entity that represents everybody is Society. Property, then, should belong to the Society.[29]

The payment of taxes on land was a recognition of the fact that the landlord is indirectly paying a "rent" to the state. Arguing from this rationale, Batlle saw the day when property would eventually be totally held by the state, if not directly, then through the taxes paid by those wishing to own land.[30]

The above vision never came to pass, and indeed both *Colorado* supporters and the *Blanco* opposition were constantly reminded by Batlle, or by his close associates, that these brave statements in no way implied the confiscation or direct socialization of the land. The operative reality of Uruguayan politics by the middle of the third decade of this century made any real attempt to push this kind of reform a hopeless task. There is no question, however, that these threats did enable the urban-based *Colorado* party to redistribute income from the rural to the urban sectors and force the landed interests to pay much of the bill for the social and other programs that are the *Batllista* legacy. It is also apparent, however, that by the mid-1920s the *Colorados* no longer had the internal unity to enable them to continue such a program of redistribution. Indeed, it was not until the late 1940s that government fiscal policy could again be used effectively to redistribute income towards the urban sectors.

The simple fact is that a political detente (or stalemate, if one wishes) had been established by the time such statements on land reform were being made. Rural interests would remain essentially untouched by the political center as long as they permitted and were willing to foot most of the bill for the programs of the urban-oriented *Colorados*. The nature of the wool and meat trade with Europe and Britain and the huge volume of such trade during the 1920s really did not make land reform a crucial issue. Consequently, it never was at the heart of the *Batllista* ideology. nor was it seen as an absolutely necessary component of its program. With benefit of hindsight, this may be seen as extremely shortsighted, but it is understandable given the political and economic reality of the period.

The Uruguayan interpreters of *Batllismo* cover the spectrum from right to left. Although one or two deny any systematic *Batllista* ideology, we agree with Aldo Solari that whatever the opinion one might have of Batlle's ideology, it seems impossible to deny that he had an ideology. It seems impossible to deny that the idea of nationalizing public services, of struggling against foreign capital in the period of English capital—of creating autonomous administrative units, and the idea of the collegial executive [*colegiado*] etc. formed an ideological whole of a certain coherence, and for which Batlle and his faction constantly struggled.[31]

Typically, the interpretations of the *Batllista* ideology reflect the particular ideological coloration of the interpreter. Thus, a deeply committed pan-Hispanist whose psychological interpretation of Uruguay leaves no doubt as to his answer to the question *¿Uruguay : ¿provincia o nación?* recognizes the basic flavor of the *Batllista* style as "bourgeois humanism, rationalism, faith in lineal and indefinite progress and a tacit utilitarian and materialist sense." He condemns this ideology as fruitless, for it turns its back on "*la nacionalidad hispanoamericana,*" and therefore fails on a cultural and philosophical level.[32]

For a sociologist like German Rama, *Batllismo* represents the rise to national power of the petty bourgeoisie through a political movement of the middle class. Hence, it is limited by the very nature of all such middle class movements.

This theme is reiterated and expanded by the young socialist writer, Julio A. Louis, in a volume entitled *Batlle y Ordóñez: Apogeo y muerte de la democracia burguesa.* For Louis, *Batllismo* is a bourgeois ideology par excellence and, like Rama, he sees it as the political expression of the middle classes. Begrudgingly conceding some important liberal-democratic accomplishments to the movement, Louis concludes that *Batllismo* did not go to the root of the problem.

However, it does not resolve the grave problems which, with the passage of time, grew worse: dependence on imperialist capital, monoproduction, domination by the latifundio, unilateral and insufficient industrial development, unfavorable exchange conditions in international markets, etc. In sum, it does not resolve any of the infrastructural problems.[33]

From a somewhat similar political perspective, Ricardo Martínez Ces condemns *Batllismo* for its inability to deal with the underlying structural problems of the society. The author runs what would now be considered a dependence theory argument. He feels that Batlle left Uruguay as he had found it, i.e., underdeveloped because of its economic structure and its dependence on the English market. His perception of this phenomenon is worth quoting extensively.

> Basically, the Uruguay of 1911 had substantially the same problem as it has today. Its underdevelopment, although they did not use this word in that epoch, was determined by its structure and "English progress." It is known that a country can in no way progress beyond that which its least productive sector, be it agricultural or industrial, will permit. If the moment arrives in which agrarian production stagnates because it has reached the maximum development permitted by the *latifundio,* in the end, it produces stagnation throughout the service and industrial sectors. . . . Uruguay has been in this situation throughout this century, occasionally alleviated by the rise in prices produced by the world wars. In addition, between 1910 and 1915, immigration increased the population from one million to one and a quarter million in round numbers. How did Batlle handle these problems? He did not alter basic structures, but he did wind the national watch so that it could function rather well for some time. To achieve this, he took what we can call a lateral road, for it passed alongside of structures without touching them. His policy consisted of creating a new investment sector, setting in motion the entrepreneurial state through interventionist politics. In this way, a series of state services were created and others nationalized, an impulse which will continue beyond his presidency and will be the soul of *Batllista* policy.[34]

Martínez Ces also has some important observations on the *Batllista* style. This style "is the result of the interpretation of the country made by the immigrant through Batlle, and of the social and economic conditions that prevailed in the first quarter of this century."[35] The vision was one of an Uruguay that could successfully escape the great problems that afflicted other countries—an Uruguay of experimentation and social justice that could play out its small but independent role with a great deal of success. This vision could be fostered because of the mass of newly arrived immigrants who found Uruguay the promised land.

It is now worth asking how the *Batllista* style could nurture and grow.
Providentialism, humanism, happiness, absence of a national problem,
its essential anti-historicism—all these had their roots in the immigration of which *Batllismo* was the political expression. *Batllismo* func-
tioned at all levels of immigration, in the highest and the lowest. In
both, the immigrant came to America fleeing societies that denied
all possibility of social mobility. To escape the life of a peasant in
the small Spanish or Italian town, to escape the cruel and rigid
military service, to escape the misery and unemployment and even
to escape one's own family and come to a country where one could
begin anew . . . were circumstances which could renew one's faith
in human kindness. Even meat, the food of the privileged classes in
Europe, could be eaten every day here. It was the national food.[36]

The need for effort and sacrifice becomes a key thread in Carlos Real
de Azúa's incisive interpretation of *Batllismo* in *El Impulso y Su Freno*.
For this foremost Uruguayan historian, the lack of a national ethic containing a sense of duty, exigency, or sacrifice is at the heart of the ultimate failure of *Batllismo*. This failure is due to a basic absence of nationalism in the schema despite the fact that there was, indeed, a good
deal of economic nationalism within its program. Nationalism implies a
deep understanding of the nation's position and role vis-à-vis other
sovereign powers. This understanding, or at least its verbal expression, is
lacking in *Batllismo*.[37] Azúa may be correct in his criticism from the
point of view of verbal style; Batlle and his party rarely used the term
nation, being satisfied with "state" or "society." However, I would argue
that the discussion of ideology in this chapter and the institutional and
power relationships that will be discussed in later chapters are indicative
of the fact that *Batllismo* was an ideology of nationalism, both in the
more formal sense in which Azúa uses it and in the deeper social sense.

As is usually the case, there is a glimmer of truth in all of the above
interpretations. The *Batllista* phenomenon was a remarkable attempt
at state-building *and* nation-building; that it ultimately failed does not
automatically mean its critics have seized on its basic achilles' heel.
Batllismo lost its creative drive because it failed or was unable, given
the preindustrial economic setting in which it operated, to change the
basic value orientations within the society. It fathered a middle class
through a commitment to social welfare and justice that were exemplary,

but the institutions it created did not grow, situated as they were in an environment in which basic values were hostile (if not antipathetic) to its value implications.

It is clear that the *Batllista* vision of the Uruguayan nation-state and the role of the individuals that compose it was conducive to the development of nationalism as a social value. The symbols with which Batlle worked, the commitment to social justice, and the economic role of the state were expressive of the desire to create a viable national community in which all could participate.

Batlle felt that Uruguay was a young nation which could make itself in whatever image it chose. His philosophy, based on man's malleability, if not perfectibility, led him to believe that a society based on social justice could avoid basic conflict. He believed that citizenship meant participation both in the fruits of society and in the management of society's affairs. His educational reforms and proposals for fuller citizen participation in political institutions reflect a desire to move beyond a merely formal conception of the citizen or of the nation into the realm of a reciprocal relationship between the two.

There are, as the discussion of the Uruguayan critics of *Batllismo* indicated, interpretations of the *Battlista* ideology that do not see it in a positive light. In a recent article entitled "Three Perspectives on the Crisis in Uruguay," M.H.J. Finch argues that Batlle's very success in meeting the challenge of the new immigrant groups and the newly created tension of industrialization served to perpetuate traditional structures and power relationships.[38] If *Batllismo* did indeed serve such a purpose, it did so not because of its internal desire or purpose but because of the environment in which it operated and the opposition it had to face.

The apparent success of Batlle and his program between 1904 and 1915 did not signify, and it never has, the lack of a counterimage of the society—an image sustained and nurtured by the landed interests. This image was to find a much fuller expression in Uruguayan literature than its *Batllista* counterpart. It would receive its greatest philosophical and literary expression in Rodó's *Ariel,* but there were other more politically pragmatic examples. The Uruguayan essayist Carlos Reyles, in such works as *La Muerte del Cisne,* reflected a view of society that was antithetical to the *Batllista* vision.

It would seem incomprehensible that in this world, where the most tyrannical determinism reigns, and where phenomena submissively succeed one another, the chimeras and romance of liberty, equality and fraternity, imagined by a *cowardly and delicate hero* have exercised such a mysterious influence over men—if it were not a known fact that they adore stories, fantasies, sweet damsels, whom the more they are deceived by them, the more they adore and are bewitched by them. . . .

No, society has never been, nor will ever be, the saintly work of the Good, of Justice or of Right. Rather it is the diabolic fetus of a vital dominant instinct, or as Marx would have it, the product of the class struggle, engendered according to him, by the evolution of interests and determinant, in addition, of the entire historical process. With some slight restrictions, it is the valid part of scientific or critical socialism, and has little to do with the sentimental utopias of a Rousseau, of the priest Meslier and of the ideologues, or the bureaucratic or fiscal agents [Batllismo or the philosophy of Henry George?] or *Utopias de los cretines,* or with other puerile forms of *socialismo vulgaris.* . . [39]

The rural interests responded to *Batllismo,* the international economic and political climate of World War I, and the heated debate surrounding the *colegiado,* with the creation of a powerful new interest group, the *Federación Rural.* The ideology of the organization is best expressed in the writings and speeches of one of its earliest and most resourceful leaders, Dr. José Irureta Goyena. His vision is one of a rural society dominated by an aristocracy capable of preserving the sense of community lost in the modernizing and industrializing cities, while at the same time acting as the medium through which the light of civilization is transmitted to the countryside.

It is necessary to appreciate the events of the urban world, to extract the consequences of its current crisis and to prevent its repetition in the countryside. It is at this point that the traditional reappears, the preventive capacity of the old rural society in which the boss was somewhat like the head of a patrimonial community. To sociologically separate is to create a wedge, to create a wedge is to disagree, to disagree is to fight. Keep your laborers at your side, invigorate with your protection the bonds of sympathy that link you to them. . . .

The ranchowner is *the* man of the area who protects the sons of the
poor and sends them to school, guards their savings and draws a profit
for them. He gives them work. He takes them to vote. He says a good
word about them to the police and defends them from arbitrary police
action. He receives the newspapers and comments on their stories.
In sum, he reflects civilization; he is the medium by virtue of which
the light of the city penetrates and slowly dominates the shadows of
the countryside.[40]

The "light of the city" of which Irureta Goyena speaks must be a
carefully selected one, for there are threats that come from that urban
world. "The idolatry of the factory does not permit the development
of the religions of the farm; as the fetishism of the city denies the noble
cult of the countryside."[41]

Batlle's anticlericalism and policy of *laicización* was a constant thorn
in the side of conservative interests. From the early poems of his youth,
which decried the false images of religion and opted for a naturalistic
atheism, Batlle relentlessly attacked organized religion, which in Uruguay
meant Catholicism. The following Easter Sunday article is typical.

The Resurrection

Today Catholics commemorate, with vigorous rejoicing, the resurrection of Jesus Christ. For them the birth of the Messiah is a miracle,
a miracle in which only the good Joseph could believe. His death,
or rather his resurrection, is also a miracle. With respect to the birth,
it would not take much effort for the town to start whispering, for
they naturally gossip about Mary's conjugal fidelity. As for the resurrection, even when children and old women still believe in ghosts,
reasonable men suppose that those that return from the grave after
dying can do so only because they have suffered a fainting-fit or a
morbid drowsiness.[42]

These attacks, and the legislation concerning divorce, separation of
church and state, and the granting of equal legal status to illegitimate
children, brought the wrath of organized religious groups and the more
conservative political forces. During the constitutional debates in 1916,
one opposition newspaper attacked Batlle for having led the assault
on religion and the family by allowing divorce "ad libitum—the road

to free love."[43] The textbooks used in the private schools, most of which were Catholic and which educated approximately 20 percent of all Uruguayans, never fail to remind the reader of Batlle's anticlericalism, and their general hostility is reflected in their treatment of his place in and contribution to Uruguayan history and politics.

Typical of these texts is a widely used secondary school history series written by a Dominican friar in the first decade of this century, updated, and still in common use five decades later. Its treatment of Batlle and his legacy is deeply revealing. The history of Batlle's second administration is covered in less than three pages, almost half of which are devoted to two footnotes on socialism and statism. The reader is reminded that Batlle returned from Europe in 1911 to assume his second presidency, "resolved to implement *socialism* in the country." Commenting on the doctrine of socialism and its principal exponents the author concludes:

(a) It is as reproachable as the passions that inspire it because it has its source in *covetousness, envy* and in *laziness.*

(b) It is *irrealizable,* because in order to establish the equality of property, it would be necessary to make all men equally strong, intelligent, hard-working and frugal.

(c) Its results would be *disastrous,* because everyone would work as little as possible if he did not have the hope of some day enjoying the fruit of his labor, and the neglect of work would bring about universal misery.[44]

A similar judgment is rendered on Batlle's nationalization program which is dubbed *"El Estatismo"* or *"Socialismo del Estado."* The author sees a parallel between such a program and the rise of totalitarianism in Europe.

The system can produce some material advantages, but it has the serious inconvenience of *suppressing competition* or *concurrence,* as well as *private initiative* and can easily degenerate into so-called *totalitarianism.* The totalitarian state requires, without admitting any form of legal opposition, the consolidation into one "block" of the totality of its citizens in the service of the state. The *fascist* and *national socialist* (Nazi) regimes, *suppressed* by the last war, were *totalitarian.*[45]

From a strictly political point of view, Batlle faced a great deal of opposition within his own party, and much of it was ideologically inspired. As early as 1911 Batlle was forced to take public opposition to the antilabor statements of his minister of interior, Pedro Mannini Ríos, who branded the labor movement as anarchist. Mannini Ríos was to break with Batlle two years later over the colegiado proposal. The Mannini faction, known as *Riveristas,* constantly fought against the collegial executive and would quickly join the anti-*Batllista* coup in 1933.

The election of only a minority of procolegiado delegates to the Constitutional Convention in July 1916 led to even greater dissension within the party. The *Colorado* president, Feliciano Viera, considered the defeat a vote against the entire *Batllista* social program. His remarks are known as the *Alto de Viera.*

> The advanced economic and social laws sanctioned during the last legislative periods have alarmed many of our supporters, and it is they who have denied us their support in the elections of the thirtieth. Very well, gentlemen: we will not advance further in the area of social and economic legislation; we will reconcile capital and labor. We have moved too quickly; let us make a halt in the journey. We will not endorse new laws of this nature and we will shelve those that are being considered by the legislative body, or, at least, if they are sanctioned, it should be with the agreement of the parties directly involved.[46]

Viera's position and the *Vierista* faction that grew up around him were not a passing phenomenon. Three years later, when Batlle sought to increase party discipline by requiring meetings of all nationally elected *Colorados* and the party executives in order to formulate policy, the reaction of Viera indicated a deep ideological hostility:

> The Colorado Party is not socialist; nor is it moving toward socialism. In my opinion, its mission, now more than ever is to reconcile capital and labor, without troubling either one, for the welfare of the nation depends on their harmony. . . . I heard about Sr. Batlle's program in all the proclamations of his followers. I am not familiar with the proposal so I cannot offer an opinion about it, but events that have occurred do indicate a tendency: above all, this kind of party organization leads to the "soviet."[47]

If Batlle was to find enemies in his own camp and among particular interest groups, he was to find a powerful and dogged opponent in Luis Alberto de Herrera. Herrera is the great figure of the *Partido Nacional* (*Blanco*) and the only politican considered Batlle's political equal. Leader of his party until his death in 1959 (outliving, and some would say out-maneuvering, Batlle by almost 30 years), he had a remarkable political career. He was actively involved on the *Blanco* side in the 1897 and 1904 civil wars; a deputy from 1905-1909 and 1914-1918; senator from 1938-1942 and 1946-1950; president of the National Administrative Council for 1925-1926 and a member until 1931; and a member of the National Government Council (the collegial executive) from 1955-1959. He was a critical participant in the 1933 coup; a chief architect of the 1934 and 1952 constitutions and of the *Blanco* electoral victory of 1958. A five time candidate for the presidency, he was the single most-voted candidate on several occasions.

Herrera's politics were nationalist in international affairs and con-servative and paternalistic in domestic affairs. He remained until his death a bitter opponent of *Batllismo* and its vision of society. Herrera's view of society was never completely expressed, although he wrote several volumes on Uruguay's independence and foreign relations. Per-haps the most widely cited example of his social philosophy involves his reaction to a 1912 *Colorado* proposal for an absentee land tax, the revenue from which would be used to eliminate matriculation fees at the university and establish *liceos* in the interior.

The *Blancos* opposed the legislation on several grounds, arguing, among other reasons, that such a tax would work a hardship on foreign capital. Herrera specifically addressed himself to the educational implications of the proposal, exposing himself to the charge that he was against the education of the poorer classes: "Enemigo que los hijos de pobres fueron doctores."[48] The parliamentary exchange does not justify such a harsh condemnation of Herrera, but it does expose his bias. As he put it:

> If the State increases the number of high school graduates by thousands, it would produce social disequilibrium. . . . A high school or college graduate or any other person with a title could not perform prosaic functions.[49]

This 1915 statement is frequently dismissed as taken out of context, yet in an editorial in *El Debate* in 1941, Herrera reiterated his position. He decried the overpopulation of the university, indicating that, while primary and even secondary and vocational training were a necessity, a university education was not needed by those now attaining it. In his opinion, the exaggerated commitment to higher education meant that many unqualified individuals were attending the university.[50]

The record of Herrera's proposals for social legislation indicates a dearth of such programs despite his pivotal position in Uruguayan political life. In his political testament to Herrera, Eduardo Victor Haedo, a key *Herrerista* lieutenant, seeks to attribute the lack of initiative on social reform to a rebuff of a Herrera-authored social package in the 1905 legislature—a weak excuse for fifty years of omission or active hostility toward programs of social change.[51]

Herrera tenaciously opposed the *Batllista* program. During Batlle's presidential administrations, Herrera and Carlos Roxlo collaborated on the newspaper *La Democracia* and took an editorial position consistently attacking the government's social and economic policy. Never sparing in its florid language, *La Democracia* condemned Batlle's divorce proposal as one which would legalize libertinism, *"que poco tardaría en surgir en mil formas depravadas."*[52]

By the late 1930s, Herrera's social conservatism was combining with a strong anticommunism. This attitude was reflected in his tacit support of Franco and the Axis powers. In a 1941 editorial, he attacked communists as being among those that conspired against the "bases of Uruguayan nationality," and called for the implementation of Article 70 of the 1934 Constitution which specifically outlawed organizations which acted in such a manner.[53]

In a similar vein Herrera attacked Uruguay's liberal immigration policies which he considered the door through which undesirable elements and radical ideas had entered the country. Realizing that Uruguay was a nation of immigrants, principally Italian and Spanish, Herrera made a careful distinction between those foreigners that "fit" into the society and those that did not.

We add that upon establishing this definition of foreigners, we are speaking of those who do not take root in what is ours either in social or traditional aspects. The case is far different, for example, with the

Spanish and Italian colonies that have so well adapted themselves to
our race and our customs.

Of our own and for our own.[54]

Herrera wrote many volumes on Uruguayan historiography, especially
as it related to the formation of the Uruguayan state. He and his followers
pointed to this literary output as proof of their nationalism. But *Herrerista*
nationalism never progressed beyond a formal juridical notion couched in
the historic symbols of state and an ideology of international legal
sovereignty.

Herrera was compelled to conduct his long political career in the shadow
of Batlle's political legacy. However, this does not mean that he could
not bend that legacy to his own needs and desires. Politics in Uruguay
after 1930 would be shaped far more by Luis Alberto de Herrera and
what he believed in than by the formal legacy of José Batlle y Ordóñez
and the vision of the Uruguayan nation that he hoped to fulfill.

The *Blanco* electoral victory in 1958 held out the possibility of significant change in national policy. Luis Alberto de Herrera's decades
old quest for control of the executive had finally met with success. His
personal triumph and the party's victory were helped substantially by
Herrera's alliance with Benito Nardone and his *Liga Federal de Acción
Ruralista* (LFAR), the official name of the political movement known
as *ruralismo*. This movement took shape and grew in strength as the
economic situation deteriorated during the 1950s. Herrera's alliance
with this movement and the sentiments it reflected are a clue to the
particularist response to the growing crisis made by the Uruguayan polity
and society. Some of the individuals who came to national prominence
through the movement had and are currently having a profound effect
on Uruguay's political life.

LFAR's founders originally perceived the movement as an interest
or pressure group acting as a spokesman for agricultural and livestock
interests. It was much later that *ruralismo* became a political faction
and considerably contributed to the 1958 victory of the National Party.
Its impact as an organized movement extended to the 1962 elections,
but with the death of its charismatic leader in 1964, *ruralismo* as a formal
organization all but disappeared. LFAR was a pressure group turned
political faction, and no movement has made better use of the
antagonisms in Uruguay between city and country, welfarism and

individualism, and the *Batllista* versus other images of Uruguayan society.

Ruralismo essentially grew out of the vision of a large ranch owner, Domingo R. Bordaberry, who as early as 1914 was attempting to organize the countryside into *ligas de trabajo*. In 1940, he established a newspaper, *Diario Rural*, and hired a young journalist, Benito Nardone, as its editor.[55] The newspaper was to remain a specialized interest group organ with a decided nonpolitical editoral stance until 1950. At this time, Nardone and Bordaberry broke with the powerful rural interest group, *Federación Rural*, over the question of the incorporation of more popular elements into the organization. *Diario Rural* now called for the creation of a new organization, the backbone of which would be made up of the small agricultural producer and rancher. It was not intended, however, that this new organization have a specific political affiliation.

In 1951 Nardone and Bordaberry established a radio station, *Radio Rural*, to act as a further stimulus in their organizational efforts. The situation was seen as a weapon through which they could organize the newly created *Liga Federal de Acción Ruralista*. The success of the station, however, went far beyond the wildest imagination of its founders. Nardone became a charismatic political figure and the first great media personality in Uruguay. By 1954 Nardone was capable of producing grand rallies in Montevideo which he dubbed *Cabildos Abiertos* in reference to the great rural protest demonstrations of the past. In the 1954 elections LFAR supported specific candidates in both of the traditional parties, but still refrained from joining the political fray in a partisan role. In 1956, however, LFAR had become disenchanted with its attachments to the *Colorado* party and especially to the Luis Batlle Berres faction within it.[56] Prior to the 1958 elections, Nardone led the organization into a completely partisan political position within the *Herrerista* faction of the *Blancos*. The movement became increasingly ideological in its persuasion.

LFAR's inclusion in the political factions that brought victory to the *Blancos* in 1958 thrust it into a prominent role in national political life. In the end, however, the movement did not live up to its promise as the spokesman of the forgotten small farmer or rancher. Nardone's electoral alliance which, on the surface, seemed so successful was more accurately a co-optation into traditional party politics and in this specific instance

into the most conservative political faction, the *Herrerista Blancos.*
The movement, which in its early days was seen as a healthy indication
of organization and mobility among the middle class ranchers and
farmers, was later to be seen in a much more pessimistic light. Solari felt
that the movement had been "converted above all into an instrument of
the upper classes and into a new mechanism to channel the interests of
the middle classes behind those of the former."[57] Germán Rama is even
harsher in his criticism:

> What is important is that this entity like the one before it has the
> interests of the large owners as its goal, and it is these owners who
> have effective control of the movement. The exacerbated nationalist
> keynote, the artificial heightening of rural-urban tension, and the
> deliberate detouring of the conflictual forces of rural society toward
> a criticism of the governors who represent the middle classes and
> urban bourgeoisie is, moreover, typical of rural fascism.[58]

Much of these criticisms, while being based on empirical political
observation, are really judgments about the movement's particular
ideological framework. Only one systematic attempt to study that ideology
is found in the Uruguayan literature. The Uruguayan sociologist, Néstor
Campiglia, analyzed the ideology of the movement through a content
analysis of a major series of Nardone's speeches, later published as the
volume entitled *José Artigas, 1764-1820.*[59]
Campiglia discussed several basic themes as indicative of the *ruralista*
ideology. These include the idealization of the *campo,* the deprecation
of the city, the exacerbation of the split between Montevideo and the
countryside, and the call for free trade. Further, Campiglia saw Nardone
dividing the world into in-groups and out-groups. In the latter category
one finds the Negro, the Indians, the Portuguese, and the colonial Spanish.
The in-group, epitomized by the Uruguayan national hero, Artigas, includes
the *gauchos* or *criollos.* The basic values of this in-group are the right to
property, the maintenance of order and security, and a deep religious faith.
The superiority of the *campo* for Nardone is best expressed in his
constant use of quotations from some of the principal founders of the
Federación Rural in 1918. Nardone was fond of quoting such men as
Carlos Reyles, Domingo Bordaberry, and José Irureta Goyena. Typical
of the type of material with which Nardone bombarded his listener or
reader is the following quotation from Reyles.

And very well: I do not vacillate an instant in saying, nor do I believe
it a paradox to assure, that the countryside has civilized the cities and
that from the fields will come one day, as from the fruit of a plant, the
autonomous civilization of Uruguay. And this is not only because the
country nourishes the entire organism of the nation with its rich
and vigorous blood, but because it enriches it morally and intellec-
tually with the vital juices of its energy and the spiritual strengths that
come from the work itself.[60]

Nardone followed the above themes to their logical conclusion. The
campo has been used and abused by Montevideo and what that city represents. Expanding on this theme of the urban-rural split, Nardone constantly spoke of the *Botudos*—the forgotten *gaucho* and small producer
of the countryside—being exploited by the *Galerudos*—the politicians and
industrialists of the city. It was this theme with which Nardone achieved
his greatest political success.

On the subject of political ideology, Nardone used a vociferous anti-
communism to attack *Batllismo* and all it stood for. The general anti-
communism of the movement is best exemplified by a volume published
in 1961 entitled *Peligro Rojo En America Latina,* which came complete
with a cover depicting a great white bear encircling North and South
America, and with its mouth and paws dripping with blood.[61] The volume
warns of communist expansion and imperialism and goes so far as to list
communist front organizations in Uruguay and detail the number of
Soviet officials found in the country along with the various cultural
activities of the Soviety Embassy and labor union activities of the Communist party. As the 1962 election approached, Nardone and his close
confidant Juan José Gari, a major exporter of wool tops, put out a magazine entitled *Mundo Americano,* whose chief slogan was *"con la democracia
y contra el communismo."*[62] In an extensive essay in this magazine, Nardone
set forth an image of a Christian America salvaging and reviving the democracy and unity destroyed by Marxism. As he sums it up:

Nationalism plays an important role after the war, when socialism
separates itself from Democracy in some countries such as Italy,
Germany and Russia, in order to form national-socialism in opposition
to the Social Democracy of Atlantic Europe and America.

The Second Great War of 1939 to 1945 destroys this movement and

the people look for the Democracy of 1846, of Considerant, with his
slogan: FRATERNITY and UNITY, which acquires definitive form
in the Encyclicals initiated with the famous *Rerum Novarum;* and
Democracy becomes integral because it helps man in all his development, in the family, in the nation and in the world, with *Quadrogessimo Anno* and *Mater et Magistrate* of Pope John XXIII.

It is Christian Democracy that erases the diabolical slogan of CLASS
STRUGGLE AND PROLETARIAN DICTATORSHIP, with the slogan
LOVE AND LIBERTY. . . .[63]

The religious theme expressed above is the constant *leitmotiv* in
ruralismo. In his most extensive political work, Nardone reminds the
reader that the socialist state stands on a tripartite foundation of socialism,
nationalism, and the anti-Christ.[64] The founders of socialism denied Christ
but espoused his ideals. They supplanted the victim of love with that of
the state. *"La armonía del capital y el trabajo—por la lucha de clases. Fué
una verdadera profanación."*[65]

Nardone carefully nurtured his Catholic image. A trip to Rome and
an audience with the Pope got first page coverage in *Diario Rural.* A trip
to the U. N. in 1961 was a great opportunity to have a much-photo-
graphed interview with Cardinal Spellman and receive an honorary doc-
torate from Fordham.

The natural enemy in Uruguay for Nardone's antistatist, antisocialist,
anticommunist, and pro-Catholic position was, of course, *Batllismo* and
its political heirs. It was through Batlle that the antithetical ideas of
socialism, statism, and anti-Catholicism were carried to Uruguayan soil.
"El Día sought a tradition which would carry it to the other side of the
Atlantic. A tradition which would enter through the port of Montevideo
and not through the footpaths of the countryside."[66]

Batlle is condemned for having bowed to anarcho-syndicalist workers'
demands inspired by the Third International in proposing his extensive
labor and social legislation. Nardone goes so far as to condemn Batlle for
forgetting his own position as an entrepreneur and proprietor. He takes
some of Batlle's own writings and presidential messages as proof of his
Marxist bent. Citing Batlle's call for state intervention in the unequal conflict
between workers and owners, Nardone concludes that such a stand is a
clear example of Marxist thought as found in *Das Kapital. "Es el mazazo
a la Libertad Económica y la proclamacion del Socialismo. . . ."*[67]

Citing Batlle's famous convention speech of 1925 concerning the gradual public ownership of the land, Nardone warns his audience that the idea was drawn from the Russian experience and that Batlle's call for public ownership is a brutally refined form of exploitation. "This is a brutal principle in which the State enchains the landowner. The latter, if he works his land, must pay tribute with his labor; if he rents it, the producer is the slave. The State is thus a new type of Feudal Lord."[68]

As Nardone saw it, Batlle was moving towards a totalitarian socialist state which is always a pagan state. As proof, Nardone offered the legislation on the separation of church and state, the laws passed banning religious objects in hospitals and schools, and the secularization of the names of all religious holidays. Batlle had replaced the private monopoly of economic liberalism with the official monopoly of the socialist state and at the same time attempted to destroy the religious basis of the society. The conclusion was obvious: "'El Día,' like all socialism throughout the world, had its source in The International, directed by the famous communist, Karl Marx."[69]

What was even more condemnable is the fact that Batlle's edifice was constructed on the back of the *campo*. His heirs at *El Día* had compounded the error by attempting to industrialize Uruguay while ignoring the essentially agrarian source of the system's wealth. The result was the disastrous economic situation in which Uruguay found itself.

The answer for Nardone lay in what he called *"libertad económica planificada."* Exactly what this would look like he never spelled out, but the call for the elimination of multiple exchange rates, the lifting of all restrictions on import and export, the return to a single member executive, the decentralization of the state industrial enterprises, the creation of a strong central bank and of a central planning agency indicate a certain lack of consistency in terms of a program. Nevertheless, certain points are clear. There would be a new reconciliation of capital and countryside which would seek to redress the grievances of the latter. However, Nardone's program at heart does not offer a picture of conciliation but rather one of equilibrium. Nowhere is this more obvious than in his discussions of wages paid to industrial workers.

The *Federal League of Ruralist Action* displays the principles of Planned Economic Liberty, which does not destroy anything, but reinforces the agricultural base and national industry.

In order to accomplish this it is also necessary to revise labor legislation, not with niggardly intentions, but with those of effective felicity. The ideological source of the International suffers from serious errors, which the Socialist State demonstrates throughout the world.

The happiness of the proletarian home does not lie in better salaries for example, but in good returns from salaries. It is worth saying that salaries must fit into the life of the country, taking into account cost and price, in order to maintain the equilibrium of the cost of living.[70]

Ruralismo dissipated as an organized movement with Nardone's death in 1964. *Diario Rural* closed but *Radio Rural* remained open. It continued to be run by Juan José Gari, using Nardone's widow as a sign of continuity. Some legislators who had begun their careers, under the auspices of *ruralismo* remained important in national and political life, and several of the *ruralista* proposals were incorporated into the new constitution. But the movement as an organized political force was finished or at least so it seemed. However, the crisis of the mid- and late 1960s produced certain unexpected benefits for those whose careers had been associated with *ruralismo*. Juan María Bordaberry, son of the founder of the movement, had become a senator under its banner in 1962 and was appointed minister of agriculture by President Jorge Pacheco Areco in the late 1960s. In a surprise move, Pacheco tapped Bordaberry for his successor as president in the 1971 election campaign. Bordaberry won and is currently president of Uruguay. This does not imply that *ruralismo* per se has made a comeback, but that the current executive authority in Uruguay has an ideological affinity to this movement and what it represented. The implications of this fact are apparent in recent events in Uruguay.

This chapter has analyzed ideological development in Uruguay in the first half of this century. Such an analysis of the symbol systems by which individuals comprehend politics in their society pointed up a dynamic tension between two countervailing systems in Uruguay. *Batllismo*, rooted in the politics and promise of the city, was an integrating nationalist ideology promoting the concepts of development, social change, citizenship, and equality. It was confronted from the very beginning, however, by a powerful counterideology, rooted in the countryside, dominated by landed agricultural interests, and espousing the concepts of tradition, hierarchy, and order. The *Batllista* vision dominated Uruguayan politics in the first three decades of the century and built the institutions which would color the society for decades thereafter. But the counterideology would slowly prevail and ultimately distort the structures created by its ideological rival. The dynamics of this process is the subject to which we now turn.

3
COPARTICIPATION: THE DEVELOPMENT OF POLITICAL INSTITUTIONS IN URUGUAY

The literature on the political process in Latin America is replete with attempts to construct models to aid in the analysis of the politics of the region. From Anderson's concept of "tentativeness" based on power capability and power contenders, to Horowitz's concept of the norm of illegitimacy, to Silvert's discussions of Mediterranean syndicalism, and to the more recent schema of the dependence theorists, the scholar is not at a loss for borrowing or adopting a schema to lend theoretical significance to the case at hand.[1] In the matter of Uruguay, however, these general frameworks seem to weaken, and the ever elusive marriage of the particular case to the theoretically general becomes more difficult. Anderson not only does not include Uruguay in the case studies in *Politics and Economic Change in Latin America,* but the country is not even listed in the index. Horowitz is forced to develop an entirely separate category for Uruguay, happily or unhappily describing it as an example of a "quasi-legitimate" state. The dependence theorists, concentrating as they do on exogenous rather than endogenous factors, are quick to incorporate Uruguay into the British sphere, but are conspicuous in never going beyond nominally assigning Uruguay to the dependence category.

There are several reasons for the difficulty encountered in putting Uruguay into a particular theoretical box. Empirically, it just didn't seem to fit—at least until recently. Theoretically, the problem has been perhaps even greater, for its image as a democratic, plural society dedicated to social justice and welfare put it closer in ranking to the accepted model of a developed Western European country: a nation with a highly competitive two party system and a long history of vigorous parliamentary independence.

The principal argument of this chapter is that Uruguay developed a mechanism for containing conflict that was more successful and, at least on the surface, more open, plural, and "democratic" than the mechanisms implied in the standard models. However, the nature of the mechanism, its historical development, and, most significantly, its symbolic and hence social meaning led ultimately to a failure of the Uruguayan political process, a failure that places Uruguay closer to the "standard" case in Latin American than has heretofore been appreciated.

The term that best describes this politics is coparticipation (*coparticipación*). The term is widely used in the political literature, journalism, and everyday conversation of Uruguay. However, it is usually narrowly confined to a description of the formal presence of the opposition party at the ministry level or in the directorship of the state corporations. As the term is used here, it includes the more narrow connotation, but seeks to go beyond it to capture the deeper meaning and process of Uruguayan politics. Indeed, it will be argued that it is a manifestation of the failure of that politics.[2]

Coparticipation has a long history in Uruguay. Formally practiced since 1872, its roots go back to the liberal-conservative civil wars to which Uruguay, like its Latin American sister republics, was heir after independence. The exhausting civil war known as the *Guerra Grande* (1846-1851), saw an opposition government established outside of Montevideo -- which effectively controlled the entire interior of the republic and laid siege to Montevideo for eight years. It was out of this struggle that the clear definition of the two traditional parties, *Blanco* and *Colorado*, emerged, and the tone of a *Blanco*-dominated interior and a *Colorado*-dominated capital was set.[3]

The tenuous peace established after the *Guerra Grande* was broken frequently. Full-scale civil war erupted in 1870 when the *Blancos* felt that they could no longer accept what they considered the exclusivist government of General Lorenzo Batlle. The conflict lasted well into 1872, and the peace settlement established the precedent for the so-called *pactos políticos* that were to become the sine qua non of politics in Uruguay. The 1872 settlement called for the naming of departmental (provincial or state) political chiefs (*jefes políticos*), in a manner that would insure that "haría recaer los nombramientos en ciudadanos que por su moderación y dema calidades personales, ofrecieran serias y eficaces garantías."[4] What this meant in practice was that politics in four departments (San José, Canelones, Florida, and Cerro Largo) would be controlled by the *Blancos*. Given the politics of the period, this meant that the *Blancos* would be guaranteed the senatorships and deputyships in the national legislature from these departments. The geographic control extended to the *Blancos* was thus being used to institutionalize and guarantee their participation in government. Their representation at the highest level in the general assembly assured that they would have at least some say in the selection of the president who, under the 1830 constitution, was chosen by the general assembly. The 1872 agreement was to be the first of a long series of party pacts which, whether verbal, written, or formally constitutionalized, would be the major method of formal institutional change in Uruguay. Coparticipation would be the major mechanism and theme within that politics.

By the 1890s the country was still divided into the *feudos partidos* established by the earlier agreement, but the *Blancos* were becoming apprehensive. They still controlled four departments, but in the interim years eight new departments had been established, and therefore their representation in parliament had been considerably diluted. In addition, the *Colorado* president from 1890 to 1894, Herrera y Obes, was beginning to practice a rather significant form of party government which was taken to imply the imminent breakdown of formal *Blanco* participation in national politics. *Blanco* uneasiness was further increased by the changes in the administration of elections sponsored by Herrera y Obes and passed in March of 1893. These changes obviously implied a lessening of *Blanco* electoral control even in those departments where they were entitled to the office of chief of police.

> As for the composition of the Electoral Juntas, according to the project made law on March 24, 1893, these will be set up so as to give decisive influence to the government. They will be composed of the President of the Economic-Administrative Junta, the Tax Director, the Administrator of Department Income, the Police Chief, three delegates from Congress elected from incomplete lists and three citizens whose names will be drawn by the other members of the body.[5]

Blanco discontent did not cease with the subsequent Borda administration. In 1896 the party abstained from the general elections, declaring:

> The previous president declared that there should be, and it was necessary that there be, an official directing influence (*la influencia directriz*

oficial). The current president, far from reacting against such nefarious practices, demonstrates, on the contrary, a tendency to use the same methods and without any signs of misgiving, shame or respect, which a magistrate should always take into account, stated in his message at the opening of the present legislative period that: "No party can truthfully say it lacks public representation, or that through government action is restrained from exercising its rights, and that all citizens enjoy the fullest guarantees of protection from the ruling institutions of the Republic." These are the words with which the first magistrate attempts to extend confidence among the people. They involve an entire electoral program of the most evil significance.[6]

The stage was thus set for a violent confrontation which broke out in March of 1897. The revolution was led by the last of the great rural *caudillos*, Aparicio Saravia. Saravia soon offered a peace settlement demanding *Blanco* control of eight departments. The demands were rejected by the *Colorados*.

After several more months of fighting, a pact was finally agreed to. Under the terms of the *Pacto de la Cruz*, six departments were unofficially placed in *Blanco* control and the president was at least morally obligated to seek electoral reform. The net result was an extension of the geographical division of the country between the two parties. The unfortunate implications of such an agreement were not lost on some of the commentators of the period.

They asked for and desired, *at whatever price,* the end of the civil war in order to end its horrors and material harm. They did not realize that to divide the country into two party fiefdoms was to make revolution and civil war inevitable, for it in fact created a state within a state.

Peace and public order are not possible without a unified national government in charge. A country with two governments, one *de jure* and one *de facto,* is a political and social monstrosity.[7]

As Aldo Solari has commented, several of the articles of agreement in the 1897 accord read like the treaties made between European nations when dividing territory after a war. One of the articles even went so far as to establish the right of a citizen of one party to leave a department, the control of which has been granted to the opposition party, and be indemnified for such a move.[8] For Solari:

> The fact that this normative system has been reproduced in the agreements of the traditional Uruguayan parties shows that instead of a national collectivity, two party collectivities existed, which were the psychological referents of their adherents, far more than nationality.[9]

The uneasy truce established in 1897 lasted until 1903, although minor disturbances did take place. However, the election of José Batlle y Ordóñez created severe consternation among the *Blanco* leaders. First, Batlle had repeatedly stated, as a senator and as the leader of the popular wing of his party, that the 1897 agreement should not be understood as a permanent arrangement. At the time of the agreement Batlle indicated that the granting of control of several departments to the *Blancos* was not a perpetual concession. In his opinion, it was valid for the life of the administration that had agreed to it; otherwise the country was condemned to perpetual division.[10] Subsequently, Batlle made clear that the coparticipation established by these pacts ran counter to his own philosophy of party government. Upon losing the presidency of the senate in 1901, he declared:

> The politics of coparticipation of parties in the government is always the result of extraordinary occurrences: such was the situation at the start of the honorable and constitutional government of Sr. Cuestas. All Colorados must respect the agreements he made and, for the honor of the party, want them to be strictly complied with. For the next electoral struggle there will not be compromises since it is not logical for the normal functioning of institutions to have anything but party government, for it is not possible for a victorious political collectivity to realize its ideals through the intervention of men from other collectivities, except when a community of interest and a total sincerity of purpose exist. The goal of the next election must be party government.[11]

Later, as president-elect, Batlle sought to clarify his position on the whole question of coparticipation. In doing so, he seemed to make a distinction between the natural right of the opposition to be part of the national government and the more detrimental type of agreement that he

saw as the result of bad faith and bad bargaining between the two traditional bands.[12]

Perhaps it was inevitable that civil war would again erupt, given
Batlle's propensity for party government. Indeed, the proximate cause
of the conflict was the sending of federal troops into *Blanco* departments,
an action that the opposition felt was in direct contradiction to the implicit understanding of the 1897 pact. The 1904 civil war culminated in
the complete victory of the *Colorado* and, hence, *Batllista* forces. It may
be considered the triumph of the city over the country, but the dialectic
between the two would not end. What had ended was the geographical
form of coparticipation of the last quarter of the nineteenth century.
There were several reasons for its demise.

The large influx of Spanish and Italian immigrants, most of whom
settled in Montevideo or its environs and were gradually being incorporated into the *Colorado* party, had shifted the power balance to
Montevideo. The conflicts in 1897 and 1903-1904 may be seen as attempts by rural interests to delay or protect themselves from the shift.
However, the insertion of Uruguay into the international (British) market,
the extension of the railroads,[13] and the pacification of the countryside
so ably carried out under Latorre, all pointed to the inevitable geographic integration of the country. The differences between Montevideo
and the interior still existed, but de facto geographical division was no
longer applicable or feasible.

The peace agreement ending the war called for general amnesty and
contained a pledge that the ruling *Colorado* party would seek electoral
reform. The man who was to lead the *Blanco* party for the next fifty
years, Luis Alberto de Herrera, called for a constitutional reform that
would strengthen the legislature, more carefully define the power of the
president, and allow for a more decentralized administration. These
proposals were obviously an attempt to soften the *Blanco* defeat and
find some new way to insure the continued political viability of the
party. Herrera specifically called for "the coparticipation of all
Uruguayans in the management of public affairs."[14] The proposal
was rejected, but obviously the question of coparticipation was not
settled. The form it would take involved certain electoral reforms and
new institutional mechanisms.

Batlle's first administration (1904-1907) and that of his hand-picked
successor, Claudio Williman (1907-1911), was a period of relative civil

calm. The *Blancos* continued to seek electoral reform and, despite some limited success in this area, remained a definite minority force in the legislature.

In 1904 an electoral measure was passed which attempted to fulfill the peace agreement and ameliorate the winner-take-all nature of the majority vote system. Under this legislation the *Blancos* were entitled to one-third of the seats from a department as long as they obtained at least one-third of the vote in that department. The mathematics of the legislation were heavily weighted in favor of the *Colorados* since only seven of the nineteen departments had a number of seats divisible by three. The *Blancos* quickly christened the new legislation the *"ley de mal tercio."* The inequity of this law was remedied under Williman in 1907, when a new piece of legislation allowed for minority representation of one-quarter or one-third of the seats in each department, provided said minority was able to get one-quarter or one-third of the vote in the department.

In 1910 the inevitable, as far as the *Blancos* were concerned, occurred. Batlle's presidential candidacy was announced and his statement of acceptance to his party convention left no doubt as to the continued viability of the old *Blanco* fears.

> I consider the theory of the politics of coparticipation erroneous when it means that the ministries should be constituted in part by men whose tendencies and opinions are contrary to that of the Executive. Under these conditions a rapid and fruitful labor is impossible, for it is controlled by men who have different and contradictory plans. The effort should be unified and not weakened by divergent or opposing tendencies. The Executive would lose the quality that must be characteristic of its office: rapid and effective execution. It would be converted into a principally deliberative body, in which the spirit of our Constitution would be subverted, for it assigns deliberative functions principally to the legislature.[15]

The announcement of the candidacy was met by two *Blanco* attempts at revolution, both abortive. The party announced its intention to abstain in the election, which at this time was considered an act preparatory to insurrection. In an attempt to placate the opposition, a new far-reaching electoral law was passed. The literature on electoral behavior contains a long-standing debate on the impact of electoral laws on parties and politics in the political system. It is not necessary to go into what has at times became a chicken and egg debate, but it is evident that certain features of the 1910 legislation did much to shape the two-party system in Uruguay.

The law further expanded the representation of minorities found in the 1907 legislation.[16] It established a limited form of proportional representation. Indeed, in the departments of Montevideo and Canelones, it reached effective proportional representation. The most important aspect of the new legislation, however, was its introducton of the mechanism of the "double simultaneous ballot." Under this system the vote cast for a candidate accrues to that candidate and his party at the same time. The separate list of candidates (*sub-lemas*) within the same party (*lema*) would be added together to determine the total vote of the party. In essence, a simultaneous primary and general election takes place. It is obvious that such a mechanism enhances splintering within a party, but allows such splintering to take place without really jeopardizing the party's total performance in an election. It may also be argued, however, that the mechanism allows for a certain amount of party unity, at least at election time. Though it was not immediately apparent, the consequence of this legislation would be all too real by the 1920s. The use of the double simultaneous ballot, the electoral legislation built-up around it, and the subsequent adoption of direct voting for the president, had important political consequences within this simultaneous primary and election framework.

The *Blancos,* whose threat of abstention got the legislation passed, still felt it was inadequate. They abstained in 1910, and indeed they did not actively participate in elections again until 1913, a fact which goes a long way in explaining the success and far-reaching nature of the *Batllista* legislation passed during this period. The *Blanco* perception of its role, expectations, and view of co-participation during this period is adequately summed up in a 1910 political pamphlet written by one of the leaders of the party, Washington Beltrán.

> We Batllistas and Nacionalistas are at opposite poles. The Batllistas believe they should govern through the Colorado Party, or rather, through their inner circle. The Nacionalistas believe that the Republic is the patrimony of all the Uruguayans and that the government should be national. . . . The Nacionalistas defend a proportional system, the

only one capable of conceding representation to all the sound forces
that give energy and life to the national organism. The Batllistas consider jobs as sinecures with which one compensates friendship or
political relationships. The Nacionalistas, on the contrary, struggle
so that these jobs will be granted without regard to affiliations, with
only experience, talent and virtue being taken into account. The
Batllistas insist that the army be Colorado. The Nacionalistas believe
that an institution supported by public funds must be genuinely
national.[17]

During the middle of his second term, Batlle stunned the opposition,
and even those closest to him within his own party, by proposing a
radical alteration of executive power in Uruguay. The heart of the proposal was a call for a collegial executive. Under Batlle's original plan,
the executive (*Junta de Gobierno*), would consist of nine men, one
member to be elected each year after an initial election in which all nine
would be chosen.

It is clear from the proposal that Batlle was attempting to insure the
hegemony of his party. The election of the first junta would be a winner-
take-all affair. Given the strength of the two parties at the time, it must
be assumed that the *Colorados* would have won. The provision for one
replacement every year meant that the *Blancos* would have to win five
consecutive elections in order to gain a majority control of the junta.
Additionally, the proposal empowered the junta to veto legislation and
return it to congress with whatever emendations it saw fit. In order for
congress to override such a veto, its vote would have to bear the same
percentage as the veto vote within the junta.

One can easily imagine the strong objections that the opposition
party made to such a proposal. What was less predictable was the enmity
aroused within Batlle's own party. Within two weeks of the publication
of the proposal, eleven *Colorado* senators signed the formal declaration
indicating that they would delay the establishment of the constitutional
convention necessary for the implementation of any change.

The Senators that have signed below, considering that a constitutional
reform must be an unequivocal expression of national sovereignty
and, given the indisputable fact that the political atmosphere does not
permit it to take place under those conditions, reiterating their feelings

of solidarity with respect to the present political situation and con-
vinced that they proceed in the interest of the country, declare:

That they will only vote for the indispensable laws necessary for the
reform if these laws offer new and ample guarantees for the popular
vote, and with the understanding that elections for a National Con-
stituent Assembly Constitutional Convention take place in 1914 on
a date and under conditions set by the legislature. Montevideo, March
17, 1913.[18]

There are two intriguing questions here: (1) why did Batlle make the
proposal, and (2) why the mass desertion within his own party? The first
question has never been satisfactorily answered in the literature. The
debate engendered by the proposal led to some interesting arguments.[19]
Those in favor principally argued that the presidency had been an office
of increasing power and the abuse of power. Thus, a plural executive
could eliminate some of the dangers inherent in a single individual's
aggrandizement of power. The argument had a nice tone, but it was
Batlle himself who, in a 1910 message, argued that the remedy to an
all-powerful executive should be found in a strengthened congress based
on proportional representation. Why the new and radical proposal?

Batlle's program was issued at a time when constitutional reform was
being favored by both parties. Two previous legislatures had voted for
it. The mechanism for establishing a constitutional convention had been
agreed to, and *Blanco* abstention made it apparent that the *Colorados*
could dominate such a reform process. However, Batlle was serving out
a second term and could not succeed himself. He undoubtedly wished
to insure his control of the party and protect the programs and institutions that had so recently been created. There is also no doubt that he
was deeply impressed by the Swiss collegial executive system, and the
proposal for such a mechanism for Uruguay certainly was not out of
keeping with his history of bold and imaginative experimentation. It is
also true, however, that Batlle's fear of displacement within the party
and of resistance to his program within his own party was quite real.
The rapidity with which an opposing *Colorado* block was established
after the original announcement of the proposal would indicate that a
growing resistance to Batlle's leadership had been long in process. Clearly,
Batlle was attempting to protect his social and political program.

Batlle's proposal was in many ways a huge tactical error. It effectively isolated his faction within the *Colorado* party and gave the *Blancos* a rallying point. In addition to congressional resistance, many of his ministers resigned. Here was the opportunity for the conservative opposition to rally its forces.

The opposition of the *Colorado* senators prevented a formal vote on constitutional reform for the two remaining years of Batlle's administration. His successor, Viera, took office and pledged to fight for the *colegiado*. In the interim, the *Blancos* had decided to enter the electoral arena and, by the time Viera was inaugurated, they had managed to capture twenty-two deputyships out of eighty-nine but were not represented in the senate. A group of pro-*Batllista* senators now controlled that house and thus the procedure for constitutional reform was finally approved. The procedure on elections for constitutional convention delegates included obligatory registration, vote by illiterates, and a secret ballot for the first time in Uruguayan electoral history. Both sides, recognizing the importance of this election for future political institutions in Uruguay, rallied their forces. The *Blanco* party found a new source of support in the *Federación Rural,* which had organized shortly before, partly due to the adverse legislation that had been recently pushed by Batlle's administration. Lending added support to the opposition were some of the key figures within the *Colorado* party, especially Pedro Mannini Ríos, who led a scathing attack against the *Batllista* reform proposals and the delegates who were sworn to fight for those proposals.

As the election approached, Batlle presented a new constitutional project which sought to placate the opposition. The new proposal, however, was essentially no different from the old one and did not decrease the struggle surrounding the upcoming election. In fact, this much more detailed plan for constitutional reform indicated a strong bias in favor of a highly centralized control of the country.[20]

The election took place on July 30, 1916, amidst the highly charged debate. The vote was a clear defeat for Batlle and the *colegiado:* a clear majority of anti-*Batllista* delegates was elected.[21]

The effect of the defeat was chilling. More than the idea of the *colegiado* had been rebuffed; there was a sense that the entire thrust of Batlle's policy and program had been rejected by the voters. Indeed, in a watershed speech to the party convention, referred to in Chapter 2, President Viera declared a halt—the so-called *Alto de Viera*—to innovative and controversial social and political legislation.[22] As one newspaper incisively observed, the disagreement involved the entire thrust of the *Batllista* program.[23]

Batlle did not give up the fight, however. He organized his strength within the legislature and was determined to force some sort of compromise upon the delegates at the constitutional convention. Among Batlle's maneuvers was a threatened third presidential term and legislative maneuvering demanding that a successful plebiscite on the new constitution should require a majority vote of all those eligible and not merely all those voting. Such legislation, given a *Batllista* abstention, would have doomed any constitutional reform.

The convention itself started off with the self-exclusion of the pro-*colegiado Colorados*. Nevertheless, the debates were far-flung and sometimes heated. Several interesting and important discussions took place. Along with a general agreement on the question of proportional representation, the mechanism of the double simultaneous ballot was well received, which was not surprising at all in view of the internal splits that had taken place in both parties. Typical of this favored attitude is the following observation:

> As is known, the system of proportional representation is by itself an abstract mathematic electoral method, which designates or expresses numeric quantities. It does not express or represent ideas, social interests, unions, public necessities or political parties.
>
> For these reasons the principle of the double simultaneous vote must be combined with it, i.e. the vote for one candidate and for ideas, for political parties, for interests, and even for unions if you wish. Only in this way can aspirations and social interests be considered represented.[24]

The majority of convention debate was taken up with the proposal for a collegial executive and other questions of central or decentralized administration. Suggestions of a social nature usually were the province of the minority party delegates, especially the socialists. Emilio Frugoni, founder of the Socialist party, led a constant but vain struggle to incorporate legislation on social and land reform into the new constitution. Perhaps his proposal on land reform was the most interesting:

> A permanent fund, formed with progressive land taxes, shall exist

for the expropriation of large estates, which will be divided. . . .

Neither the State or municipalities will be able to give away public land.

In accordance with necessity and social interest, the law will limit the number of hectares the individual citizen can acquire.[25]

It is interesting to note that much of this sort of program was incorporated into the *Colorado* party platform during the 1920s. At the time of the proposal by Frugoni, however, they were easily defeated.

The fact of the matter is that the convention, despite some interesting debate, was working in the shadow of the *Battlista* abstention and the constant maneuvering by Batlle. After several months, ideas had been aired but any real compromise was far off. Then on June 16, 1917, the dam broke. The *Colorados* and *Blancos* had reached a private accord, the so-called Pact of the Eight, concerning the new constitution.

The reaction from the anti-*Batllista Colorados* was severe. They generally denounced the pact as an antidemocratic agreement made behind closed doors between two specific factions of the traditional parties.[26] Nevertheless, with the support of the *Batllista* wing of the *Colorados* and the Herrera-controlled *Blancos,* the acceptance of the private agreement was assured on the floor of the constitutional convention. The remaining work of the convention was in reality a pro forma ratification of the agreement.

The constitution resulting from the pact created a bicephalous executive. The presidency was not eliminated, but its functions were limited to the conduct of foreign relations and the preservation of internal order and external security. A *Consejo Nacional de Administración* was created to deal with all the other activities of the state. It consisted of nine members with a two-thirds representation of the majority party and one-third of the minority. The president and the council were to be elected by popular vote, the former serving for four years and the latter for six, with the council renewable by thirds every two years. In addition, the secret ballot, proportional representation in the chamber of deputies and senate, and the formal separation of church and state were established.

Many *Blanco* politicians accepted the pact, and hence the new constitution, because they honestly believed that they had succeeded in a now two decades old quest for institutional coparticipation. Administrative power was now in the hands of a nine member council in which they were guaranteed a one-third representation even if they never became the majority party. In a remarkable book, *Ante la neuva constitución,* Martín Martínez, a principal *Blanco* jurist and politician and a member of the original group of eight that agreed to the pact, presented a strong argument for its acceptance.

In Chapter 7, entitled *"La Coparticipación,"* Martínez argues that the *Consejo Nacional de Administración* must be considered a secondary achievement when compared with the strengthening of parliament, electoral guarantees, and municipal autonomy. Nevertheless, he feels that minority representation on the *consejo* represents the birth of a true interdictive power for the *Blancos:* "[T] he role of the minority in the Council of National Administration [*sic*] can be similar to that of the same minorities in the legislature—critical watchdog more than collaborator."[27]

Coparticipation for Martínez does not imply a politics of fusion. Its significance lies in the attempt to distinguish between politics and administration. Under the new charter, important aspects of administration had been at least separated from direct presidential control, if not influence. This was crucial for an antistatist like Martínez. In arguing for the acceptance of the pact before the constitutional convention, he described the growth of the state as follows:

> Many years ago Carlos María Ramírez compared the President of the Republic and his nineteen department political heads to an octopus which, with its tentacles, absorbed the civic energy of the country, or at least immobilized it. Today these tentacles number a hundred because the state is no longer only a politician and policeman; it is an impresario in all kinds of functions as well; it is an intendant, electrician, prepares to be a railroadman, a colonizer, and I don't know how many other things.[28]

The role of the state could not be rejected, but for Martínez it should be depoliticized.

> Coparticipation must take place in all the secondary spheres of public administration, in posts that do not affect political guidance. This is the practice in the great model nations. What does the administration of welfare or roads have to do with Blancos or Colorados, *Whigs* and *Tories?*[29]

The Martínez conception of a depoliticized administration and an interdictive power for the minority ran up against the reality of bureaucracy
and politics in Uruguay. Both parties realized that a key to the electoral
struggle of the future would be, in part, the public employee. The question of public employment and the manipulation of such employment as
election time drew near was a strong issue during the constitutional
debates. The lack of accurate statistics on the subject makes exact analysis difficult, but some evidence of the importance of the phenomenon,
even as early as the first quarter of the twentieth century, is available.

In 1900 the total number of public functionaries was estimated at
20,000.[30] This was at a time when there were less than 75,000 registered voters and the individual vote was public. Although new legislation
and electoral laws saw the size of the electorate quintuple over the
next fifteen years, the question of the public employee and control of
his vote would still remain a crucial political issue. Martínez cites a
figure of 40,000 in 1918 for all public employees including the army,
police, central government administration, and decentralized state
enterprises.[31]

Several sessions of the drafting committee on the constitution were
taken up with the question of a politicized public payroll. During a debate
in the full assembly, the socialist delegate Mibelli raised the issue by commenting, "Our country is perhaps one of those most singularized by the
phenomenon of a growing bureaucracy. It is a real illness which has been
given the name of 'employmentmania.'"[32] All political factions realized
that the constitutional acceptance of the state enterprises and the proposals for an ever-increasing role for this type of organization meant that
the control of employment in the public sector would be a powerful
political tool. *Blancos* and *Colorados* lent their support to a deliberately
vaguely worded constitutional article on the state enterprises because it
meant that each would have the possibility to control at least part of
the spoils of administration. The *Colorados* felt that it fit comfortably
into the scheme of industrial socialization, while the *Blancos* felt that
an independent state system of enterprises would at least give them the
possibility of preventing the opposition from monopolizing public employment.

Mibelli's statement on employment was followed by a direct appeal
to the *Blancos* to support the minority parties in an attempt to nationalize public employment by adopting a civil service examination
system.

Public employment, under a system of competitive examination, would be for all. If one were to interpret the famous phrase that the Nacionalista Party proclaimed in its street demonstration and in its newspaper, "The fatherland is for everyone," a correct interpretation would be that public employment, the nation's jobs, should be for all its citizens. I hope that the Nacionalista Party, so amply represented in this Assembly, will keep this formula in mind so that it can be definitively realized through competitive exams. . . .[33]

This proposal was rejected by both major parties, and the wording of Article 100 on *entes autónomos* was deliberately vague. The directorships of the *entes* would be plural in nature and it was understood that, since these directors would be appointed by the *Consejo Nacional de Administración,* a minority voice would always be in the hands of the *Blancos,* who would thus control some patronage. In essence, then, the coparticipation inherent in the adoption of a semicollegial executive system was being extended to the public employment sector.

The literature on development places much emphasis on institution-building and institutional differentiation and specialization. The structures and institutions in existence in Uruguay by the time of the 1919 constitution, and those created and built in the ensuing decades, helped give Uruguay its image and reputation as a modern system. I do not share the optimism of that perception. The institutional coparticipation of the 1919 constitution may be seen as a step forward, but the politicized bureaucracy and administration were not. If the state is to act as an impersonal arbiter and all citizens are equal before it, then the instruments through which the state acts must not be comprehended or used in a parochial political manner. Unfortunately, this was not to be the case. Each of the two traditional parties more and more saw the state and its apparatus as something to which they were entitled. This essentially antinational attitude was justified or rationalized in the name of coparticipation.

The sharing of power without the concomitant vision of the state as the synthesizing artifact in society does not make for effective national institutions. The record of Uruguayan political life since 1917 and especially since the early 1930s indicates that the trappings of modern society are not enough without the emphatic vision necessary for true national life and the courage to make budding national institutions viable.

The period immediately following the installation of the new constitution on March 1, 1919, saw a further estrangement of the *Batllista*

faction from other forces within the *Colorado party*. Batlle sought to
ameliorate the split by preserving some semblance of party discipline.
The mechanism through which he sought to accomplish this was his call
for an *"Agrupación de Gobierno."* According to the plan, a commission
consisting of the president, *Colorado* counsellors, all *Colorado* deputies
and senators, and the members of the National Executive Committee of
the party would meet periodically to discuss and formulate the party
program. The proposal met with extensive opposition from the anti-*Batllista*
factions.[34] Batlle responded with a call for the completion of the party's
social program, reminding all who would listen that there was much
work to be done in order to eliminate social injustice.[35]

The president and council elected in 1919 were selected by the
general assembly under a transition procedure established in the constitution. The following year, elections took place to renew one-third of the
council, and the vote was 93,000 for the *Colorado* party and 85,000 for
the Nationalist (*Blanco*) party.[36] The election was much closer than
anyone had expected and was a portent of the electoral equality of
the two parties throughout the 1920s.

The first public election for president took place in 1922 and the
result was a *Colorado* victory, but a narrow one. José Serrato defeated
Herrera by a vote of 123,000 to 117,000.[37] The dual executive and
the partial renovation of the legislature and the council every two years
meant that there would be eight national elections between 1922 and
1934. The closeness of these elections highlights two crucial aspects of
Uruguayan politics: the nature of party coalition and electoral laws, and
the frenetic search for votes.

The 1910 election law had made it possible for different factions of
the same party to combine their votes in an election provided that they
ran under the same *lema* (title or slogan). While this aspect of the law was
not of real importance at that early date, it became crucial with the splits
in the parties from 1916 on . In effect, by the 1920s the *Colorado* party
was really split into several parties—Batlle's, the *Riveristas* under Mannini
Ríos, and the *Vieristas*.

The switch of civil strife to the electoral battlefield made honestly
regulated elections and clarified electoral laws a political practicality if not
necessity. Thus, an electoral law was passed in 1924 that established an
electoral court (*Corte Electoral*) to oversee all aspects of the electoral

process. In 1925 another law was passed recognizing the factionalization of the parties and regulating the use of party *lemas* and *sub-lemas*.[38] The significance of this legislation may be seen in the fact that the *Blancos* gained the majority on the council in 1925 by a national vote of 119,000 to 115,000, due to a splinter group within the *Colorados (Partido Colorado Radical)* that refused to run under the *Partido Colorado lema* and thus cost the party the 7,000 votes that would have meant a victory instead of a defeat. Reversing this occurrence, the *Blancos* under Herrera lost the presidency in 1926 by a vote of 141,581 to 140,055, due to the defection of a liberal group that left the *lema* and polled 3,844 votes.[39] In both of these instances, despite some cries of fraud, there was a willingness to accept the outcome—no mean accomplishment in the Latin America of the 1920s.

The close victory margins and the frequency of elections made for a frenetic search for votes. It was soon apparent to all that political patronage would now make the difference between victory and defeat. The growing state bureaucracy, which increased 50 percent in size between 1920 and 1930,[40] was both a source of votes and a payoff for the loyalty of party factions. Hard evidence of the scope and extent of such political patronage is difficult to obtain. We do have, however, the observations of important officials of the period. Luis C. Caviglia, a *Colorado* member of the council during the 1920s, reported:

> One will discuss whether, in accord with doctrine, the appointment of a janitor can be considered a party act, but as is public and notorious, that is exactly how it is considered. It is useless to pretend that the author of the declaration has wished to exclude from the so-called Colorado solutions precisely one which while not constituting the principal function of a government, is, definitively, the principal preoccupation of those that govern, to the point of making high administrative positions difficult and disagreeable.[41]

One finance minister resigned in protest over the lack of a standard of merit or seniority in the promotion of public employees.[42]

The debate over the regulation and control of public employment soon touched on the entire question of coparticipation. The Nationalist party, led by Herrera, constantly argued that coparticipation implied a fusion politics which meant that neither party should control public

employment. Batlle took strong exception to such a point of view and
stated that the representation of the minority party on the national
council did not mean a fusion politics, but only meant that there would
be minority representation in national government. He carefully dis-
tinguished between the coparticipation which was the forced result of
the dictatorships of the nineteenth century and the institutional coparticipation of the twentieth, but he continued to insist that this in
no way implied that the majority party did not have the absolute right
to rule under a system of party government.[43]

José Batlle y Ordóñez died on October 20, 1929. That same month
the stock market crashed in New York. Both events had important
political consequences for Uruguay.

Until 1929 Uruguay had been riding the crest of a worldwide
economic expansion. Imports had tripled in the period from 1900-1930
and government expenditures had shown a similar growth.[44] With the
onset of the world economic crisis, Uruguayan exports fell precipitously.
From 1930 exports fell from one hundred million to seventy-eight million pesos.[45] Beef exports dropped 60 percent and wool exports dropped
65 percent.[46] The crisis soon saw the increased organization of interest
groups along class lines. The large banking and commercial interests formed
the "Committee of Economic Vigilance," and in the same year a new
national labor confederation was founded.

The presidential elections of 1930 took place in the midst of this
growing economic crisis. Compounding the situation was the loss of
Batlle's leadership and ability to unify a highly fragmented *Colorado*
party. A split developed even within the *Batllista* wing, with the majority
supporting Gabriel Terra for the presidency, but those closest to Batlle
(the *El Día* group) supporting the candidacy of a relatively unknown
neutral *Colorado*. The political maneuvering became almost unbelievable.
The *Blancos,* suffering from their own internal division, offered two
presidential candidates, Herrera, and André Lamas.[47] Terra won by
15,000 votes.

During the first year of Terra's administration, division within the
two parties increased and the economic situation deteriorated rapidly.
Terra, elected as a *Batllista,* soon turned his back on this tradition and
began to campaign strenuously against the council form of government,
stressing its inefficiency and cumbersomeness in the face of the economic
situation. Terra's abandonment of the *Batllista* program was not out of

character. In a 1928 prologue to the volumes *Socialismo en el Uruguay,* by Juan Rodríguez, Terra offered the following judgment on Batlle's policies:

> We have brought into practice a great part of the program that Karl Marx formulated in his postulates of international communism and that he counseled to the proletariat of all countries—that they should move forward once they have violently taken public power and should make themselves into dictators.[48]

At this time there was a growing realignment of forces between the two parties, with Terra and the *Riveristas* seeing themselves allied with the *Herrerista Blancos* against the orthodox *Batllistas* and "Independent *Blancos.*"

The results of the realignments and maneuvering was an undeclared war for control of the state bureaucracy and patronage. Several legislative proposals were offered, the most blatant of which called for the appointment of public employees by their political party affiliation under a formula of proportional representation determined by the voting strength of the parties in the last election.[49] The proposal was actually legalized in October of 1931. The law called for the establishment of a seven-man board of directors for each of the state *entes* and the appointment of all employees and laborers by party affiliation in proportion to the strength of the two parties in the previous election. A separate act passed at the same time called for the appointment of day laborers to all public works projects in the same proportional manner.[50]

At its baldest, this legislation implied the total politicization of public employment and bureaucracy in Uruguay. Thanks to the *Batllista* programs, the state was indeed a vital force in Uruguayan economics. In 1933 the operating budget of the state *entes* was 36 million pesos out of a total national expense budget of 58 million pesos.[51] The period from 1930-1932 showed an increase in public employment from 30,000 to 52,000.[52] It is not surprising that the legislation has always been labeled the *"Pacto de Chinchulín"* (Pork-Barrel Pact).

One of the features of the pact was *Blanco* acceptance of a state monopoly on oil refining and the production of alcohol and cement. In fact, the law creating ANCAP (*Associación Nacional de Combustibles, Alcohol y Portland*) was passed during the same session in the chamber of deputies as the law on public employment. ANCAP was to become the single largest state enterprise in terms of budget and number of employees. Its creation was hailed as an act in the public interest and defense of Uruguay. Although the original proposal was clothed in such a justification several years before, it is obvious that the intent of its creation had little to do with the defense of the public interest. The *Pacto de Chinchulín* and the creation of ANCAP were manifestations of a desperate search for advantage that was soon to mire Uruguayan politics in dictatorship. For these agreements were not really between the two major parties as much as between factions within each of the parties. The 1931 agreements were actually directed against Terra and Herrera. The Terra-Herrera alliance at the time of the coup in 1933 was, among other things, directed against the opposing factions in both parties.

The 1933 coup was carried out in the name of constitutional reform. Terra had found a hostile majority in the legislature which was unwilling to call for constitutional amendment or give him approval for a consultative plebiscite. Thus, after months of building tension and threats of insurrection, Terra dissolved the legislature and the National Administrative Council and declared himself in sole authority.

The constitution promulgated under the Terra dictatorship of 1934 had the ideas and models of the 1930s as one source of its intellectual foundation. Given Vargas in Brazil, the 1932 coup of Uriburu in Argentina, Mussolini in Italy, and José Antonio Primo de Rivera in Spain, it is not surprising that corporatist ideas and institutions were part and parcel of the discussions surrounding the new constitution. Several clearly corporatist projects were submitted, one of which called for a "corporative assembly" made up of the principal professional and economic branches of the economy. These and other overtly corporatist solutions were rejected. This is not to say, however, that there was not strong sentiment in favor of such a solution. In an honest appraisal of the situation, the constitutional commission of the constitutional convention summed up its reasons for not submitting any corporative projects:

In Uruguay, where democratic ideals are profoundly rooted in the mass of citizens, it is evidently impossible to speak of establishing a "corporative government" as in other countries. Perhaps some day a happy formula will emerge which permits the conciliation of democracy with the indubitable advantages of a firm organization of labor by the state. But such a formula is yet to be found.

Therefore, the constitutional commission has not attempted to study plans for the corporative organization of the state. It has considered the republican and democratic organization of the Uruguayan state, with its powers constituted by means of universal suffrage, beyond discussion.[53]

Admiration for some fascist solutions was publicly stated, however. A favorable judgment on the Mussolini regime was offered by Dr. Ghigliani, a Terra lieutenant and major architect of the coup. He argued that the changing conception of liberty employed by the Italian state under Mussolini was a lesson that should not be ignored.[54]

There are many factors that hindered the birth of a full-blown falangism in Uruguay, not the least of which was the leveling effect of the *Batllista* ideology and social program. However, the basic reason for the rejection of an overtly corporatist solution is to be found in the ideology of the two parties and the balancing mechanisms still operative between them. A key *Herrerista*, Martin Echegoyen, rejected a corporatist parliament on the following grounds:

> What do the parties do with social interests? They seek a certain equilibrium between them, a minimum harmony—reconciled at times in favor of certain interests, but never in a manner which totally obscures or mutilates the others that make up the social framework. We might say that the parties effect a stabilization of social forces and of the interests of the state.

> As one commentator has said, if interests are exclusively represented, they would oppose each other without having anything in common to bring about a reconciliation. In sum, the parties avoid more dissolution than they cause.[55]

In effect, Echegoyen argued that to represent interests directly would mean the destruction of the traditional parties. The survival of the two traditional parties was, from the point of view of Realpolitik, a necessity. The two factions that had engineered the coup did not trust each other, yet neither could destroy the other. Once again, the constitution would be a pact between the parties, more exclusivist than in 1918, but still a pact. The ideological justification would be the historic role of the two parties.

> Confronted with reality, we have had to perceive the existence through-out history of two great traditional parties, that have represented and represent the overwhelming majority of public opinion. This reality should not be, nor can it be, ignored.
>
> With the collaboration of these two great parties, the business of government will be easy and lasting, because it will rest on the base of a permanent majority, homogeneous in governmental action. . . .[56]

This sentiment was reiterated by Herrera.

> There is simply the deep desire to stay close to these historic groups and to permit the one victorious in the urns to rule, while the other controls its action, according to the situation that events dictate. . . .
>
> What we have desired is simply to affirm the principle that in the government of Uruguay, exclusivism is not permitted, public positions are open to all, and those that govern are obliged to seek collaboration from the sectors that have sizeable public support. That is the whole question.[57]

Here lies the crux of the matter. The models of fascism, falangism, or corporatism favor a one-party system. One of the common threads of the Mussolini, Vargas, Primo de Rivera, Franco, and Perón regimes was a tendency toward the identity of the ruling party with the state. The symbols of Uruguayan politics, the history of its political institutions and of its mechanisms for political change made a one-party political solution impractical if not impossible. The two-party mold could not be broken. Corporatist politics in Uruguay were therefore never as obvious as in the other systems. Indeed, it was unique in that it was built upon a highly competitive two-party model. It is not suggested that politics in Uruguay is therefore any less corporatist in its intent or its effect, but only that it is less superficially corporatist in formal structure.

The 1934 constitution eliminated the dual executive and reestablished the single executive office of the president. In addition, proportional representation was eliminated in the senate with that body divided equally between the two coup factions (15-15). Executive power was to be shared between the president and a strengthened council of ministers consisting of nine members. Parliamentary approval of ministerial nominations insured that three of the nine ministries would belong to the minority party, i.e., Herrera's faction. The net effect was to preserve a collegial system.[58] The old council had been eliminated, but the structure of the new senate and the guarantee of minority ministerships implied close cooperation and shared decision-making. One can argue that the real difference between the 1918 and 1934 constitutions was that in 1918 coparticipation was between the two parties, but in the 1934 charter it was restricted to one faction in each of the parties. Further evidence of this fact can be found in the new articles on the state *entes* and decentralized services. These activities now were run by boards of three or five members, and these boards had to be approved by the council of ministers and three-fifths of the senate. Thus, Herrera's faction was guaranteed minority representation on all directorates. In essence, the 1931 pact had been informally constitutionalized.

There were several aspects of the 1934 constitution that did hint of a falangist bias. Perhaps the most interesting is Article 52 on labor.

It is the duty of every inhabitant of the Republic, without prejudice to his liberty, to apply his intellectual or physical energies in a manner which will redound to the benefit of the community, which will endeavor to afford him, with preference to citizens, the possibility of earning his livelihood through the development of some economic activity.[59]

Work (labor) is seen as a duty. This is the way to translate *deber* and the way the official Pan American Union text of the constitution translates it. The wording of the article and its choice of terms is remarkably similar to the 1927 Labor Charter in Italy and echoed in the Spanish Labor Charter of 1938.[60] Preference for job opportunity was given to citizens, and the framers made it even more apparent that some citizens were more equal than others. Thus, while citizenship could be suspended for participation in organizations that "through means of violence tend to destroy the fundamental bases of nationality," such action could only be taken against naturalized citizens.[61]

The constitutional plebiscite was held on April 19, 1934. Out of 422,000 eligible voters, 222,000 voted in favor and only 10,000 voted

against. Abstention was over 40 percent, due to the refusal of the
Batllista-Colorados and Independent *Blancos* to participate in the
ratification process.[62]

In addition to the corporatist and exclusivist aspects of the constitution, the legislation and institutions created by the Terra regime betray
its bias. On July 12, 1934, in conjunction with its protectionist economic
policy, the government created a *Comisión Honoraria de Contralor de
Cambios.* This organization was transformed several months later into a
commission with direct control over imports and exports. Representation
on the commission was restricted to leaders of the industrial and business
communities, which were organized by economic function. Much the
same type of organization was found in the *Consejo Superior de Trabajo*
which was established one week after the coup.

The regime also passed laws amending the penal code to include crimes
against the state and several pieces of legislation which attempted to control the nature and function of strikes. A printing law passed in 1935
restricted the press in matters concerning state security, the image of
the state, or the support of individuals found guilty of acts against the
state. A rather curious decree, issued May 15, 1934, authorized special
Italian courses in the *Escuela Superior de Guerra.* In education, control
of secondary schools and university preparation was removed from
university auspices and put in the hands of a newly created autonomous
ente.

The regime's reaction to the Spanish Civil War was also indicative of
its ideological position. As the Spanish situation intensified, sentiment
in Montevideo seemed to be clearly in favor of the republican side,
and demonstrations to that end were planned. It was obvious to most
that these demonstrations, in addition to conveying support for the
Loyalists, were clearly anti-Terra in their implication. Consequently, legislation was passed requiring previous authorization for any public act
concerning the politics or activities of any foreign nation (June 2, 1936:
Ley 9, 565).

Despite the promulgation of the new charter, the political climate
remained unstable amid the continued opposition and electoral abstention
of the *Batllistas* and Independent *Blancos.* World politics and potential
realignments in Uruguay caused consternation among the coup forces.
Consequently, they moved quickly to solidify their advantage. In May
1934 a new electoral law, *Ley de Lemas,* was passed which put the

slogans and symbols of the two traditional parties in the hands of those factions that had majority representation in national office.[63] Of course, this honor fell to Herrera in the *Blanco* Party and Terra in the *Colorado* Party.

As the 1938 elections approached, the Herrera-Terra axis sought to prevent any coalition party or "Popular Front" from challenging their position. Thus, a series of constitutional amendments was passed by the General Assembly in 1936 and approved by plebiscite in 1938.[64] These amendments prevented an electoral coalition from forming among the opposition while allowing Terra and Herrera to combine their electoral forces if they so chose. As it turned out, an antigovernment coalition was not seriously attempted and Terra chose not to combine his *Colorado* strength with Herrera. Instead, Terra offered the *Colorado* voter a choice: his son-in-law, Alfredo Baldomir, or his father-in-law, Eduardo Acevedo Díaz. Once again, the *Colorados,* having a better sense of the voting implication of the double simultaneous ballot than the *Blancos,* were offering the voter a chance to choose among *Colorado* candidates. The result of the election was a huge *Colorado* victory. Their two candidates, Baldomir and Acevedo, polled 121,000 and 97,000 votes respectively, while Herrera, Herrera, as the only major *Blanco* candidate, polled 107,000.[65]

On the occasion of the fourth anniversary of the 1933 coup, the *Blanco* leadership made a series of speeches that are helpful in measuring the ideological perspective of the group. The year was 1937, and the threat of "Popular Front" and communist expansion was a constant theme in all the speeches. But behind the rhetoric on the issue lay an attempt to explain and justify the events of March 31, 1933. The collection of speeches is perhaps the most synthetic statement of the *Blanco* supporters of the regime and their views on state and society. Those views are delineated in a speech by the *Blanco* representative, Pedro P. Berro.

> Therefore, situations exist in which paramount reasons of hygiene and social order (with regard to public services) justify the nationalization of certain activities. But the crazy, unchecked statist ends by choking the sources of production, dampening the development of the economic forces of the country, and removing all incentive for private capital and labor.
>
> What can be done in the face of the complexity of the phenonomenon

that modern life brings, overturning classical principles of the economy?
. . . we know that the old individualism proves insufficient to resolve
the ever more difficult and intricate situations that international
exchange and the overproduction derived from the formidable development of modern technology incite. But we also know, at the same time,
that official direction of the economy also leads to grave errors and
confusion.
Socializing without nationalizing—here is the economic formula of
the future. Neither the old individualism, nor the obsessive forms of
State socialism.[66]

The familiar corporatist theme of the reconciliation of labor and capital,
the recognition of an economically active state, the rejection of classical
individualism and collectivized socialism are all here, along with the now
traditional rejection of the *Batllista* program. In another discussion Roberto
Berro praised the return of a "sincere nationalism instead of exotic
ideologies."[67] He offered a corporative image of a Uruguayan society in
which individuals, while remaining loyal to their traditional party, will
"march toward the future in parallel lines."[68]

As mentioned above, the 1938 election, taking place amidst a degree
of economic improvement, indicated that the Terra-Herrera alliance was
no longer an equal partnership. The *Colorados* received 61 percent of
the vote and the *Blancos* only 32 percent. The newly elected president,
Alfredo Baldomir, son-in-law of President Terra and his chief of police
in Montevideo at the time of the 1933 coup, did not consider the
Herreristas as equal partners. Additionally, the increased voter turnout
indicated, among other things, that the *Batllista* wing of the party was
no longer capable of keeping the faithful in a position of abstention
vis-a-vis the government.[69]

The outbreak of World War II and the general sympathy for the allies
exhibited by almost all groups, with the exception of the *Herreristas,*
was a signal to Baldomir that he could break the alliance without a threat
to his own position. By 1940 he was publicly soliciting suggestions for
constitutional reform. A reform commission was established in the
congress and in 1941 a constitutional junta of the political parties was
formed. The 15-15 composition of the senate, however, doomed any
attempted proposals. The Herrera group opposed a reform which was
indeed intended to destroy the equal participation of the two coup

factions. They warned that the reform was exclusivist in nature and could compromise the peace of the republic.[70] In addition, the procedure for amending the constitution, established in 1938, made a legal route exceedingly difficult. As the situation deteriorated and the election scheduled for March 1942 approached, the hint of coup in the air became heavier and heavier. When it took place on February 21, 1942, with the acquiescence of all groups except the *Herreristas,* it was considered a foregone conclusion and was accepted more readily than its 1933 counterpart.

Baldomir dismissed parliament and invited all factions to join in the deliberations of a *Consejo de Estado* to act as a legislative and consultative body. On May 29 Baldomir presented his constitutional reform proposals to the Council of State, decreeing these proposals constitutional and indicating that they would be considered promulgated if they were ratified (by the majority of those voting) in a plebiscite to be held the following November.

The constitutional changes were no surprise, being essentially those proposed in the 1940-42 period. They consisted of a few amendments which did away with the 15-15 senate and the imposed coparticipation in the cabinet and directorships of the state *entes.* The senate was to now be elected by proportional representation, with the entire country as a single constituency. Ministers would still have to be approved by the General Assembly, but enforced minority representation in the ministries was deleted. The same would *not* hold in the appointment of directorships to the state enterprises. Essentially, then, the enforced Herrera-Terra coparticipation was eliminated and the abstaining groups of the 1934-42 period, the *Batllistas* and the Independent *Blancos,* were reincorporated into electoral and political life.

The last of the above accomplishments required intricate legal maneuvering. The *Ley de Lemas* of 1934 had put control of party slogans, labels, and symbols in the hands of the *Terristas* and *Herreristas.* A 1939 amendment to this law had declared that the use of emblems and slogans belonged to the majority of the party, but had, through some rather byzantine language, allowed the abstaining *Batllista Colorados* to return to the fold with a *Batllismo sub-lema.* In an effort to gain Independent *Blanco* support for the 1942 constitution, Baldomir had decreed an amendment to the 1939 law (July 13, 1942: *Ley* 10, 192) allowing the Independent *Blancos* to run under their own *lema* by simply adding

the word "independente" to the title *"Partido Nacional."*[71] This assuaged
the faction for the moment, but was to become an important point of
contention in the 1952 constitutional debates.

As for corporatist elements in the 1942 constitution, there was a
strong attempt to implement the *Consejo De Economía Nacional,* the
creation of which was authorized in section IV of the 1934 constitution.
The constitutional reform commission in the General Assembly discussed
the establishment of such a body and suggested that it include the representation of economic interests and interests of a professional and
social character. In addition, it was considered desirable that the body be
divided into functional sections, grouped "on the basis of large industrial
activities, such as livestock, agriculture, construction, transformation,
extractive industries, credit and monetary exchange, commerce, transport,
real estate, the liberal professions, science, and the arts and culture."[72]
The list was meant to be suggestive, and it was left to the legislature to
determine the exact functions and composition of the body.

Not unexpectedly, several of the minority parties on the left vocifer-
ously opposed the project. Communist party representatives indicated
that an already complicated reform should not be burdened with a
project of such a clearly fascist nature and one which would establish
corporative representation.[73] Ultimately, an article empowering the
legislature to create a *Consejo de Economía Nacional* was included in the
1942 constitution, but that power was never used. Thus, the formal
language of corporatist politics did not enter the constitution, although
politics and public activity betrayed a continual subnational and particularist bias.

The result of the entire experience from 1931-1942 was the infusion
of the budding national secular institutions with a fragmented, particularist style. A second and equally pernicious result was to establish
the traditional parties, their emblems and symbols, as a device to be
manipulated by key elites. The coparticipation established by the 1933
coup was justified by a false and exclusivist image created by and for
men and groups whose policies and politics were and would remain the
most overtly corporatist of any faction in Uruguayan politics. The frequent and closely fought elections of the 1930s, in a period of economic
expansion, had dampened some of the *particularismo* of Uruguayan
politics. The economic decline and coup obligated the political elite to
return to an ideology and rhetoric of party traditionalism. The require-

ment of identification with party in order to identify or demonstrate loyalty to nation was now to be a tenet of Uruguayan politics.

The style set in the 1930s was to become the predominant mode of politics in Uruguay. The invocation of the two parties as the *patria,* the failure to move beyond the incomplete set of institutions created by Batlle, the coldly pragmatic fluctuation between types of national execu tive power, and the eventual economic standstill have their roots in the politics of the 1930s.

In order to understand Uruguayan politics in the late 1940s and early 1950s, one must look at the industrial boom that took place between 1935 and 1955 and especially after World War II. Aside from the meat packing industry, there was little in the way of true industrialization in Uruguay before Batlle's death in 1930. With the exception of one or two major textile enterprises, industry in Montevideo was of the artisan or handicraft variety. If the great success of *Batllismo* was its incorpo- ration of the middle class into national political life and the integration of the immigrant and popular class into Uruguayan society, that society as of 1930 was not an industrialized, mechanized one, and few people were performing skilled industrial functions.

The industrial growth which began in the late 1930s changed this picture. Fortunately, we have some good quantitative evidence of the change. The 1930 industrial census indicated a total of 6,570 industrial establishments employing 54,143 workers. The figure had grown to only 65,900 workers by the time of the industrial census of 1936. However, by 1948 the figure had exploded to almost 110,000 and became 141,000 by 1952. The growth of industrial employment between 1936 and 1956 was as follows: [74]

	Workers	Employees
1936	79,725	10,463
1956	195,413	40,123

During these same two decades, electrical consumption increased by some 500 percent while petroleum consumption increased by some 1,000 percent. [75] Industrial production more than doubled between 1935 and 1955. [76] Similarly, the total value of manufacturing production measured in 1961 pesos had grown from 2.25 billion in 1936 to 3.8 billion in 1948, and 7.5 billion by 1955. [77]

There is also good indication that a large percentage of workers were employed in large manufacturing establishments. The 1961 industrial census for Montevideo, where approximately four-fifths of all industrial activities in Uruguay take place, showed that some 49 percent of the workers were employed in plants employing 100 or more individuals. These large establishments represented only 1.6 percent of the total number of industrial enterprises in the city.[78]

This post-World War II industrial growth reflected, as it did throughout Latin America, a conscious attempt at import substitution.[79] Key areas of expansion involved the food processing, textile, and clothing industries. Of some 200,000 industrial workers in 1960, 56,000 were employed in food and beverage industries, some 46,500 in clothing and textile industries, and some 15,000 in the key service industry of transportation.[80] These industries were highly protected through tariff, subsidy, and exchange mechanisms. Their growth and expansion were heavily tied to the fiscal and monetary policies of the government—a *Colorado* government run directly or indirectly by the most important *Colorado* politician since José Batlle, his nephew Luis Batlle Berres. To a greater extent than is generally realized, the policies and leadership of Luis Batlle Berres in Uruguay parallel that of Perón in Argentina, but without the army and some of the unpleasant facets of *Peronismo*. His commitment to protected industries and a subsidized agricultural sector created much enmity with the livestock interests.[81] Unquestionably, Batlle Berres was the benefactor of industrialization in Uruguay. He created the most powerful political faction in the country (List 15) with the support of the industrial urban and working class. This class benefitted from the relationship: from 1948 to 1954, while the cost of living rose some 58 percent, wages in 31 trade unions were up 110 percent.[82]

The neo-*Battlista* ideology of Luis Batlle Berres is apparent in his defense of state enterprises and the nationalization of the remaining British-owned utilities. Batlle Berres, like his great-uncle, saw the entreprenurial role of the state as a defense against *"grandes consorcios internacionales."*[83] The buying of the water works and remaining private railroad lines was defended as the culmination of the peaceful socialization begun by José Batlle.[84] The style and policies of Batlle Berres were anathema to the rural-backed *Blancos* and the conservative, preindustrial welfarism of the orthodox *Batllistas*. It is in this context that the 1952 constitutional reform should be understood.

The motives behind the sudden agreement on the need for constitutional revision are complex and varied. The orthodox *Batllistas,* now led by Lorenzo and César Batlle, sons of "Don Pepe," had proposed the implementation of a totally collegial executive (*colegiado integral*) during the 1946 electoral campaign. For this faction, the achievement of the *colegiado* was almost a religious dream.

The *Blancos,* led, as always, by Herrera, found themselves as far from presidential power as ever after the 1950 elections. Herrera had received 92,000 more votes than his nearest *Colorado* rival, but the total vote showed the *Colorados* winning by the huge margin of 433,000 to 255,000. The aging leader, now thwarted in his sixth try for the presidency, was sorely tempted to support a collegial reform that would guarantee him at least part of the executive branch.

In addition, the rift between Luis Batlle and José Batlle's sons was widening. "Luisito" started his own newspaper in 1948 (*Acción*) and backed a separate and victorious list in the 1950 election. He served as president from 1947 to 1950 after the death of Tomás Barreta. The victory of his list in 1950 and the threat of *continuismo* that this implied were probably too much for both the more conservative *Colorados* and the *Herrerista Blancos.*

The 1951 constitutional reform debates centered on the question of coparticipation. The discussion followed the usual political lines. The orthodox *Batllistas,* perhaps best typified during the debate by González Giúdice, an almost religious disciple of Batlle and coauthor of *Batlle y el Batllismo,* trotted out the historic arguments in favor of the *colegiado.* The *Herreristas,* attempting to justify their zigzags on the issue, argued that the 1934 constitution had created an effective coparticipation and that what was needed now was once again the constitutional guarantees of such participation. In the words of one *Blanco* leader:

> I have declared and reiterated that we do not admit nor do we wish coparticipation as a good-natured act of the President, of the one who governs, but that we want it as a right, by constitutional mandate. I have been constantly trying to emphasize this concept, and today I see by the explanations of Deputy Batlle Pacheco, that his father (Batlle) had the same thought.[85]

The small ideological parties and some dissident elements within the

Blancos and *Colorados* strongly opposed the reform. They all harshly attacked the politicization of administration and the implied monopolistic coparticipation of the two traditional groups. A socialist deputy argued that the worst feature of the new constitution was its enforced coparticipation between the two traditional parties. This coparticipation was not meant to bring about effective control in government but was to be a device to distribute bureaucratic posts.[86]

Under the new constitution the executive consisted of nine members, with six seats going to the majority party and three to the next most voted party. Equally significant was the arrangement concerning the directorships of the state services and industrial enterprises. In a constitutionalization of the 1931 *Pacto de Chinchulín*, the five-member boards of the *entes autónomos* were divided three to two between the two major parties, thus assuring the division of patronage between *Blancos* and *Colorados*.

A succinct and systematic condemnation of the new constitution was offered by the *Unión Cívica* (a Christian Democratic party) representative, Venacio Flores. Submitting a dissenting report as a member of the constitutional commission of the Chamber of Deputies, Flores argued that the proposed change "subordinates the constitution to the parties and pushes the government away from institutions toward party committees."[87]

Another member of Flores' party attacked the ideological foundations of the pact which formed the basis of the 1952 reform.

> For me, the primordial end of the reform is given in the terms of the pact subscribed to by the parties. There is a phrase in it that has a transcendency and a profound significance. When the accord or party pact refers to the dispositions that are required in order for votes to be accumulated by *lema,* the test indicates: ". . . in this manner the cohesion of the parties that historically have influenced and influence the unfolding of the life of the nation will be maintained." This phrase encompasses a much debatable position—one which is controvertible, but is nevertheless a position, and one which is reiterated although a little more obliquely in many discourses and manifestations.[88]

The almost total coparticipation that resulted from the 1952 constitution represented a meeting of minds among the more traditional power groups in the society and effectively dampened the "Luisito" phenomenon and some of its implications. It is more than coincidental that the 1933 coup and subsequent constitution created a coparticipation that effectively halted the nationalist and reformist program of José Batlle y Ordóñez, while the 1952 reform was to brake the industrial populism of Luis Batlle Berres, again through the mechanism of coparticipation.

The inability to import during World War II and the boom created by the Korean War gave Batlle Berres the resources with which to build and sustain the protected industries and pay for the welfarism that he expanded to the urban lower class. But, by the mid-1950s, it was apparent that the surge in construction and industrial development was built on a weak foundation, the agrarian sector. There are several key factors in this weakness. First, the artificial protection of the new high-cost industries, coupled with subsidy and price supports for certain agricultural products, was in great part paid for by the export sector. The continued strength of this sector was therefore essential to the protection and growth of the industrial sector and the capital intensive agricultural sector. Second, given the small internal market in Uruguay, the limited economy of scale that would be practiced in Uruguayan industry necessitated the optimum growth of the internal market, especially interior urban centers. The stagnation of the livestock sector limited the growth of this internal market. Third, industrialization had increased Uruguay's dependence on the importation of fuel, capital equipment, and raw materials, and had created a built-in necessity for the purchase of these products. Stagnation in the export sector, which prior to significant industrialization would have been met by a concomitant reduction in imports, now implied a disastrous slowdown in industrial production and capacity. In other words, industrialization, contrary to what was believed, actually increased Uruguay's dependence on the primary sector of the economy.[89]

The deteriorating economic situation was not helped by internal political squabbles. The split between Luis Batlle and the more conservative *Colorados* led to a deeply divided collegial executive, while economic stagnation helped produce a spiraling inflation. The cost of living doubled in the 1955-1959 period, a situation that Uruguay had never before come close to experiencing.[90] This inflation caused a drop in the value of the peso from 3.77 to the dollar in December 1955, to 9.58 to the dollar in December 1958.[91] At the same time the cost of living increased at the following rates: 1956—6.7 percent; 1957—14.7 percent; 1958—17.5 percent; and, 1959—39.5 percent.[92]

By the time of the 1958 elections, the urban masses saw their purchasing power diminishing rapidly, the agrarian sector was organizing itself politically to reverse what it considered discriminatory government policies, and the *Colorado* party was deeply split. The 1958 election subsequently swept the *Blancos* into executive power (control of six of the nine seats on the *colegiado*) for the first time in ninety-three years.

It was clear to most individuals that new policies, offering effective national solutions, were needed. The *Blanco* victory held out the illusion that such policies would be forthcoming. But, what should have been apparent, and quickly became so, was that the nature of coparticipation and its effect on government institutions and industrial enterprises had long since precluded the exercise of an impersonal nation-state capable of exercising power in an effective national manner.

The election was a response to a growing crisis, but the results of the election were a continued particularistic and clientelistic politics. The net result was that the state corporations would now be run by boards of three *Blancos* and two *Colorados* instead of three *Colorados* and two *Blancos*. In spite of some abrupt changes in monetary and fiscal policy which quickly proved ineffectual, things would proceed as before, except that the nation was headed for more serious economic, political, and social problems.

4
CLASS AND NATION
IN URUGUAY

The heart of any corporatist system is the particularist columns or pillars
into which it compartmentalizes society and the class-bound politics in
which it holds the individuals found within these pillars. Indeed, corporatist politics is subnational (or antinational) to the extent that it denies
the function of an impersonal synthesizing state to which all individuals
can pledge their ultimate loyalty. Obviously, the above description is
ideal-typical; there is slippage from the pure form in any empirical case.
The columns are simply not that neat, individuals find themselves in
more than one pillar, varying degrees of individual mobility do exist, and
true "nationals" do emerge. But systems that fall into the general family
of those that are corporative demonstrate an acute inability to create a
viable and innovative nation-state in which there is a reciprocal loyalty
between the state and its citizens. While the citizen may give the state
his loyalty, the state cannot give the citizen its loyalty, for it cannot act
as his impersonal arbiter.

When we turn to Uruguay, the use of a corporatist template seems,
at least at first, to be in error. This homogeneous European middle
class country, with a long tradition of civil two-party politics and, despite
its fifteen years of economic decline, one of the highest standards of
living in Latin America, hardly seems a proper example of class-bound,
subnational, corporative politics. The "Switzerland of South America,"
a "utopia," an "integrated society" are just a few of the terms used by
foreign observers. Even the Uruguayan observers constantly remind the
reader of the gifted and unique aspects of Uruguayan society. Thus, in
his volume, *Las Clases Medias en el Uruguay,* Antonio Grompone concludes:

> The social structure of Uruguay is characterized by the dominance of
> the middle classes; in number, in economic activity, in mentality,

problems, ideals, Uruguay is a middle class country. . . .

Synthesizing then, Uruguay is, as we said before, a country in which members of the middle class, urban as well as rural, and those who have direct ties with governmental activities, predominate in everything. This explains the idiosyncracies of their mentality and the social interest that appears in the resolution of particular types of conflicts—political, economic and social.[1]

Real de Azúa, combining the physical with the social, paints the following picture:

"Country of closeness," we have sometimes called our nation: "physical closeness,"—a small area and a nature (as our greatest poets say) within man's reach; "social closeness,"—everything is relative, if you will, but effective, if you compare life style and concentration of wealth with those of other Latin nations.[2]

These observations, foreign and domestic, are partially valid; yet at the same time they are incomplete, or, what is worse, misleading. Insofar as they are valid, they remind us of the unique qualities of the Uruguayan case. Insofar as they are incomplete, they force us to seek a more inclusive and theoretically significant explanation. Uruguay was an integrated society with a high degree of equilibrium. It now finds itself in a pathological stasis: the middle class city-state, that "integrated utopia," has disappeared. What has replaced it is built on a legacy of corporative, subnational politics.

In this chapter we will argue that the ideological and institutional matrices prevailing in Uruguay have been and are incapable of providing for the economic integration and maturation conducive to the degree of social mobility associated with a fluid class situation. Additionally, it will be demonstrated that horizontal (geographic) integration has been incomplete, if not a failure. The historical split between Montevideo and the interior has been exacerbated, and the city-state that is Uruguay has been unable to overcome the economic and political tensions traditonally associated with this split.

The failure to integrate Montevideo and the interior into a viable national community is apparent in a wide range of indicators. Uruguay had one doctor for each 843 inhabitants according to the 1963 census, a figure which compares favorably with many developed nations. Yet, the figure for Montevideo was one doctor for each 489 persons, while outside the departmental capital the ratio was one to 2,145 persons.[3] Infant mortality statistics show much the same disparity. While the overall figure in the 1955-1959 period was 49.9 per 1,000 births, the figure for Montevideo was 33.6, while in the interior it was 61.6. Significantly, comparing the 1950-1954 period with that above, the mortality rate increased from 33.6 to 38.6 in Montevideo and from 50.6 to 61.6 in the interior.[4] Nationwide figures for 1960-1966 show no improvement.[5]

The concentration of industry in and around Montevideo is extreme; 78 percent of all industrial production takes place in or around the capital.[6] The port of Montevideo is the site of almost all the export and import trade. It is not surprising, therefore, that a late 1950 estimate concluded that over 8,700 of Uruguay's 14,200 professionals exercised their functions in Montevideo and that this figure did not make allowances for those individuals who, while formally practicing in the interior, live in Montevideo.[7]

A wide disparity exists between lfestyle in Montevideo and the interior. While 65 percent of Montevideo households report the use of a refrigerator, the figure for the urban interior is 49 percent and falls to 30 percent for communities of 250 to 2,500 dwellings. While 95 percent of Montevideo households had radios, only 77 percent of interior households had them.[8]

Demographically, the usual effect of urbanization and adoption of a middle class life style is apparent in the differences between the metropolitan center and the interior. While 25 percent of the Montevideo population is 15 or under, one-third of the population of the rest of the country falls into this category.[9]

Life chances of individuals born outside the capital are considerably different, educationally and occupationally, from those born in the capital or abroad. In one study of a Montevideo *liceo,* the students' fathers were asked about their geographic origins, schooling, and occupations. Correlating education and geographic origins produced an interesting picture. (See Table 1.)

As Table 1 illustrates, those individuals born in Montevideo have a higher

Table 1
Geographic Origin and Education of
Fathers of *Liceo* Students

Origin	Education							
	S.P.	P.I.	P.C.	L.I.	L.C.	B.	U.I.	P.M.
Montevideo	1.2	34.4	46.3	8.5	1.2	1.2	1.2	0.3
Interior	6.6	46.2	34.0	6.2	4.5	1.7	0.4	0.4
Foreign	5.7	31.1	48.1	10.4	2.9	0.9	—	0.9

Legend: S.P. = No schooling. P.I. = Incomplete primary schooling. P.C. = Completed primary school. L.I. = Incomplete secondary schooling. L.C. = Completed secondary education. B. = Completed all preuniversity training. U.I. = Some college. P.M. = University degree.

SOURCE: Germán W. Rama, *Grupos sociales y enseñanza secundaria* (Montevideo: Arca, 1968), p. 80.

level of education than those born in the interior or on foreign soil. The differences in educational levels, however, are not really as great or as internally consistent as are those concerning the occupational category of these individuals. (As will be seen below, general educational levels are significantly higher for those living in Montevideo than for those living in the interior.)

While it must be remembered that these parents were reflective of a lower working class neighborhood, there is a significant occupational advantage for those born abroad or in Montevideo, as opposed to those born in the interior.

As Table 2 indicates, while 75.5 percent of those born in the interior are classified as workers or service personnel, the figure for those born in Montevideo is 47.2 percent and for foreign born, 53.8 percent. Similar differences emerge when one looks at self-employed versus salaried categories. Almost 40 percent of those foreign born are self-employed, while only 25 percent of those born in Montevideo and less than 14 percent of those born in the interior find themselves in this category.

These urban-rural differences are a manifestation of an economic and

Table 2
Geographic Origin and Occupation
of Fathers of *Liceo* Students

Socio-professional category	Geographic Origin (in percent)		
	Montevideo	Interior	Abroad
Farmers	2.3	1.0	1.9
Farm Workers	— —	1.7	0.9
Industrialists and merchants	23.0	12.8	36.8
Upper strata	1.5	2.1	— —
Middle strata	6.1	1.7	2.8
Employees	19.5	15.2	3.8
Workers	37.2	44.1	42.5
Service personnel	10.0	21.4	11.3
Inactive	0.4	— —	— —

SOURCE: German W. Rama, *Grupos sociales y enseñanza secundaria* (Montevideo: Arca, 1968), p. 82.

political system which, while it catered to the population of the mega-lopolis, left the social, economic, and political structures of the interior virtually untouched. Land tenure patterns, the contribution of the beef and wool producers to Uruguay's foreign exchange earnings, and the clientelist politics of *Blancos* and *Colorados* among the urban voting mass have all contributed to the dialectic between city and country. Thus, an analysis of the agrarian sector of the economy will help us to understand the meaning of the urban-rural dichotomy and the failure of national integration on this horizontal dimension.

Although Uruguay is bereft of oil and other important subsoil resources, it is blessed with an arable soil covering 88 percent of its surface, 70 percent of which is tillable.[10] The manner in which this natural resource is used, however, tells much about the system. Most of the land area of Uruguay is devoted to the raising of livestock. With a population of less than three million, the country finds itself host to almost nine million cattle and twenty-two million sheep.[11] Impressive as these figures may seem, they pale when one considers that in 1908, with a population of one million, the country had a similar number of cattle and five million more sheep than it currently possesses.[12] One result of these statistics can be seen in the percentage of beef that is available for export.[13]

Years	Export (Pct.)	Internal Consumption (Pct.)
1935/1937	45.5	54.4
1950/1952	36.9	63.1
1960/1962	29.1	70.9

Extensive open pasture (free-grazing livestock production) has meant that of approximately 16,500,000 hectares of available land, 14,500,000 or 86 percent of the total are devoted to the raising of livestock, and only about 8 to 9 percent to other agricultural pursuits.[14] Additionally, only approximately 3.6 percent of the land is improved.[15] Whether land and livestock are abused, misused, or underutilized, the singular fact remains that over 90 percent of Uruguayan exports are directly related to the primary sector of the economy. (See Table 3.)

Table 3
Profile of Uruguay's Exports During the 1950s

	Millions of Dollars	Percent
Wool (dirty and washed)	73.3	39.5
Spun wool and fabric	30.1	16.2
Meat and meat by-products	30.8	16.6
Hides and bristle	16.9	9.1
Flax and oil of flax	9.6	5.2
Other agricultural products (natural and processed)	22.6	12.2
Other	2.2	1.2
	185.5	100.0

SOURCE: Centro Latinoamericano de Economía Humana, *Situación económica y social del Uruguay rural* (Montevideo: Ministerio de Ganadería y Agricultura, 1963, p. 94.

When we turn to the ownership of this vital sector of the Uruguayan economy, a picture of severe concentration emerges. The 1966 agricultural census indicated that there were approximately 79,000 agricultural livestock enterprises. Of these, over 65,000 or more than 82 percent were less than 200 hectares in size and represented approximately 14 percent of the exploitable land area. At the other extreme, however, some 1,200 establishments or 1.5 percent were over 2,500 hectares in size and represented over one-third of the total agricultural land area.[16] One investigation of ownership comes to the conclusion that some 600 families controlled 55 percent of the land, while another such investigation found that some 500 families controlled one-half of the arable land.[17]

Land tenure patterns also affect investment and ownership. Absentee ownership is reported for over one-third of livestock operations, while it is less than 4 percent in dairy, fruit, wine, and crop operations.[18] Investment in productive improvements was also found to be lowest in livestock operations, representing some 29 percent of the value of such operations.[19] Lack of investment, long-term improvement, or balanced use of resources is also a function of land-holding patterns. Some 40 percent of all productive land is rented and not owned,[20] a legal relationship to the land which has been shown to be detrimental to investment, planning, and use. Despite the increase in direct ownership between 1951 and 1966, one should not conclude that effective entrepreneurship is on the rise. As one North American expert observes:

> The evidence marshalled in this analysis supports the hypothesis that land purchases have protected the investor against inflation. There is also good evidence to support the hypothesis that much of this investment has been speculative in nature and has sought land purchase opportunities in areas requiring minimal input of managerial time and production-increasing technology. Although investment in additional land has been a sound decision on the part of the individual investor, from the standpoint of the development of the economy, it is a nonproductive investment.[21]

The ownership pattern becomes more meaningful when we look at the occupational and political correlates of the activity of the sector. Less than 20 percent of the economically active population in Uruguay are employed in the primary sector, and this sector is responsible for approximately 15 percent of the gross national product. These figures compare favorably with those of many developed nations; yet, like so many statistics in Uruguay, what on the surface appears to be an indicator of development is really a manifestation of underutilized human and natural resources. The fact is that extensive cattle and sheep raising, primitive methods, and low productivity have meant that even fewer people can make a living from the land. Since the early 1950s there has been a continuing depopulation of the Uruguayan countryside. (See Table 4.)

Table 4
Evolution of Uruguay's Rural Population

Year	Rural Population	National Population	Rural Population as Pct. of National Pop.
1916	269,756	1,295,400	20.8
1930	330,849	1,703,700	19.4
1937	342,359	1,881,400	18.1
1951	453,912	2,228,700	20.3
1956	413,859	2,401,800	17.2
1961	389,850	2,575,500	15.1
1966	327,821	2,748,700	11.9

SOURCE: Centro Latinoamericano de Economía Humana, *Situación económica y social del Uruguay rural* (Montevideo: Ministerio de Ganadería y Agricultura), p. 280. The 1966 figure is taken from Instituto de Economía, *Uruguay: Estadísticas Básicas* (Montevideo: Universidad de la República, 1969), p. 165.

The individuals who have left the countryside have usually emigrated to interior towns and cities and eventually to Montevideo. The important point is that they have not left because of the increased mechanization or modernization of agriculture and livestock raising, but because the methods employed and the increasing stagnation in the sector have reduced employment possibilities. This stagnation is demonstrated by the figures in Table 5.

The lack of growth in the livestock sector has been the significant factor in the desertion of the countryside. The only systematic attempt to study internal migration in Uruguay indicates that there is a strong correlation between migration and the practice of extensive livestock

Table 5
Evolution of Livestock Production, 1935-1964

Product	Average Annual Rate of Growth (Pct.)	Average Per Capita Rate of Growth (Pct.)
Beef	-0.10	-1.42
Lamb	-0.39	-1.66
Pork	0.92	-0.34
Wool	1.71	0.39
TOTAL	1.00	-0.30

SOURCE: Instituto de Economía, *El proceso económico del Uruguay* (Montevideo: Universidad de la República, 1969) p. 63.

raising. As the author of the study concludes: *"El latifundia está en la base de la migración hacia Montevideo."*[22]

It is, of course, difficult to determine with exactitude the effect of the owner-production relationship on class structure. However, we do have some interesting statistics on the effects of large scale traditional livestock enterprises on rural poverty. One study of the rural slum areas, known in Uruguay as *rancheríos*, shows a strong correlation between the type of agrarian enterprise and the existence of these rural slums with their rural *Lumpenproletariat*. A census of *rancheríos* taken by the university extension department showed that 196 out of 278 were located in areas of extensive livestock raising, while only 29 were found in areas which were exclusively devoted to agricultural or vinacultural pursuits.[23] The study found that some 28,000 of the 33,000 individuals in these shanty-towns were living in areas devoted to either livestock raising or minifundia agricultural production. Thus, minifundia and latifundia here combine to create rural misery.

A curious anomaly results. The sector of the economy that is responsible for approximately one-fifth of production and one-fifth of employment and has actually shown a very poor performance record in the last decades is still the sector on which Uruguay is absolutely dependent for its international exchange earnings. The landed interests in Uruguay continue to be the focal point of the economy and thus a crucial pillar within the society. Indicative of this is the image of the nation imparted both pedagogically and ideologically. Solari comments on a diffuse and pervasive ideology that supports and favors the rural sector—an ideology that constantly reminds all who listen that the wealth of the country depends on the land, that it is in the efforts of those men tied to the land that the energetic impulse of the country lies. This vision of the system is apparent in the texts used in the primary and secondary schools. Solari reports the following concerning two widely used texts:

> In one, 32 pages are dedicated to the economic activity of Uruguay; only 2-1/3 are devoted to non-agriculturally related industry; of 25 illustrations, 23 are dedicated to agricultural activities (Cayetano di Leoni y Santa di Lorenzo, *Geografía Escolar* de 4° y 5° ano, 3ª ed., Montevideo, 1957); in the *Texto Unico* for the fifth year 12 pages are dedicated to agricultural activities and only half a page to industry.[24]

One indication of the political strength of rural interests has been their ability to delay the implementation of important social and labor legislation for rural workers. The Statute on Rural Workers was not passed until 1946, and retirement provisions for rural workers were not implemented until 1943, some 24 years after similar legislation was passed for workers in industry and commerce. Effective enforcement of minimum wage legislation for rural workers was not implemented until 1943, again many years after such legislation was passed.

However, this does not mean that the livestock interests have always gotten their way. The import substitution boom of the late 1940s and early 1950s was accomplished and in good measure subsidized by the export sector of the economy. The industrial populism of Luis Batlle Berres included fiscal policies that were clearly detrimental to wool and beef producers. Government taxation of these export producers was accomplished by means of exchange rate manipulations, the so-called *política cambiaria.* Under this system, the exporter was paid at a peso to dollar rate that was lower (and at times much lower) than either the official financial rate or the free market rate. This was true for meat exports throughout the postwar period and especially in the early 1950s.[25] The wool exporters did not feel the squeeze until after the boom for wool created by the Korean conflict had passed and the government found it necessary to retain a greater share of the international price in order to maintain its revenue base.[26]

It is apparent that the livestock sector was at a disadvantage when compared with the industrial sector and the producers of certain agricultural products. Production indices for wheat, corn, and linseed oil show significant gains in the postwar period. A modernizing agricultural produce sector supported by subsidy and preferential exchange rates was reaping benefits along with the protected and subsidized industrial branch of the economy. By the late 1950s livestock interests were putting pressure on government to change its fiscal policies and were threatening to withhold their products from market. In addition they were taking a renewed interest in direct political activity, especially within the *Blanco* party. The upset *Blanco* victory in the 1958 election and the abrupt change in fiscal and monetary policy are in no small way reflective of the exercise of political power by the traditional agrarian interests.

An examination of the educational institution in Uruguay makes the failure of horizontal and vertical integration increasingly apparent. While the exact nature of the relationship between education and development or education and democracy can be and indeed is hotly debated, it cannot be denied that the educational institution both reflects and can help change or maintain the existing class structure of a society. Education is one of the prime factors in social mobility, and access to and successful completion of various levels of the educational matrix is certainly one of the principal screening processes by which the potential if not actual distribution of goods and services in society is determined.

The formal educational structure in Uruguay closely resembles that of continental Europe. After six years of primary school, the student proceeds to a secondary education which may be academic or vocational in nature. The academic tract in secondary education is divided into two cycles: the first four years (*liceo*), and an upper cycle of two years of more specialized preuniversity training (*preparatorio*). The successful completion of *preparatorio* grants the student the *Bachillerato* and enables him to enter a faculty of the university if he or she so desires. All public education in Uruguay from primary school through university is free.

The extensive commitment to mass education made under Batlle and the extension of schooling in the interior has given Uruguay one of the highest literacy rates in the Third World. Approximately 10 percent of the population is illiterate,[27] the lowest figure in all of Latin America. However, there is a good deal of fluctuation in this rate from a high of

16 percent in rural areas to a low of 5 percent in Montevideo.[28] Over 90 percent of those students of primary school age (6-12) are attending school. In the early 1960s, over 50 percent of the 14-year age group were in school compared to 69 percent in France. When we reach the 17-year age bracket, the figure has fallen to 22 percent but still compares favorably with a French figure of 28 percent.[29] Nevertheless it should be pointed out that approximately one-third of all students do not complete their primary education.[30]

The growth and penetration of primary schooling, however, has been impressive. From a total enrollment of 24,000 in 1880, the primary school population grew to 55,000 by 1906 and doubled to 114,000 by 1914. At the time of Batlle's death in 1929, approximately 175,000 students were enrolled in primary schools.[31] From 1930 to 1963 the index of those attending primary schools in urban areas had gone from 100 to 228. For schools in the urban interior, the index shows a similar increase from 100 to 239.9. The total enrollment in rural schools, however, has remained practically static, moving only from an index of 100 in 1930 to 107.3 in 1963.[32] This last statistic is reflective of the educational differences between the urban and rural population at all levels of instruction. (See Table 6.)

Table 6
Education and Place of Residence
(in percentages)

Education Level	Total	Montevideo	Urban Interior	Rural
No schooling	10.7	6.2	12.7	18.7
Primary	70.3	67.7	71.6	74.8
1st cycle secondary, partial or complete, and/or vocational training	13.8	18.3	12.7	3.9
Beyond 1st cycle of secondary	3.8	6.1	2.2	0.9
Other	1.4	1.7	0.8	1.7

SOURCE: Aldo Solari, Néstor Campiglia, and Germán Wettstein, *Uruguay en Cifras* (Montevideo: Universidad de la República, 1966), p. 43.

What the figures in Table 6 mask, however, is the relatively low efficiency of the system. Some 23 percent of urban primary school children repeat at least one year of the primary school cycle. The figure in rural areas reaches a high of 37 percent.[33] Of the approximately two-thirds of the students who eventually do get through their primary education, one-fifth go into a vocational training track and two-thirds go on to an academic secondary education. This leaves some 13 percent who, though graduating from elementary school, do not go on to any higher education. This 13 percent, however, consists of 7.7 percent of those students in urban public schools, but 48 percent of those students in rural public schools.[34]

When we turn to secondary education in Uruguay, we find that class as well as geography become key factors. The penetration of secondary education in Uruguay has been explosive in the twentieth century, and especially in the last three decades. While the index of primary school matriculation from 1950 to 1965 rose some 41 percent, the figure for secondary matriculation is 167 percent.[35] An analysis of the percentage of the secondary school age population actually attending school shows an increase from 11.2 percent for those born between 1930 and 1933 to 30.9 percent of those born between 1946 and 1949.[36] However, once again an analysis of repetition and desertion within the secondary cycle sheds light both on the nature of the system itself and the impact of class factors on that system.

The figures available for 1961 for *liceos* in Montevideo indicate that one-fifth of the students repeated at least one year of the secondary education cycle.[37] In that same year, a study of secondary education performance in general indicated that there was a clear class factor involved in the phenomenon of repetition. As Table 7 illustrates, there was a correlation between the socio-professional category of the students' fathers and the repetition rate.

One study of primary schools in Montevideo shed further light on this problem.[38] Dividing the schools into A, B, and C categories on the basis of drop-out rates, graduation rates, and intelligence test scores of the students, the investigator found a significant relationship between social class and educational performance. While the distribution of the student population by school year was close to normal in the A category schools, with 19 percent in the first year and 14 percent of the student body in the sixth year, in those schools classified in category C, 26 percent of the students were found in the first year, and only 8 percent

Table 7
Grade Repetition and Social Class

Category	Percent of Repeaters
Upper strata	19.4
Middle strata	23.3
Employees	24.7
Skilled workers	31.2
Specialized workers	33.3
Laborers	48.6
Domestics, waiters, etc.	50.0

SOURCE: Ministerio de Instrucción Pública y Previsión Social, Comisión de Inversiones y Desarrollo Económico (CIDE), and Comisión Coordinada de los Entes de Enseñanza, *Informe Sobre el Estado de Educación en el Uruguay,* Tomo Primero (Montevideo, 1966), p. 15. Adopted from an unpublished study by Antonio Grompone, Aldo Solari, E. Tuwana, and Germán Rama entitled *El rendimiento de enseñanza secundaria.*

of the student body was found in the sixth year.[39]

An indication of the socio-economic difference between students in level A and level C schools is found in the fact that, whereas 18 percent of the fathers of level A school students were classified as workers, 68 percent of the level C school students' fathers fell into this category.[40] Another study of all *liceos* in Montevideo found that while the lower classes were represented by 27 percent of the students in the first year, this percentage fell to 13 by the fourth year.[41]

In his study of *Liceo* 13, German Rama found additional confirmation of the relationship between class and education. While the overall drop-out rate in Montevideo for the first cycle of secondary education was 22.4 percent, the rate for *Liceo* 13 was over 40 percent.[42] The top-rated *liceo* in Montevideo had almost as many students in the first year as in the fourth year—374 to 308—but *Liceo* 13, situated in a lower working class neighborhood, had 272 students in the first year class but only 98 students in the fourth year.[43] Thus, while only 36 percent of the students in *Liceo* 13 managed to get to the fourth year of the cycle, some 56.9 percent of the students were able to do so in Montevideo in general.

When we turn to an internal analysis of the effect of social class on education performance in *Liceo* 13, the expected pattern emerges. The class composition of the student body changes as we progress from the first year to the last year. Whereas those students whose fathers had job classifications as workers or *personal de servicio* made up 55.6 percent of the student body in the first year, the percentage fell to 40.8 percent by the fourth year. While 17 percent of the student body in the first year had fathers in the highest socio-professional categories, by the fourth year these categories represented 34.7 percent of the total class.[44]

There is obviously a clear relationship between social class and the student's success in secondary school. The significance of this fact is clear. The democratization of education in Uruguay, the extension of the educational system to more and more people, and the commitment to free public education has, taken as a whole, not been enough to overcome the effects of social class. Not only has secondary education in Uruguay remained the property of the middle classes, but the percentage of those students completing the first cycle of secondary education and going on to the second, or of those students completing the second cycle and going on to faculties of the university, has actually remained the same or declined slightly in the period 1942-1963. The number of students completing the first cycle as a percentage of the total number of students enrolled has remained between 12 and 13 percent between 1945 and 1963, but the number of students who have completed the preparatory cycle of secondary education and enrolled in a faculty of the university has dropped from 18.4 percent in the 1942-1944 period to 13.2 percent in the 1961-1963 period.[45]

There was a significant rise in the number of individuals completing both cycles of secondary education in the post-World War II period. However, since the mid-1950s, the number of students actually completing the second cycle has remained almost stationary, while the number matriculated in the cycle has shown a gradual but steady increase. In other words, while there was probably significant individual mobility through secondary education in the 1945-1955 period, such mobility has since decreased. Many more individuals have access to secondary education and many more individuals are completing the process of secondary education than did in the past, but the percentage completing this level of education has not changed significantly and, in the past few years, the absolute numbers of those completing the process has remained stationary.[46]

The University of the Republic is Uruguay's sole institution of higher learning, and all of its schools and faculties are located within the city of Montevideo. As parochial and monolithic as this might at first appear, there is nevertheless a great deal of difference in the style and academic excellence of its various divisions. Additionally. the university, at least in terms of matriculated students, is not an exclusive or small institution.

The University is divided into 12 faculties and 10 schools, with some 8.5 percent of the student body enrolled in the schools and the remainder in the more traditional *facultades*.[47] In 1960 total enrollment was some 15,300, and it is currently estimated that some 18,000 Uruguayans are matriculated in the University.[48] The 1960 figure gives a university population of 610 per 100,000 population, one of the highest figures in the world.[49] However, these statistics can be misleading.

The university in Uruguay, as in most systems, is a certifying mechanism for new elites and the continued maintenance of older elites. The degree of mobility found in any system can in part be measured by the geographic, social, and occupational pool from which university students and graduates emerge. From a geographic perspective, it is apparent that those whose schooling takes place in Montevideo have a much greater propensity for entering the university. Of those entering the university in 1961, only 16 percent had completed their secondary education outside the capital. In 1968 some 23 percent of the entering students had attended *preparatorio* in the interior.[50]

In the class entering in 1961, 30 percent of the students had attended private elementary schools. The figure reached 36 percent in the 1968 entering class.[52] These percentages fall off at the secondary school level, but private school students are considerably overrepresented in the university population. While only 14 percent of the school population attend private secondary schools, 28 percent of those students entering the university in 1968 had attended such schools.[52]

Turning to the social and economic background of the student population, we find some interesting patterns. In terms of family education, an important statistic emerges. Whereas only 1.5 percent of the Uruguayan population over 30 years of age had four or more years of university education, some 17.2 percent of those students entering in 1968 had fathers with this level of education.[53] The vastly superior educational level of parents of incoming students is reflected in Table 8.

Table 8
Educational Levels of the General Population Aged 30 and over
and of the Parents of Those Entering the University in 1968

Educational Level	General Population	Father	Mother
No data	0	0.6	9.5
No schooling	15.3	1.6	1.3
Incomplete Primary	44.8	15.1	14.5
Complete Primary	24.6	30.1	39.0
Incomplete Secondary, Technical and other	10.9	22.7	23.2
Complete Secondary and at least some university	4.4	29.9	21.5

SOURCE: Universidad de la República: Oficina de Planeamiento, *Censo de estudiantes ingresados en 1968: Proceso de reclutamiento en la Universidad de la República* (Montevideo, 1968?), p. 64. Hereafter cited as *1968 University Census*.

If we go back yet another generation to the paternal grandfathers of incoming students, we find that some 12 percent had at least some University education.[54] The percentage of adult males in the grandfathers' generation that had some university education could not have exceeded 2 percent.

Specific economic data on the students' families indicates a not un-expected profile. Of those students entering in 1968, the fathers' occupations fell into the following sectors of the Uruguayan economy: 12 percent of the fathers were engaged in the primary sector, 20 percent were engaged in private industry, 28 percent in the private end of the tertiary sector, 11 percent were classified as independent professionals, and an unusually high 28 percent were occupied in public administration or in one of the state industrial enterprises.[55] Breaking down these occupations by income and prestige, the pattern emerges as follows: 31 percent of the fathers were considered to be in upper occupational strata, 58 percent in middle occupational strata, and 11 percent in the lower occupational strata.[56] As a point of comparison, the 1961 entering class showed a 37.45, and 16 percent breakdown.[57] It appears that during the 1960s the student population showed a slight decrease in those coming from upper income homes, a substantial increase in those coming from medium income homes, and a slight decrease in those coming from the lowest category.

The above data and categories do not, of course, allow very fine distinctions. Fortunately, however, we have a more detailed attempt to analyze the class composition of university students. In a study done in 1960 using a seven category occupational scale and comparing the results with a general stratification study of Montevideo, an interesting picture emerged. (See Table 9.)

Reorganizing the categories found in Table 9 into three broader groups is helpful. Taking categories 6 and 7 as indicative of the upper class and the upper middle class, we find that whereas some 12.4 percent of the heads of households in Montevideo fell into these categories, over 37 percent of the students in the university were in households from these categories. Taking categories 3, 4, and 5 as indicative of the medium and lower strata of the middle class, we find a closer correlation between the percentage of this strata found in the general stratification study and their participation in the university. While these categories made up 33.7 percent of the households in Montevideo, they represented 46.7 percent of the university population. Again, the middle class is overrepresented, but not that greatly. Turning to the two lowest categories, we find a severe underrepresentation in the university. While these categories were found to represent over 46 percent of all the households in Montevideo, only 12.2 percent of the 1960 student population came from these households.

The severe overrepresentation of the upper strata of the occupational scale and the severe underrepresentation of the lowest strata of this scale seem to corroborate the fact that the university in Uruguay is above all at the service of the middle and upper classes in the country. As in the case of secondary education, the democratization of higher education has not significantly meant an opening of the doors of such education to the lower strata of society. Additionally, when we turn to the career paths chosen and the number of students who actually receive university degrees, an even more elitist and static profile emerges.

If the university is viewed as the certifying institution for traditional elites, it is also looked to as the training ground for those skills and technical occupations which seem to be necessary in a modernizing situation. The profile of the Uruguayan university, however, does not lead one to the conclusion that it is fulfilling this second function. Uruguay's univer-

Table 9
Distribution of University Population According to
Parents' Socio-Occupational Category

Scale	University	Montevideo stratification sample
7	6.7	2.2
6	30.6	10.2
5	4.3	13.7
4	32.7	9.4
3	9.7	10.6
2	8.6	16.9
1	3.6	29.7
0	2.8	7.1
No Data	1.0	0.2

OCCUPATIONAL LEGEND:

7 — Large farmers and ranchers (over 2,500 hectares); industrialists and merchants; highest levels of public and private administration.

6 — Medium-sized farmers and ranchers, medium-sized industrialists and merchants, university professionals.

5 — Teachers; technicians, etc.

4 — Small farmers and ranchers; artisans and small shopkeepers; lower level supervisors in public and private administration.

3 — Employees.

2 — Foremen, ranch bosses, skilled workers.

1 — Salaried rural labor, peons, domestic employees, line soldiers and police.

0 — Economically inactive.

SOURCE: Ministerio de Instrucción Pública y Previsión Social, Comisión de Inversiones y Desarrollo Económico (CIDE) and Comisión Coordinada de los Entes de Enseñanza, *Informe Sobre el Estado de Educación en el Uruguay,* Tomo Primero (Montevideo, 1966), p. 318. Hereafter cited as *Informe Sobre Educación.*

sity has the highest proportion of students enrolled in law or medicine of all the universities on a continent known for its overemphasis on these liberal professions. Uruguay had over one-half of its students enrolled in the law or medical faculties in 1960.[58] There have been some changes in enrollment patterns in the last decade, with significant increases in agronomy and engineering between 1960 and 1968. In this same period, medical school enrollment has merely reflected the increase in general student enrollment. However, enrollment in law has increased from 20.6 percent of the total to 27.1 percent. Thus, in 1968 the law, medical, and dental faculties still were responsible for 45 percent of total student enrollment.[59]

One measure of a university's performance is how many professionals it turns out and how long it takes these individuals to complete their university education. The typical curriculum in most of the faculties of the Uruguayan university would ideally require five to six years to complete. However, statistics for 1964 indicated that over 33 percent of the students registered in the faculties of the university were still in school beyond the projected number of years for completion of their course of study. Some 14 percent of the students had actually been attending the university for ten years or longer. Almost one-fifth of all the medical students fell into this category.[60]

In spite of a significant increase in enrollment in recent decades, the number of degrees awarded has remained essentially static. As can be seen in Table 10, while the number of new matriculants increased from 2,402 to 5,017 between the 1942-1944 and 1957-1959 periods, the number of graduates of the university has not shown any significant change in those 20 years. Since matriculation has increased without a concomitant increase in the number of graduates, the university has been able to produce only one graduate for every 20 students enrolled. With a 1960 enrollment of some 15,000, the annual number of graduates was as follows during the early 1960s:[61]

1960	507
1961	951
1962	741
1963	818
1964	724
1965	771

These statistics make it difficult to believe that the university has played a significant mobility function in recent years. Additional significance of the above figures may be seen in calculations, based on available census and university data, which indicate that a small minority of individuals in any

Table 10
Incoming Students and Number of
University Degrees Conferred

	Years	No.	Pct. (Incoming Students/ Degrees Conferred)
Incoming students	1942-44	2,402	
Graduates	1947-49	1,344	56.0
Incoming students	1945-47	2,897	
Graduates	1950-52	1,220	42.0
Incoming students	1948-50	3,198	
Graduates	1953-55	1,365	42.7
Incoming students	1951-53	3,816	
Graduates	1956-58	1,437	37.7
Incoming students	1954-56	4,228	
Graduates	1959-61	1,370	32.4
Incoming students	1957-59	5,017	
Graduates	1962-64	1,432	28.5

SOURCE: Ministerio de Instrucción Pública y Previsión Social, Comisión de Inversiones y Desarrollo Económico (CIDE) and Comisión Coordinada de los Entes de Enseñanza, *Informe Sobre el Estado de Educación en el Uruguay*, Tomo Primero (Montevideo, 1966), pp. 296-297.

age bracket actually receive four or more years of university education. More important, the percentage receiving such an education does not increased significantly in any age category.[62]

Age	Percentage
20-24	.36
25-29	1.4
30-34	1.8
35-39	1.7
40-49	1.7
50-64	1.3
65+	.8

Further calculations have enabled us to evaluate fairly accurately the percentage that each age category actually contributes to the number of university-trained persons in Uruguay.[63]

Age	Percentage
20-24	3.0
25-29	12.0
30-34	16.0
35-39	14.0
40-49	24.5
50-64	21.8
65+	7.3

The University of the Republic emerges as an institution that has fallen short of the social and intellectual role one could expect it to play in an integrated national community dedicated to basic equality of opportunity. It is an institution which caters to the upper and middle classes of Montevideo. It has not turned out an appreciably greater number of graduates in recent decades and those that it does produce are trained in the more traditional professions. The university is not producing highly trained, scientifically equipped professionals capable of innovative contributions to the society. It has essentially perpetuated existing class relationships and acted as a certifying mechanism for the conferring of status within a set of traditional norms and values.

What does our discussion of urban-rural differences and the promise and performance of the educational institution tell us when placed against an overview of social class in Uruguay? In answering this question, it is helpful to look at the global estimates of class structure. Below are some of the more important estimates made by Uruguayan observers:[64]

		Upper Class (Pct.)	Middle (Pct.)	Lower (Pct.)
Grompone	(1949)	5.0	68.0	27.0
Ganón	(1953)	5.0	71.0	24.0
Ganón	(1966)	5.0	60.0	35.0
Solari	(1957)	5.0	75.0	20.0
Solari	(1964)	2.3	32.0-50.0	47.0-66.0
Rama	(1960)	2.0	31.0	67.0

The most salient feature of all of the estimates is the large proportion of the population that is included in the middle sectors or middle class. Even the lowest estimate, 29 percent, would place Uruguay very high among Third World nations and would be equalled in Latin America only by Argentina. The Uruguayan profile would rival that of almost any country in the world and, if accurate, is approximately equal to that of mid-century Britain.

The 1964 Solari figures are based on the only full-scale stratification survey ever done in Montevideo.[65] The internal range of Solari's estimates depends on where one decides to make the cut between the lower middle class and the lower class. However, the real value of this study does not lie in its ability to determine the relative size of social classes in Uruguay accurately, but rather in its ability to give us some hard information on intergenerational mobility patterns. Indeed, using Max Weber's concept of class as the life chances of the individual, mobility patterns may give the observer the most accurate reflection of changing class distributions within a society.

The 1959 study involved male heads of households in Montevideo. Several interesting patterns emerged from a merely cursory analysis of its results. In the first place, there was a very crucial change in the occupational profile of the previous generation as compared with the current generation. While agricultural and livestock occupations accounted for 37 percent of those employed in the father's generation, it represented only 2 percent of the present (1959) generation.[66] A second major finding concerns a progressive increase in salaried employment. The increase in those working for a salary as opposed to being self-employed is marked, and holds true even when only non-agricultural employment is considered. (See Table 11.)

Comparing the occupational categories of the present to those of the preceding generation indicates that the drop in agricultural occupations has been principally absorbed by unskilled labor and service jobs (as shown in Table 12).

Thus, when agricultural activities are excluded, the pattern that emerges indicates that middle level and professional occupations are actually underrepresented in the present generation. (See Table 13.)

What do such findings indicate when placed against an overview of class structure and the nature of the Uruguayan economy? The stagnation of the primary sector has meant that many have been pushed out of

Table 11
Independent and Salaried Employment
Through Two Generations

Type of Employment	Previous Generation		Current Generation	
	Including Agricultural Employment	Excluding Agricultural Employment	Including Agricultural Employment	Excluding Agricultural Employment
Independent	60.3	43.7	26.4	25.6
Salaried	39.7	57.0	73.6	74.4

SOURCE: Aldo Solari, "Sistema de Clases y Cambio Social en el Uruguay," in *Estudios sobre la sociedad uruguaya*, Vol. II (Montevideo: Editorial Arca, 1965), p. 123.

Table 12
Occupational Profile Through Two Generations

Occupational Category	Previous Generation	Current Generation
Farmers	33.3	1.3
Major industrialists and merchants, liberal professions, upper strata.	6.8	9.7
Minor industrialists and merchants, middle strata and technicians.	9.6	12.8
Artisans, employees.	20.4	27.1
Workers, agricultural laborers, service personnel.	29.9	49.1

SOURCE: Aldo Solari, "Movilidad Social en Montevideo," in Solari, *Estudios sobre la sociedad uruguaya*, Vol. I (Montevideo: Editorial Arca, 1965), p. 95.

Table 13
Occupational Profile Through Two Generations
(Excluding Agricultural Employment)

Occupational Category	Previous Generation	Current Generation
Major industrialists and merchants, liberal professions and upper strata.	10.8	9.9
Minor industrialists and merchants, middle strata and technicians.	15.2	13.0
Artisans and employees.	32.4	27.6
Workers and service personnel.	41.6	49.5

SOURCE: Aldo Solari, "Movilidad Social en Montevideo," in Solari, *Estudios sobre la sociedad uruguaya,* Vol. I (Montevideo: Editorial Arca, 1965), p. 95.

rural areas and have migrated to the capital. The fact that internal migration to Montevideo has been less a factor of opportunity "pull" than a lack of opportunity "push" may be seen in the fact that it is the departments with extensive livestock raising that have been the prime areas of internal migration. From the 1930s through the 1950s, these migrants at least could get unskilled laboring jobs in the expanding industrial sector or on public service work projects. However, the failure of import substitution and the subsequent stagnation of the industrial and construction sectors meant that many of these individuals at the lower end of the socioeconomic scale were unable to find the outlet and mobility channels that formerly existed. At the same time that this process was being carried on, the middle classes in Montevideo were experiencing a greater and greater dependence on public sector employment to maintain their position. The independent middle class of the 1920s and 1930s had, by the mid-1950s, been replaced by a dependent middle class which found its one great source of employment and its only chance for economic security in the government bureaucracy and the state industrial enterprises.

The nationalization of certain public services under Batlle, state intervention in banking, insurance, and in certain industrial activities meant that by the middle of the century, the 22 public corporations generated some 30 percent of the gross national product.[67] The Uruguayan budget for 1965 represented some 25 percent of the gross national product, and the state paid approximately 40 percent of all salaries in the country.[68] The economic stasis experienced by Uruguay since the mid-1950s is in almost diametrical opposition to the growth statistics of the public sector. In 1958 it was estimated that there were some 170,000 public employees.[69]

Looking at the relatively brief period of 1955-1961, we find that the annual rate of growth in employment in the private sector was .9 percent, while the rate in the public sector was 2.6 percent—almost three times as high.[70] Furthermore, older workers were increasingly taking advantage of and becoming eligible for the early retirement provisions that were part of Uruguay's social and labor legislation. The retirement rolls, therefore, were increasing some 5.6 percent annually during this same period. By 1961 some 278,000 individuals were collecting retirement or old age benefits at a time when the total economically active population was approximately one million.[71]

The exhaustion of the state-sponsored industrial boom which took place between 1945 and 1955 put an additional burden on a public sector that had traditionally been seen as a source of employment. It was not that government jobs paid well, but they offered something that an increasingly depressed middle class sought—security. The middle class father could look towards his early retirement provisions while the son sought, in becoming an *empleado público,* security of income and a socially acceptable white collar position. It was in the desire to maintain its middle class status that the Uruguayan family exacerbated an already powerful clientelist politics. What emerged was a reinforced and strengthened network of personal and particularistic accommodation. Public and private individuals did not relate to an impersonal state, but rather to their personal and especially political contacts. The parties thus were incapable of becoming more or less than the *"oficinas de reclamos,"* that Solari has so aptly dubbed them.[72] They were also incapable of becoming the integrating mechanisms through which national policies and priorities could be established and carried out. The state under these conditions could not become the synthesizing institution through which effective national community can be built. As Solari concludes,

Rather than as a secular artifact destined to resolve social conflicts at the highest level, the state is conceived in a paternalistic manner, as the one who must keep the vigil in order to, in the last analysis, sustain everyone. . . .[73]

The most significant aspect of the maze of data to which the reader has been subjected is the picture of institutional and economic stagnation which emerges and the implications of that stasis. The increased pressure on the state, through the good offices of the traditional parties, to absorb those entering the job market and maintain resources to support welfare and retirement benefits was symptomatic of a growing crisis.

By the first decade of this century, Uruguay, like the majority of Latin American nations, emerged as a capitalist society. Unlike most of these nations, however, Uruguay had managed to ameliorate the tension between class and nation which is both cause and consequence of the rise of the nation-state under capitalism. While the emergence of the modern state required an impersonal marketplace and new levels of individual freedom, both implemented by the newly created loyalty to the social nation, the very success of the process produced the urbanization, bureaucratization, and centralization that engender particularist class loyalties. This strain between loyalty to the social nation and loyalty to class was bridged historically by the concept of social mobility which, while recognizing class differences, held up the state as the impersonal regulator of a marketplace of opportunity for all citizens.

In such a way the problem of equality and inequality were fused, for the notion, which many call a belief and others label ideology, holds that although persons may be born into socially unequal places, the national community would provide the avenues or fields of equal opportunities through which these persons, given the capacity and the will, could overcome or break through their ascribed structural position.[74]

As long as the myth of social mobility bore resemblance to reality, i.e., as long as individuals saw the system pay off in terms of a better life or at least the realistic hope for a better life, then the strain between class and nation could be held in check. But the evidence indicates that

Uruguay's stagnation was making it increasingly difficult to keep the myth viable and thus ameliorate the contradiction.

The exacerbation of the historic tension between class and nation did not mean that Uruguay had to follow a particular path, but it did imply the need to seek solutions. Essentially, these options fell into three categories. The country could do nothing and hope to move forward through fortuitous circumstances, e.g., a Korean War type boom or the discovery of oil in the Río de la Plata. The nation could attempt basic reforms, especially in its economic and political institutions. Last, existing power relationships and interests could be preserved, even at the cost of continued stagnation, through increasingly authoritarian measures. Many people hoped for the first solution, some worked for the second, but most acquiesced or participated in the third. The causes, consequences, and implications of the path taken are the concerns of the concluding chapter.

5
URUGUAY IN THE 1960s AND 1970s: A REQUIEM FOR DEMOCRATIC NATIONALISM

The history of Uruguay from the mid-1950s to the present is one of economic decline, increased social and political tension, deepened and widened ideological division, erosion of civil liberties, and most recently, the destruction of constitutional government. What originally spurred my interest in Uruguay was a fascination with its past and present image and the reality behind these images. I wished to determine how and why a nation that was regarded as so different from and superior to its sister republics could so quickly "fall" and come to resemble them.

To answer these questions, I have tried to describe and analyze Uruguay's development in the first half of this century. I looked at its ideological and institutional configurations as well as the effect of these configurations in the building of an egalitarian national community. In this chapter an attempt will be made to synthesize these various themes. Such an exercise will explain recent occurrences in Uruguay, thus demonstrating the validity of the conceptual scheme employed throughout this study.

Events in Uruguay in the last twenty years have been revealing. The failure of the nation's leaders to implement effective national policies abetted the deteriorating economic situation and consequently exacerbated social and political tensions. Thus, the nation's leaders were faced increasingly with the question of the kind of community they would build and the quality and terms of membership in that community. How they met this challenge is the essential focus of this chapter.

The import substitution and export boom enjoyed by Uruguay during World War II and extended by the Korean conflict had run its course by the mid-1950s. The 1958 national elections took place in the midst of a deepening recession. Voter dissatisfaction with the *Colorado*-dominated *colegiado* was expressed in a victory for the *Partido Nacional* which, by winning the November 1958 election, took majority control of the executive for the first time in ninety-three years. The *Blanco* victory was seen by many as a repudiation of *Batllismo* and a call for significant change. It was certainly a victory for rural interests against the urban oriented industrialization policies of the *Colorado* party. By the end of 1959, the *Blanco* administration accepted the guidelines which the IMF had been pressing on Uruguay for several years. The measures included the elimination of Uruguay's multiple exchange rate, the removal of restrictions on imports, and the reduction of taxes on the export sector.[1]

These new policies were clearly designed to benefit and stimulate the primary sector. The anticipation of their adoption had stimulated production and driven up the value of land. But such fiscal and monetary measures did not prove capable of overcoming the structural reality of the rural sector. The large absentee-owner and the small producer did not respond in the expected manner to the new incentives, and the lack of improvement in the international export markets further inhibited the expected effect of the new policies.

The administration's emphasis on the agriculture sector and its laissez faire policies meant that the previous support for the precariously built industrial sector was withdrawn. The consequent downward swing in industry and construction coupled with the disappointing agrarian performance marked the beginning of sustained economic stagnation. This stagnation, combined with the huge government payroll, welfare, pension, and social security expenditures, spelled the onset of serious inflation. At the time of the 1962 elections, inflation was running at 35 percent a year, a high figure for a society whose currency had been as stable as the dollar throughout the 1940s and early 1950s and for an economy which had not experienced an inflation greater than 15 to 18 percent in decades.[2]

The 1962 elections thus took place under a growing pessimism concerning the *Blanco* administration's ability to turn the economy around. While they had won control of the *colegiado* by 120,000 votes in 1958, they managed to retain control by only 24,000 votes in 1962.[3] The second *Blanco* administration, despite the excellent diagnostic report developed by the national technical staff assembled in the early 1960s and the five-year plan produced by this body in 1965, accomplished little.[4] The economy reacted as expected to this lack of effective policy and continued to decline as inflation continued to soar.

The failure of a *Blanco*-dominated government to spur the Uruguayan economy and the death of major political figures in both parties (Herrera in 1959, Luis Batlle Berres and Benito Nardone in 1964) increased the feeling of frustration and drift. The economic situation was becoming desperate. The cost of living, which had doubled between 1945 and 1955, doubled again between 1959 and 1962, again between 1962 and 1964, and increased another 100 percent in 1965.[5] The gross national product had remained stationary during these years and, on a per capita basis was actually declining.[6] As labor found its purchasing power seriously threatened, union unrest increased and the more than 200,000 individuals on retirement or old age pensions found their security threatened by the galloping inflation.

Under these circumstances there was a growing impetus for yet another constitutional reform. The *ruralistas* and the *Herrerista Blancos* had favored the abolition of the plural executive since 1958. As the situation worsened in the 1960s, many politicians of all political persuasions increasingly called for constitutional reform as the answer to Uruguay's problems. Apparently, it was easier to blame the failure to develop and execute effective national policy on a multi-headed executive than to remember who created that executive and to recognize that the factional nature of Uruguayan party politics made coherent action by the executive or legislature difficult. Thus, the *colegiado* was made the scapegoat for the failure of national leadership, and "constitutionalitis" became the surrogate for effective national leadership.

The 1966 constitution was one more attempt to change without changing. Once again the nation's political leaders agreed to a political pact, and sold to the electorate a constitutional reform holding out the promise of a new start for Uruguay.

The idea was easily sold to the voters, but not without some indication of conflict along class lines. An opinion poll conducted three months before the November 1966 plebiscite and regular elections showed that, while 71 percent of the public as a whole was in favor of reforming the constitution, 85 percent of those respondents classified as upper class favored the reform.[7] Differing class perception of the effect of a reform is signified by the fact that while 46 percent of the upper class respondents thought the reform would help the country overcome its economic crisis, only 29 percent of the lower class respondents expressed a similarly favorable opinion.[8]

By the time the debates on constitutional reform took place in the General Assembly in August 1966, each major political faction had its own version of a new charter.[9] The debates, as usual, reflected the ideological and power position of the various groups, but something important was missing. Instead of calling a constitutional convention or conducting extensive debate, the formal debate in the General Assembly only lasted through a few lengthy sessions which covered a span of only several days. These discussions centered on the failure of the collegial executive and the need for a streamlined presidential system, but did not offer any proposals concerning basic reform of economic structures. Except in the statements of some minority party spokesmen, there was no longer preoccupation with a greater vision of the society. The philosophical discussions that had accompanied the adoption of a mixed executive system in 1919 and a totally collegial system in 1951 were absent. Absent too was any discussion of the nature of the national community or of the purpose of the national enterprise. What was left was a merely mechanical debate on the structure of a new presidential system which would include some new planning and fiscal agencies to coordinate a still unimplemented development program.

The most significant aspect of the 1966 reform was a return to a presidential system, with the chief executive serving a five-year term concurrent with the legislature.[10] In an attempt to bolster the streamlined "developmentalist" image of the new government, several new organs were created. A Social Security Bank (*Banco de Previsión Social*) was established to coordinate the almost chaotic administration of retirement and social security funds. In addition, a central bank was established to help coordinate monetary and fiscal policy, and an Office of Planning and Budget was created as a technical planning arm of the executive branch.

In an apparent attempt to depoliticize the public administration of state enterprises, the old 3-2 division of the directorships of these organizations between the *Blancos* and *Colorados* was eliminated, but the requirement of a 60 percent confirmation vote implied that the two traditional parties would continue to split the assignments. Congress was also empowered to change the procedure of designation of directors in the future if it so desired.

There is a curious and telling addition to the 1966 constitution concerning land expropriation and indemnification. Articles 231 and 232 empowered the legislature to nationalize land but required that the necessary funds be established to pay for the land taken, that such payments must be made within ten years, and that the government could not take the land until it had paid the owner a minimum of one quarter of his total indemnization. Here was a clear attempt by landed interests to constitutionally protect themselves from future land reform programs. It is indicative of the forces being served by the new charter.

The constitution was easily approved by a plebiscite held concurrently with the November 1966 elections. In the presidential election the *Colorado* party handily defeated the National party.[11] The president-elect was a retired army general, Oscar Gestido, who enjoyed a reputation as an honest and capable administrator. Unfortunately, he died less than a year after assuming office, and his relatively unknown vice-president, Jorge Pacheco Areco, a former editor of *El Día*, assumed the office. Pacheco quickly established his own identity and the firm hand with which he intended to rule. One week after taking office, he issued a decree outlawing the Socialist party and several small leftist and anarchist groups. The leftist newspaper, *Epoca,* and the Socialist party's newsweekly, *El Sol,* were also permanently closed.

On June 13, 1968, Pacheco instituted a limited state of siege by invoking the so-called *Medidas Prontas de Seguridad* (Prompt Security Measures), a form of emergency power granted by the constitution to the president acting with the appropriate ministers.[12] Exercising this power, the president ordered the militarization of striking bank workers and declared a freeze on prices and wages. The congress, which could nullify these measures, chose not to do so. With the exception of a brief period in the second quarter of 1969, Pacheco used (and some would say abused) these special faculties throughout the remaining four years of his administration. In addition, on two occasions an acquiescent congress suspended all constitutional civil liberties, once for twenty days following the assassination of U. S. police agent Daniel Mitrione (August 1970), and again for forty days after the kidnapping of British Ambassador Geoffrey Jackson (January 1971).

The systematic erosion of civil liberties during the Pacheco administration is well documented. Freedom of the press was hampered by a July 4, 1969 decree which established prior censorship on reports concerning guerrilla activity. On December 1 of that year, the government banned the use of seven words concerning the guerrillas (such terms as comandos, células, delincuentes políticos), and the leftist press retaliated by dubbing the Tupamaros "los innombrables." In April 1971, it was announced that only official police communiques on the guerrillas could be published. Finally, a decree issued December 14, 1971, established censorship of all printed matter that dealt with "themes of armed violence, of rural and urban guerrillas, of the tactics and strategy of insurrection in Latin America and on other continents and, in general, of anything that develops the theory of armed subversion."[13]

Charges of police brutality and torture became frequent in the later years of the administration. In 1970 a bipartisan senate congressional commission investigating such charges concluded that

> The application of tortures in different forms is a *normal, frequent, and habitual occurrence* and that, among officials of recognized abilities, individuals have infiltrated who use their public positions to give free rein to their perverse instincts. It is also clear that the High Command lacks energy and courage, if it is not at times an accomplice, in transforming the prisons into places where the human being undergoes tortures incompatible with our democracy, our style of life and degree of civilization.[14]

The continued failure of the administration's economic policies—inflation was 135 percent in 1967 and was reduced to 67 percent in 1968 only through the imposition of a discriminatory wage freeze—and its growing reliance on force and repressive legislation brought it into increasing conflict with traditionally autonomous groups in the society.[15] Most important among these were organized labor and university students.

As indicated in our discussion of *Battllismo,* there was significant labor union activity in Uruguay by the turn of the century. Unions have been an important feature of the political landscape throughout this century. They lost the favored status they enjoyed under *Batllismo* during the Terra dictatorship in the 1930s but regained wide latitude and organizational freedom during and after the Second World War, organizing the General Workers Union in 1942 and the Syndical Confederation of Uruguay in 1951. The deteriorating economic situation during the late 1950s and early 1960s saw a move toward the creation of a more powerful national organization, culminating in 1966 with the establishment of the National Workers Convention (CNT). The increasing dependence on public employment, the huge government payroll, and retirement and social security payments created a situation in which public employees and, increasingly, private workers, found it necessary to make direct demands on the government. These demands invariably involved salary increases to offset the loss in purchasing power that accompanied the spiraling inflation. (Table 14 illustrates this declining real income.)

Table 14
Index of Salaries in Selected Activities, 1957-1967
(1957=100)

Year	Industry and Construction	Public Employment	Commerce	Total
1957	100.0	100.0	100.0	100.0
1958	97.3	97.2	95.2	96.9
1959	90.5	89.3	88.3	89.7
1960	90.0	89.5	86.9	89.7
1961	94.8	73.0	95.9	84.6
1962	97.1	72.8	103.8	86.5
1963	96.3	65.8	102.8	82.7
1964	90.2	67.1	97.0	80.1
1965	85.0	61.8	89.9	74.6
1966	94.5	52.6	89.0	73.8
1967	91.4	60.2	90.9	76.5

SOURCE: Instituto de Economía, *El Proceso Económico del Uruguay* (Montevideo: Universidad de la República, 1969), pp. 274, 330.

One group in particular bore the brunt of the higher cost of living. These were the individuals living on retirement or old age pensions. Real median income for pensioned individuals declined precipitously from a base of 100 in 1963 to 47.9 in 1970.[16] Basically unorganized, this group did not have the instrument of direct pressure available to the workingman.

The strike became the increasingly frequent tool of labor to better its position. Total man-days of labor lost through strikes is estimated at 1,200,000 per year during the 1950s, but jumped to 2,500,000 for 1963.[17] As inflation skyrocketed in the mid-sixties, major strikes and work stoppages became an everyday fact of life in Montevideo. Transportation workers, bank clerks, and the heavily unionized workers of the state industrial and service enterprises were particularly active. The militarization of bank employees in 1969 and the use of troops to break a power and utility workers strike in 1968 were just a few of the repressive measures taken by the Pacheco government against these more militant unions within the communist dominated National Workers Convention.

The traditionally antiestablishment position of the university was also exacerbated by these trends. Uruguay's University had a long history of leftist political activism, and increased university demonstrations in support of striking workers and memorial services for fallen guerrillas deeply disturbed the government. Pacheco's administration made no secret of the fact that it believed the University, and especially its Medical, Architecture, and Fine Arts schools were directly supportive of the guerrillas. The university-run hospital and other university buildings were the scene of extensive search operations whenever the guerrillas pulled off their growing number of kidnappings.

This interinstitutional strife had been compounded for several years by the emergence of a new and important political force—urban guerrillas. The existence of an organized revolutionary movement officially calling itself the *National Liberation Movement—Tupamaros* was an indication that growing divisions could not be contained at the institutional level and were spilling over into basic value conflict concerning the nature of the national community. It is not by chance that the most widely used *Tupamaro* slogan was *"Habrá patria para todos o patria para nadie"* which translates as: "There will be a fatherland for all or a fatherland for none."

Many commentators were surprised by the appearance of a revolutionary guerrilla movement in Uruguay. They felt that the literate, sophisticated, relatively democratic, and still relatively comfortable society was not the kind of sea in which revolution normally spawns. What they overlooked was the fact that it is these very conditions which would impel more and more individuals to challenge an increasingly repressive and privileged regime and enable these individuals to make such a challenge effective.

The best information available indicates that the *Tupamaros* were organized in late 1962 or early 1963 around a nucleus of disenchanted members of the Socialist party.[18] Their founder was Raúl Sendic, then

a 36-year-old law student and militant member of the Socialist party
who had been active in the organization of the sugar beet and sugar
cane workers in Uruguay's northeast. The name *Tupamaro* has two possible derivations. The most widely accepted explanation is that the
name was derived from Tupac Amaru, an Indian chief who led an un-
successful rebellion against the Spanish and was rewarded for his efforts
by being drawn and quartered in Cuzco's main square. Another explanation argues that the name was taken from Uruguayan history, the term
having been used in the 1820s and 1830s for the rebel bands that continued to attack the large landowners after the defeat and self-imposed
exile of the nationalist hero, Artigas.

In any event, the *Tupamaros* remained in a totally clandestine organizational phase until 1967 when they made their position and motives
public:

> For these reasons, we have placed ourselves outside the law. This is
> the only honest action when the law is not equal for all; when the
> law exists to defend the spurious interests of a minority in detriment
> to the majority; when the law works against the country's progress;
> when even those who have created it place themselves outside it, with
> impunity, whenever it is convenient for them.
>
> The hour of rebellion has definitively sounded for us. The hour of
> patience has ended. The hour of action and commitment has com-
> menced *here and now*. The hour of conversation and the enunciation
> of theory, propositions and unfulfilled promises is finished.
>
> We should not be worthy Uruguayans, nor worthy Americans, nor
> worthy of ourselves if we do not listen to the dictates of conscience
> that day after day calls us to the fight. Today no one can deny us
> the right to follow this dictate, wherever it might lead. No one can
> take the sacred right of rebellion away from us, and no one is going
> to stop us from dying, if necessary, in order to be of consequence.[19]

The opening paragraph of this statement merits particular attention.
The *Tupamaros* indicate that they are profoundly aware that the rule of
law is a basic instrument through which an effective national community
is built and that the perversion of this instrument dooms the creation of
an egalitarian national community. They thus take the position that they

must place themselves outside the law in order to build a viable nation-state. Their position is deeply nationalist. Indeed, one may argue that the *Tupamaros* were the only effective nationalist voice in Uruguay in the late 1960s and early 1970s.

The ideology of the movement has never been espoused in an explicit, coherent, single statement, although several documents, communiques, and interviews do give some basis for analysis.[20] The *Tupamaros* believe in an independent, integrated, national community for Uruguay and affirm that such independence and integration can only be built through socialism. The blueprint for socialism is vague, but includes nationalization of the banking and export apparatus and a thorough land reform program, including expropriation of large and underutilized holdings.

They also believe that the political and economic power holders in a capitalist, dependent nation like Uruguay will not relinquish power peacefully, and therefore conclude that armed revolution is necessary. Violence is seen as a necessary tactic of this revolution, but is not promoted as an end in itself. The movement's spokesmen also believe that the final victory will require mass action and that *Tupamaro* activity promotes this possibility by (1) pointing out the corruption and inefficiency of the regime, and (2) demonstrating that the *Tupamaros* are a parallel power within the nation, thereby raising the consciousness of the public. Organized labor and the university and high school populations are seen as the most available sources of mass support for the guerrillas.

It might be added as a final consideration that the *Tupamaros* were always aware of potential foreign intervention and the demonstration effect offered by Brazil. In a document written in March 1972, the point is made that Brazil offered "an example which our local oligarchs might want to imitate"—a prophetic observation.[21]

During the mid-and late 1960s, the *Tupamaro* strategy and ideology became defined, and their impact became apparent. Adopting an urban focus based on the obvious demographic and political reality that is the Uruguayan city-state, the movement embarked on an escalating series of robberies to secure money and arms. By 1969 the guerrillas had added political kidnapping to their arsenal and in 1970 kidnapped and assassinated Daniel Mitrione, a U. S. AID official working with the Uruguayan police. During the remainder of 1970 and 1971 the guerrillas pulled off several spectacular kidnappings and robberies, and in September of the latter year freed, in one jailbreak, all of the one hundred plus guerrillas being held by the government. However, instead of pressing its advantage, the movement decided on a temporary truce while it supported the newly created leftist coalition, the *Frente Amplio*, in the November elections. It is in this context of increased confrontation, growing repression, and the new leftist alliance that the 1971 election should be understood. The election would be a strong test of the Uruguayan political system, and its implications and effects would be profound.

The 1971 elections were complicated, as usual, by Uruguay's electoral peculiarities.[22] Uruguay's constitution and electoral laws (the so-called *Ley de Lemas*) provide for a congress elected by strict proportional representation and a president elected by means of a simultaneous primary/election through the mechanism of the "double simultaneous vote."[23] This system enables the ballot cast for a presidential candidate and his faction (*sub-lema*) to accrue to that candidate and to his party (*lema*) at the same time. The most voted candidate of the most voted party attains the presidency (Article 151). What this has meant in the highly factonalized world of Uruguayan politics is that the two traditional parties usually present several presidential candidates. This splintering has not led to electoral suicide since, as explained above, the party is credited with the votes of all presidential candidates who agree (and are permitted) to run under the general party title or label (*lema*). In practice, then, the *Blanco* and *Colorado* parties could more accurately be depicted as electoral cartels than as parties in the traditional sense.

The 1971 election saw the usual multiple candidacies. The *Colorados* offered five, and the *Blancos,* three, presidential aspirants. But the voter was faced with a new and, for many, radical third party alternative in the *Frente Amplio.* This coalition of socialists, communists, Christian Democrats, independents, and dissident factions of the *Colorados* and *Blancos* had emerged as a serious alternative by March of the election year. Its legality and ability to contest the election gave rise to several constitutional questions.

The 1966 constitution, in a continuing process of incorporation of the long-standing series of electoral and party legislation, makes a careful distinction between "permanent" and "accidental" parties.

Article 79 specifically states: "To be considered permanent, a party must have participated in the preceding national election and must have attained parliamentary representation." As a new electoral group, the *Frente* could not qualify as a permanent party and would thus be denied the right to accumulate the votes of its various factions (*sub-lemas*), a right reserved to permanent parties by Article 79. Forced to run a unified list of candidates for congress, the *Frente's* various factions would have jeopardized their individual identities. More important, they would have been unable to determine their individual electoral strength and contribution to the ticket. Such determinations would be crucial in the upcoming election and the future political moves of the factions. The only way to overcome this prospect was to run under the *lema* of a permanent party. This was accomplished when Juan Pablo Terra, leader of the small but active Christian Democratic party (P.D.C.) and a strong proponent of a third party alternative for Uruguay, was willing to lend his party's *lema* to the coalition.

The *Frente* ran a single presidential candidate, although its status as a permanent party enabled it to offer several if it so desired. The delicate nature of the coalition prevented such a move. The Uruguayan voter is well aware that through the "double simultaneous vote," his ballot for one candidate can help elect another presidential aspirant within the same party. Several of the leaders of the leftist coalition would have caused many potential voters to desert the *Frente* if they were presidential candidates. Consequently, a nonaligned retired general, Liber Seregni, was put forth as the sole *Frente* presidential candidate. The political leaders of the various leftist groups agreed to head the senate lists of their respective factions (*sub-lemas*) within the *Frente Amplio*.

Another crucial election issue involved a plebiscite on a presidential succession amendment. Under the constitution, Pacheco could not succeed himself, but a constitutional amendment permitting him to do so had been placed on the election agenda after the pro-Pacheco forces obtained the requisite signatures of 10 percent of the eligible voters (Art. 331, Sec. A). To be adopted, the amendment (and with it Pacheco's reelection) needed the majority support of those voting in the regular election. (It received almost 440,000 votes, far short of one-half of the votes cast.) The voter could cast a ballot for a general succession amendment or one indicating his support for Pacheco's specific reelection. In addition, of course, he could cast a separate ballot for one of the regular presidential candidates. In the opinion of qualified observers, President Pacheco's reelection campaign was a brilliant political move, for although the succession amendment had little chance of passing, the President's active electoral presence undoubtedly helped his party. As will be discussed below, it also enabled considerable manipulation of the vote count.

The campaign itself was accompanied by a level of violence unparalleled since the civil war period at the beginning of the century. A right-wing youth group called Uruguayan Youth on the March (JUP, *Juventud Uruguaya en Pie*) conducted many public meetings and demonstrations which led to violence against several local political headquarters of *Frente Amplio* factions. Campaigning in the interior, General Seregni was attacked by one knife wielding individual, and on the same day an eleven year old boy was killed by a stray bullet apparently aimed at the General's motorcade. During the campaign period, the homes or offices of several leftist academics and politicians were damaged by explosive or incendiary devices. In addition several violent confrontations were reported between right- and left-wing youths in the secondary schools.

As election day approached, the ideological rhetoric, always prominent in Uruguay's electoral politics, took on a strident and divisive tone. Newspapers warned the Jewish community, among others, that a vote for the *Frente Amplio* was a vote for the Russian bear and the anti-Semitism and other aspects frequently associated with communist politics. These ads implored the voter to vote for one of the traditional parties, stating that to do otherwise was to vote against the future of electoral democracy. Two days before the election, conservative *Colorados* and *Blancos* joined together in a large demonstration in "defense of democracy." It is worth noting that the liberal *Blanco* presidential candidate (the only liberal out of the eight presidential candidates of the two traditional parties) refused to associate himself with the demonstration and requested that his supporters remain at home and not participate.

The heated political climate in which the campaign took place was not cooled by the election itself. A huge turnout was insured by a government decision to enforce (for the first time) the obligatory voting clause in the constitution. A fine of five dollars would be imposed on nonvoters, and salary or pension payments would be delayed for those

who did not vote. In a ninety-five degree late spring heat wave, pro-
cedural delays at voting stations required the government to obtain a
four hour extension of voting hours. Fearing these possible delays and
challenges, the *Frente Amplio* had urged its supporters to go to the
polls early.

The snafus, delays, and extension of voting hours may be considered
acceptable facts of life during an election. What must be far more
seriously questioned is the vote count itself. Early returns indicated the
expected pattern: a heavy *Colorado* plurality in Montevideo with the
usual *Blanco* advantage in the interior. The *Frente Amplio* received a
not unexpected 30 percent in Montevideo but did so poorly in the interior
that its total national vote was a disappointing 18 percent.[24] It was clear,
with less than half the vote counted, that the *Frente* had done poorly.
Attention quickly turned to the narrowing *Colorado* lead, which fell
below 11,000 as more votes were tallied from the interior. But surprisingly,
after a confusing halt in the preliminary counting procedure, the *Colorado*
lead held up, despite the late returns from the traditionally *Blanco*-
dominated interior. President Pacheco's handpicked candidate, Juan
María Bordaberry, was unofficially declared the winner as the *Colorado*
party outpolled the National party whose reformist candidate, Wilson
Ferreira Aldunate, was actually the most-voted candidate, having received
26 percent of the vote to Bordaberry's 24 percent.

Wilson Ferreira Aldunate was prevented from winning the election
by a determined *Colorado* president and the aquiescence of conservative
Blancos who did not wish to see their own party's liberal presidential
candidates elected, even if it meant that their party was defeated. There
is strong evidence to support this view beyond the irregularities mentioned above. The amending ballot supporting Pacheco's reelection was
deliberately almost identical to the regular Bordaberry ballot. Voting
procedures enabled the citizen to put both the ballot for amendment and
his regular election ballot in the same envelope. Given the large number
of reform ballots cast (several hundred thousand), it is not difficult
to believe that several thousand Pacheco ballots found their way into
the regular *Colorado* tally. (One observer estimated that some 35,000
extra ballots could have been credited to Bordaberry in this manner, over
two and one-half times more than the winning margin.) Indicative of this
possibility is the fact that more votes than registered voters were reported
in several dozen election districts. Additionally, a few weeks after the

election, several bags of uncounted ballots turned up in a paper pulp
plant outside of the capital. Charges of irregularity were politely raised
by the *Blanco* leadership, but Ferreira Aldunate and his supporters were
left to their own devices in terms of investigating or strenuously denouncing such irregularities.

The Uruguayan electoral court (*Corte Electoral*) did not officially
certify the election results until February 19, 1972, less than two weeks
before the new administration would take office and over two and one-
half months after the elections themselves. The official count was as
follows:

Colorado Party	681,624
National Party	668,822
Frente Amplio	304,275

Bordaberry won by some 13,000 votes in an election in which over
88 percent of the eligible voters (the highest turnout ever) cast ballots. In
a postelection press conference the president-elect hinted at the future
course of his government, indirectly reaffirming the ideological roots we
described earlier in this study. Bordaberry declared his *"afinidades ideólogicas
con el gobierno brasileño,"* criticized liberal church activity, and attacked
university autonomy.[25]

On March 1, 1972, Bordaberry was sworn in as president. He was chief
executive of a nation which, as relatively late as 1968, lacked one of the
most common elements of a hardening, right-wing, neofascist political
picture—the active political involvement of or intervention by the military.
But this situation changed rapidly.

During the Pacheco administration there had been one serious political
crisis that involved the military. On June 24, 1969, in the face of major
strikes growing out of the continuing inflation and wage freezes, the
president reimposed a limited state of siege under the *"Medidas Prontas
de Seguridad."* The administration closed the leftist newspaper *Extra* and
arrested scores of labor leaders, but the strikes continued. In early August,
Pacheco decreed the militarization of private bank workers who had been
on strike since July 2. He further indicated that under such militarization,
workers who refused to stop their strike would be subject to a court martial. The Uruguayan congress prepared to vote on a nullification of the
militarization decree. On the eve of this vote, Pacheco conspicuously

visited several army, navy, and air force installations in and around Montevideo. In addition, in an appearance before parliament, Defense Minister Antonio Francese reminded his audience: "I am not here as a minister, but as a general; the armed forces are the guardians of the nation's institutions."[26] The president's action and the minister's statement had their effect. Congress did not vote on the militarization, apparently not willing to test the administration's implied threat to ignore or close congress with the support of the military.

On September 9, 1971, immediately after the spectacular escape of 109 *Tupamaros* from the Punta Carretas Penitentiary, President Pacheco put the army in control of all antiguerrilla activity. This important new role for the army did not have an immediate impact because of the truce declared by the *Tupamaros* in the months surrounding the November 1971 elections. The *Tupamaros* ended the informal truce on April 14, 1972, with the assassination of several officials in various sections of Montevideo. The president immediately asked for and received a declaration of "internal war" against the *Tupamaros*. In essence, Uruguay was placed under martial law, and all constitutional guarantees of individual liberties were suspended.

The military, given carte blanche and unhampered by judicial or constitutional restraints, proceeded to employ repressive techniques that moved far beyond those that any administration had dared to employ in any systematic or sustained manner. The use of torture and drugs were weapons which the *Tupamaros* could not withstand. In the ensuing months, the army enjoyed almost total success against the guerrillas, all but destroying their infrastructure, capturing hundreds of active supporters, and detaining thousands of other suspects.

I would here hazard the hypothesis, with the advantage of hindsight, that the decision to support the *Frente Amplio* and refrain from their usual activity from October 1971 to April 1972 was a fatal mistake for the *Tupamaros*. Apparently faced with the problem of expanding their base, the *Tupamaros* took a calculated risk and supported the effort of the various liberal groups that made up the *Frente*.

But, as the guerrillas themselves emphasized, they did not believe that the revolution could be made in Uruguay through elections. Permitting elections to take place in an atmosphere controlled by the Pacheco government and allowing his handpicked successor to take power in relative calm put them at a disadvantage. In addition, since the jailbreak in September, the armed forces had been placed in control of antiguerrilla operations and had been permitted to gear up for their role, unchallenged, since then. Thus, the dramatic *Tupamaro* escalation on April 14 was met by a firmly entrenched new administration backed by a well-equipped and adequately prepared military which needed but three months to crush the guerrilla movement—a movement which found itself abandoned by the liberal groups that it had surfaced to support in the elections.

In the midst of its success against the *Tupamaros,* the government passed an omnibus security bill which represented a final blow to freedom of the press and is deeply revealing of the ideological proclivities of the regime. Dusting off and amending a press law passed under the Terra dictatorship in 1935, the new law made a whole host of journalistic activities criminally punishable by military courts. Under the legislation, editors, publishers, and the actual authors of articles that deprecated the nation, defended persons sought for or accused of crimes, or disseminated false information, were liable to three months to two years in prison. The *Ley de Seguridad del Estado,* in which the new press legislation was included, established harsh penalties for all subversive activities and conspiracy to commit subversive acts. Those charged with these crimes would be tried in military courts. In addition, the law also empowered the president to suspend or deny the right of public assembly if such assemblage tended to bring about or encourage the "alteration of public order."[27]

The government also moved against the autonomous structure of education. In the past, it had limited its reprisals against the university and secondary schools to a cutting of funds for scholarships and operating expenses. This policy was reflected in the changing priority for education in the national budget. While total current peso expenditure increased 5.8 times between 1968 and 1973, the education budget only increased some four times. During this same period, defense expenditures multiplied by 12. While the education component of the budget fell from 24.3 percent to 16.6 percent between 1968 and 1973, the military component increased from 13.9 to 26.2 percent.[28] As student unrest filtered down to secondary school students, the government moved to abolish the autonomous councils that governed secondary, primary, and vocational education. Legislation was proposed that would restructure these governing bodies in the hope that this would depoliticize the school system. The previously autonomous councils would be replaced by five-member boards with three members selected by the president and two by congress. Student and teacher strikes were in effect outlawed by a prohibition on activity which "might impede or deny the right of study."[29] A curious but telling clause betrays the organic and corporatist bias of the bill's creators. This clause provides for the suspension of the assistance allowance paid to families with school children if the child proves to be a discipline problem. The attempt to hold the family as a unit responsible for the conduct of the child is a deeply organic attempt to control political unrest in the schools.

The new legislation and legislative proposals were met with a growing number of strikes and demonstrations. The education bill provoked sit-ins and strikes by faculty and students from the university through the primary schools. Doctors and health and hospital workers struck over new national health insurance proposals and in support of several prominent doctors arrested and detained on charges of guerrilla-related activities.

As inflation approached 100 percent, public and private employees struck for an adjustment in salary. In response to this unrest, the government floated several proposals to limit the right to strike and restructure the communist-dominated unions. At the same time, it also pushed the education bill through the legislature.

Adding to this already tense situation was a military anxious to flex its new muscle after its dramatic success against the *Tupamaros*. The armed forces quickly moved to institutionalize their role in the political process. In July 1972 over 500 officers met and issued a strong statement condemning congressional charges of armed forces brutality against prisoners. The officers declared such attacks to be an unpatriotic smearing of the defenders of the nation. Later in the year, during the growing military anticorruption campaign, a *Colorado* senator, Jorge Batlle, was arrested and detained for 24 days after attacking the military's authority to conduct investigations of corruption.

During the second week of February 1973, the army and air force (joined later by the navy) openly rebelled against President Bordaberry's selection of Antonio Francese as Minister of Defense. Actually, the Francese appointment was merely the excuse for a quasi-coup. The military were really formally announcing their intention to oversee national policy. It appeared that the president would be forced to resign, but an accommodation was soon reached. Bordaberry would stay in power, but government policy would be supervised by a newly created National Security Council clearly dominated by the military.

The ideological foundations of the military action appeared, at first blush, to be of a left-nationalist variety. The commanders issued a communique calling for a *"revolución a la uruguaya,"* and demanded a host of reforms.[30] The reforms included reorganization of the public administration, distribution of land, stimulation of the export sector and employment, and investigation of illegal economic activities. The statement indicated that the armed forces' activity against the *Tupamaros* had made them conscious of the deep problems facing the country and that, with this new awareness, they had decided to give a firm directon to the solving of these problems.

In spite of the rhetoric, the military proceeded to act with vigor only in regard to its anticorruption campaign. As for students and the unions, after promising to stay out of these problem areas, the army quickly backed the president's clearly repressive legislation. The military's support for the State Security Law and the proposed Law of the Consolidation of the Peace indicated that they were clearly in agreement with the president on the need for such measures.

The Law of the Consolidation of the Peace (originally proposed with the harsher but perhaps more accurate title, *Ley de Estado Peligroso*) would have established a virtual police state in Uruguay. The heart of the proposal empowered military courts to order the "indefinite detainment of persons whose conduct suggested they might be inclined to commit crimes against the state, persons who had legally or illegally assisted others accused of planning to commit crimes against the state, persons who frequented the same places as persons accused of committing crimes against the state, and persons who might be associated with subversive elements through possession of some object which had belonged to the subversive elements."[31] The bill's preamble, seeking to justify such measures, condemned the *Tupamaros*—who had been all but destroyed by this time—as demonstrating "instincts of special ferocity, genuine criminal delirium, the flowering of inherited tendencies, subhuman fear and vengeance peculiar to psychopathic personalities."[32]

The "ideal conception of Uruguay" that the military sought thus involved a heightened sense of security first, and a drive to root out corruption second. In their own words, they seek the "recovery of national moral values, patriotism, austerity, idealism, generosity, honor, abnegation and strength of character."[33] Noticeable is the lack of a specific call for social change. It is not surprising that the principal

leaders of the military's February thrust into politics were described
as "puritanical nationalists," and one was called a "believer in the
rural mystique."[34] One cannot turn the clock back to a mythical age
of the noble *gaucho*, especially when he erects a police state to
oversee his attempt.

On March 22, 1973, the armed forces issued a communique condemning the nation's politicians for their failure to help the president and
military in their efforts at national reconstruction, reminding the public
that the *Tupamaros* had attempted to "destroy the very base of our
nationality."[35] A few weeks later, the military demanded that congress
lift the immunity of Senator Enrique Erro whom they charged with
complicity with the *Tupamaros*. While the legislature balked over this
demand, the military issued an ominous communique (May 14, 1973)
strongly condemning congress for its failure to fight corruption and
subversion and for its attacks on the armed forces.[36] The situation reached
the boiling point in late June when the Chamber of Deputies declined
to institute impeachment proceedings against Erro and the senate voted
to investigate charges of torture levelled against the armed forces.

This growing tension between congress and the presidential-military
confluence culminated in a military-backed presidential coup in the early
morning hours of June 27, 1973. Bordaberry closed congress, prohibited
the dissemination of any information implying dictatorial motives to the
government, and empowered the police and armed forces to take whatever measures necessary to ensure continued public services.

In his message to the nation that same night, President Bordaberry
blamed the inefficiency, corruption, and misuse of privilege by congress
for his actions. He singled out the Erro matter as the crux of the situation.
Calling Erro "the symbol of the infiltrated enemy," Bordaberry argued
that the failure to lift his immunity "represents the decay of the spirit
of struggle against sedition."[37] Actually, this matter was the tip of the
iceberg. In point of fact, the congressional majority that Bordaberry had
painstakingly assembled in 1972 (another example of coparticipation)
through a series of agreements and political payoffs to several *Blanco* and
Colorado factions had broken down by May 1973 with the adoption of
an independent position by several legislators. Thus, the administration
no longer had the necessary votes to continue the now year-old suspension of civil liberties and could not count on passage of some of the
legislative proposals discussed above.[38] In addition, more and more con-
gressmen were actively denouncing and attempting to investigate military

involvement in politics and charges of torture of prisoners held under military jurisdiction.

Bordaberry's message affirmed his government's commitment to "legitimate private interest," welcomed foreign capital, and rejected "all ideology of Marxist origin that attempts to thrive on our difficulties, that intends to take advantage of the generosity of our democracy in order to present itself as a doctrine of salvation while ending up as an instrument of totalitarian oppression."[39] In his message to congress declaring that body's dissolution, Bordaberry used the same arguments and included the actions of the labor unions and educational institutions in the list of structures that had been "penetrated" and suffered from "the conspiracy against the nation."[40]

In response to the closing of congress, the National Workers Convention issued a call for a general strike. The government responded by declaring the labor organization illegal. The strike lasted for fifteen days but was broken by government action which included the arrest of scores of union leaders, the call to military service (mobilization) of some technically skilled individuals, and finally, a decree permitting public and private employers to fire summarily anyone who did not report to work. The government also moved against the political opposition. The presidential candidate of the *Frente Amplio,* retired army general Liber Seregni, and several of his aides were arrested, as was the president of the *Partido Nacional.* Several leading politicians went into exile in Argentina and vowed to maintain organized opposition to the regime. Action against the public at large was limited until the night of July 9, when a peaceful demonstration by several thousand opponents of the regime was violently dispersed by the police and army with several individuals shot, scores injured, and hundreds arrested. The Catholic and Protestant churches in Uruguay deplored the situation, and the Uruguayan Episcopate declared that "all order imposed by force, that is not founded on justice, sooner or later engenders violence."[41]

It is obviously difficult to make a definitive judgment on the ideological axis of the new power holders in Uruguay, but some telling evidence is available. In an interview granted to an Argentine reporter five days after the coup, Bordaberry indicated that the old unionism would not be tolerated, for the government had liberated the unions from the "dictatorship that communism exercised over them." He announced that the banks would not be nationalized and that land reform would be carried out almost exclusively through incentive tax policies.[42]

But Bordaberry's most interesting comments concerned Brazil. He indicated that "we have a certain attitude of sympathy for the Brazilian regime, and I have sometimes said we have points in common." When pressed on the nature of these points, Bordaberry responded: "They are anti-communism in the defense of democracy. Moreover, we have an ample border with Brazil which makes it possible for us to develop a policy of economic integration."[43] It appears that the president had no qualms about using Brazilian political methods and in turning Uruguay into a client-state of Brazil.

The most overtly ideological statement in the aftermath of the take-over was issued by the Minister of the Interior, Colonel Nestor Bolentini. In his statement of the objectives of the new government, the Minister evoked a strongly neofascist image of a future Uruguayan society. He saw the immediate task of government as one of establishing "the continuity of work." Once this was accomplished, the government would pursue its goal "to normalize the tripartite relations between workers, enterprises, and the State—to establish a method which, supported by dialogue and understanding, permits the peaceful subsistence of the three sectors and their harmonic action in pursuit of common objectives."[44] Here we have a 1973 version of the centuries old falangist (corporatist) ideal of a society built upon and regulated through the functional operation of its essential pillars or sectors. The symbol system from which he borrows is laden with the traditional corporative concern for work, duty, and harmonious relations between the key pillars of society, plus the added vision of rural virtue and anticommunism.

Bolentini recognizes that there are "recalcitrants" who may not share or approve of this goal, but they must understand that "in Uruguay, there is no place for extremisms." There is only room for "*orientalidad*," that is, a recognition of a superior Uruguayan "national interest, the interest of the people themselves."[45] Unfortunately, the Minister forgets that the national interest will now be defined by an ever more narrow and ideologically circumscribed group which is in the most profound sense antinational, for it precludes the development of an egalitarian national community.

It is fitting that Bordaberry, his ministers, and the military chiefs have given such early and clear clues to the nature of their regime at both the operative and intellectual levels. Throughout this study I have examined the relationships between values, ideology, and institutions as they affect the construction and maintenance of the nation-state. Having looked at

Uruguay's political, ideological, and institutional development in this century, I conclude that nationalism as a social value is necessary for the development of an effective nation-state. The emphasis here is on the word "nation." It is not denied that the state (although probably not a very efficient one) can exist in the absence of nationalism as a social value. It is denied that an egalitarian national community can be built without such a value commitment.

Uruguay's *Batllista* experiment, as limited or bourgeois as it may have been, was an attempt to build a viable nation-state. The democratic nationalism which it propounded and the policies and institutions which it established gave the Uruguayan citizen a standard of living, a freedom of conscience, and a quality of membership in the social nation that would be difficult to equal in many systems. The turning-away from that commitment in the 1930s put Uruguay on an ever more precarious course in which the *Batllista* legacy survived as a structure whose facade slowly crumbled as leadership groups tried to maintain their own position and their control of the state without the necessary commitment to the national community which effective action required.

It has been nearly two years since the June 1973 coup, two years in which the new leaders of Uruguay could begin to flesh out their vision. The record of this period, however, is mostly one of increased repression: the further suppression of civil liberties and freedom of the press; the prohibition of labor unions and most political parties; an interference with the university that has brought Uruguay's only institution of higher learning to a standstill; and the continued imprisonment of thousands of men and women in jails, military garrisons, and prison camps. The economic situation, bleak at the time of the coup, has turned even more sour. The response to this situation has been a growing frustration within the armed forces and the continued juggling of Bordaberry's cabinet. In addition to this general drift, however, a strategy has emerged which can provide us with greater insight into the nature of corporatist regimes.

Until recently, many had seen in the economic success of the Brazilian regime a justification of corporatism as a developmentalist ideology. There is no doubt that twentieth-century corporatism recognizes the reality of the Industrial Revolution. However, in the Uruguayan case, we see the ability or even desire of one such regime to forego development and even destroy forces of production in the name of preserving existing power relationships. After two years in power and with the added prodding of the oil crisis, it appears that the Uruguayan military and supporting civilian interests are prepared to abandon any meaningful attempt to modernize the industrial sector. Rather, the image of an agrarian state has an ever increasing hold on the imagination of the leadership.

As these men see it, the future is an Uruguay that is one big *estancia* importing its industrial needs from its northern neighbor, i.e., Uruguay as an agrarian client-state of Brazil. Uruguay's current decision-makers are not troubled by the fact that this scenario has meant the wholesale writeoff of middle and lower class families historically tied to the secondary and tertiary sectors of the Uruguayan economy. Tens of thousands of these families have emigrated in the last few years, and, aside from some mild government skittishness concerning this mass exodus, the official attitude seems to be predominantly one of good-bye and good riddance.

The present rulers of Uruguay claim to be building or reconstructing a viable nation-state. In the short run, they are probably capable of strengthening the Uruguayan state, but their ideas and actions indicate they have no interest in and are incapable of constructing the social nation. Thus, their actions deny and will continue to deny membership in the national community to a large number of Uruguay's citizens.

The construction of an egalitarian national community is a difficult process and, as anyone familiar with political history knows, that process is fraught with failure and regression. In its own way, Uruguay was seeking to build such a community at the beginning of this century. Not unexpectedly, the nation was faced with economic and political problems which inevitably tested the commitment to the process of democratic nation-building. As the economic situation deteriorated, Uruguay's leaders and their publics were increasingly faced with a crucial choice. Now, more than ever, they had to decide clearly between a particularist politics of privilege and class and a nationalist politics that would promote the development of an egalitarian national community. They chose privilege and class and proved again that such a choice, especially in the face of economic difficulties, inevitably means that the nation suffers. In addition, the military, so long an apolitical institution, decided to play the role that we have grown accustomed to in this century—that of undertaker in the death of the social nation.

The advantage of employing this theoretical framework, however, goes far beyond the ability to evaluate the present Uruguayan regime. In doing this study, one of the conclusions I have reached is that it is theoretically important, diagnostically necessary, and methodologically possible to look at what men and, particularly, political elites say about politics, programs, and the visions they hold for their societies. The symbol system they employ is a clue to the society they would build. The dismissal of speeches, debates, editorials, and like material as rhetoric is a facile way to dismiss these important tools for analysis and prediction. The social scientist does so at peril to his diagnostic and explanatory models. Analysis on the basis of values and ideology places men at the center of political causality, while the material and structural limits on his thought and action are recognized. The political scientist has all too frequently employed frameworks which at best place human beings on the dependent side of the causal equation and at worst eliminate them altogether by talking exclusively about "forces," "requisites," "structures," or "functions."

It is also clear that, beyond the fact that the symbols employed by a political generation are reflected in the institutions it erects, these institutions delimit the changes that a subsequent or competing ideology can effect. This was increasingly evident as one viewed the tension between the institutions created by *Batllismo* and its political and ideological opponents, who found themselves saddled with its legacy even as they attempted an authoritarian solution in the 1930s.

We are, in effect, arguing that the framework is not static, that its dynamism is made understandable through historical analysis and at the same time brings processes into sharper focus. Thus, Uruguay's strong two-party tradition, coupled with a particularist and subnational value stance of the leaders of these parties, made coparticipation an excellent mechanism by which to accommodate tradition and the balance of political forces to the needs of political groups. The nature of political reform and the various constitutional experiments are more clearly understood in this context, and their increasingly antinational implications become more obvious.

This analysis also points up the close relationship between the two key instrumental institutions in society, the polity and the economy. These have been closely tied in Uruguay since the triumph of *Batllismo*. Modernization and the development of an effective nation-state thus implied for Uruguay (and, one suspects, elsewhere) a synthesizing political institution not nearly as differentiated from other institutions as the development literature leads one to believe. It is an institution which is charged with a function that crucially determines the class structure of the society and hence the development of an egalitarian national community. Perhaps it is this last measure which should be employed in determining a given polity's development.

The relationship between nationalism and development requires a deeper analysis of the relationship between nationalism and capitalism. The development of capitalism required the liberation of men from the soil and the creation of urban centers of production. The concept of citizen (one of the city) flowed from this requirement as did the need for a new value to integrate the complex transpersonal world that capitalism both required and developed. The emergence of secularism, rationalism, and science were part of the picture, but underlying the changing value structure was the emergence of nationalism as a social value. Just as empathy allowed the individual to relate to an increasingly complex and impersonal world, nationalism allowed for a societal-wide institutional power reflection of empathy. Thus, nationalism became one of capitalism's principal contributions to man's potential for development.

The nationalism nurtured by capitalism holds out the promise of an egalitarian national community, but the structures and power relationships of modern capitalism block the creation of such a community. We are thrust back and faced with the tension between class and citizenship discussed in the first chapter. Capitalist politics are essentially class-creating politics. As such, capitalist societies reach a point in their development when, having solved or being capable of solving the basic problem of the production and distribution of goods and services, they must face the tougher question of social justice and equality for all citizens. Such societies can decide whether or not they will move beyond the politics of class. Unfortunately, most have opted to preserve and protect existing distinctions and power configurations at whatever cost to the society as a whole and to many of its citizens.

In this light, it is not surprising that the last decade has witnessed a significant convergence of political systems in Latin America. Nations that were considered so disparate in their political, social, and economic development suddenly find themselves easily placed in the same analytic category. The political systems of Brazil, Bolivia, Uruguay, and now

Chile can be described accurately as authoritarian, corporatist, military regimes. Reducing the problem to a simple but profound dichotomy, these nations have chosen dictatorship over democracy. Conflict in all of them could not be contained at an institutional level and quickly escalated to class and ideological confrontation, which raised the basic value question involving the definition of national community, i.e., the question of who is and who is not entitled to membership in the social nation. By answering this question in an essentially exclusivist and repressive manner, the regimes that have emerged espouse a curious view of politics: the depoliticization of the social polity. The overt attempt to depoliticize society that has accompanied the polemics and practice of all of these regimes is final proof that corporatism is a political ideology and not merely a schema for public administration. The attempt to do away with "politics" through force, repression, and torture and the reading of fellow citizens out of existence are profoundly political acts.

This depoliticization, which appears to be a primary goal of all corporatist regimes, is an ominous and misguided reading of the nature of community. The rejection of formal democracy, which is a sine qua non of such regimes, actually implies the rejection of politics as the conflict inherent in the making of normative choices concerning the goals, means, and distribution of product in a given society. It is only with the logic of such rejection that the corporatist could attempt to build a nation (community) without citizens. But as the Greeks concluded millenia ago, it is impossible to create a viable open community without the participation of the individuals who compose it in the conflictual process through which citizens decide their fate.

Politics should be desired for its affective and instrumental value to the individual and his society. Neither a purely utilitarian calculus nor a coldly corporate technocracy are capable of sustaining political systems in which men enjoy full citizenship and the nations in which they live have the openness to guide their destinies rationally; yet these are the routes that are increasingly chosen. Thus, Uruguay's path is not an isolated phenomenon, peculiar to that country. The events of recent years make it painfully obvious that the choice Uruguay has faced equally confronts the modern and emerging nations of this world.

NOTES

Chapter 1: The Theoretical Framework

1. Two of the more interesting discussions on the concept of ideology may be found in Reinhard Bendix, "The Age of Ideology: Persistent and Changing," in David Apter, ed., *Ideology and Discontent* (New York: Free Press, 1964), and George Lichtheim, "The Concept of Ideology," in his *The Concept of Ideology and Other Essays* (New York: Vintage, 1967).

2. See especially Daniel Bell, *The End of Ideology* (New York: Free Press, 1962). For the best collection on the issue, see Chaim T. Waxman, ed., *The End of Ideology Debate* (New York: Clarion Press, 1969); especially Joseph La Palombara's "Decline of Ideology: A Dissent and an Interpretation," pp. 315-341, reprinted from *American Political Science Review* vol. LX, no. 1, 1966.

3. In David Apter, ed., *op. cit.*, pp. 47-76.

4. See especially Ernst Cassirer, *An Essay on Man* (New York: Bantam, 1970), and Suzanne Langer, *Philosophy in a New Key: A Study of the Symbolism of Reason, Rite and Art* (New York: Mentor, 1969).

5. Cassirer, *op. cit.*, p. 29.

6. Geertz, "Ideology as a Cultural System," in David Apter, *op. cit.*, p. 56.

7. Walker Percy, "Symbol, Consciousness and Intersubjectivity," *Journal of Philosophy* 55 (1958), pp. 631-41, cited by Geertz, *op. cit.*, p. 61. (Emphasis in original.)

8. Geertz, *op. cit.*, p. 62.

9. *Ibid.*, p. 63.

10. Mannheim, *Ideology and Utopia* (New York: Harvest Books, 1936), pp. 57, 59.

11. Talcott Parsons and Edward A. Shils, eds., *Toward a General Theory of Action* (New York: Harper Torchbook), 1962 (1951).

12. *Ibid.*, p. 395.

13. Robert Lane, *Political Ideology* (New York: Free Press, 1962), p. 44.

14. Clyde Kluckhohn, "Values and Value Orientation," in Parsons and Shils, *op. cit.*, p. 433.

15. In David Apter, ed., *op. cit.*, pp. 206-261.

16. For an interesting discussion of legitimacy and stability as they are affected by authority patterns in a society see Harry Eckstein, *Division and Cohesion in Democracy: A Study of Norway* (Princeton University Press, 1966).

17. Hans Kohn, "A New Look at Nationalism," as quoted in Urban G. Whitaker, Jr., ed., *Nationalism and International Progress* (San Francisco: 1960), p. 21.

18. Carlton Hayes, *Essay on Nationalism* (New York: 1926), p. 235.

19. Carlton Hayes, *The Historical Evolution of Modern Nationalism* (New York: 1931), cited in Anthony D. Smith, *Theories of Nationalism* (New York: Harper Torchbook, 1971), p. 196.

20. *Human Nature in Politics* (New York: Knopf, 1921), p. 286, cited in Deutsch, *Nationalism and Social Communication: An Inquiry into the Foundations of Nationality,* 2nd ed. (Cambridge, Mass.: The M.I.T. Press, 1969 [1953]), p. 22. (Deutsch's italics.)

21. *A Study of War* (Chicago: University of Chicago Press, 1942), vol. 2, p. 999, cited by Deutsch, *op. cit.*, p. 23.

22. Deutsch, *op. cit.*, p. 177.

23. *Ibid.*, p. 97.

24. *Ibid.*, pp. 152-153.

25. Gerth and Mills, eds., *From Max Weber: Essays in Sociology* (New York: Oxford University Press, 1958), p. 172.

26. "The Strategy of the Study of Nationalism," in Silvert, ed., *Expectant Peoples: Nationalism and Development* (New York: Vintage, 1967), pp. 3-38.

27. *Ibid.*, p. 17.

28. *Ibid.*, p. 19.

29. *Ibid.*, p. 27.

30. *Ibid.*, p. 22.

31. Daniel Lerner, *The Passing of Traditional Society* (New York: The Free Press, 1966), p. 50.

32. *Ibid.*

33. Introduction by S. M. Lipset in *Class, Citizenship and Social Development: Essays by T. H. Marshall* (New York: Doubleday, 1964), p. 9.

34. E. H. Carr, *Nationalism and After* (London: MacMillan, 1968), p. 2.

35. *Ibid.*, p. 10.

36. *Ibid.*, p. 18.

37. Silvert, *op. cit.*, p. 32. I would not, however, argue that the process of national identification, modernization, and development

is unilinear or unidirectional, but rather that the strength of the social value of nationalism can significantly shape the scope and direction of change.

38. "Toward a Theory of Spanish American Government," *Journal of the History of Ideas* XV (1954), p. 72.

39. "Recent Research on Latin American Urbanization: A Selective Survey and Commentary, *Latin American Research Review* I (Fall 1965), p. 41.

40. K. H. Silvert, "The Costs of Anti-Nationalism: Argentina," in Silvert, *op. cit.,* p. 360.

41. Irving Louis Horowitz, "The Norm of Illegitimacy: The Political Sociology of Latin America," in Horowitz, de Castro, and Gerrasi, eds. *Latin American Radicalism* (New York: Vintage, 1969), p. 12.

42. Howard J. Wiarda, "Toward a Framework for the Study of Political Change in the Iberic-Latin Tradition: The Corporative Model," *World Politics* XXV (January 1973), p. 215. Another interesting but conceptually confused attempt to describe the cause and nature of corporatist politics may be found in Rogowski and Wasserspring. *Does Political Development Exist? Corporatism in Old and New Societies,* Sage Comparative Politics Series, 01-024 (Beverly Hills; Sage Publications, 1971).

43. "The P.R.I. and the Mexican Political System," M.A. thesis, New York University, 1968. In this study I used the term *controlled pluralism* to describe the phenomenon.

44. Ronald C. Newton, "On 'Functional Groups,'–'Fragmentation' and 'Pluralism' in Spanish American Political Society," *Hispanic American Historical Review* L (February 1970), p. 16.

45. *Ibid.,* p. 17.

46. Parsons and Shils, eds., *op. cit.,* p. 78.

47. *Ibid.*

48. *Ibid.,* p. 82.

49. Glen H. Dealy, "Prolegomena on the Spanish American Political Tradition," *Hispanic American Historical Review* XLVIII (February 1968), p. 51.

50. Franciso José Moreno, *Legitimacy and Stability in Latin America: A Study of Chilean Political Culture* (New York: New York University Press, 1969), especially Chapter I, "The Colonial Heritage."

51. "Fundamental Law Behind The Constitution of the United States," in Conyer Reed, ed., *The Constitution Reconsidered* (New York: Columbia University Press, 1938), reprinted in Macridis and Brown, eds., *Comparative Politics: Notes and Readings* (New York: Dorsey, 1968), p. 399.

52. Anne Freemantle, ed., *The Papal Encyclicals in Their Historical*

Context (New York: G. P. Putnam's Sons, 1956), p. 173.

53. *Ibid.,* p. 174.

54. *Ibid.,* p. 232.

55. Richard L. Camp, *The Papal Ideology of Reform* (Leiden: E. J. Brill, 1969), p. 39. From *Divini Redemptoris,* March 19, 1937.

56. Ralph Bowen, *German Theories of the Corporative State* (New York: McGraw-Hill, 1947), p. 6n.

57. The recognition of this influence is apparent in the increased literature on corporatism that has made its appearance in recent years. The January 1974 issue of *The Review of Politics* (vol. 36, no. 1) was devoted entirely to the subject, carrying the title *The New Corporatism: Social and Political Structures in the Iberian World.* Of particular interest in this issue is Philippe Schmitter's article "Still The Century of Corporatism?" While Schmitter plays down the valorative and cultural dimensions of corporatism in favor of a more structural interpretation, his own training and experience as a Latin Americanist compel him to concede that "it is, of course, quite conceivable at this early stage of research into these matters that what I have found to be a set of interrelated institutional practices coalescing into a distinctive, highly covariant and resistant modern system of interest representation may be quite limited in its scope of applicability, for example only to Iberian regimes. . . ." Schmitter thus recognizes the importance of the cultural context of corporatism in spite of his structural and cross-cultural inclinations on the subject. For an interesting recent volume that works within this cultural matrix while recognizing the crucial structural and class consideration involved see Lawrence Littwin, *Latin America Catholicism and Class Conflict* (Encino, California: Dickenson Publishing Company, Inc., 1974).

Chapter 2: *Batllismo* and Its Opponents: Ideology in Twentieth-Century Uruguay

1. As one observer summed up the nineteenth-century record of Uruguayan politics: "An inventory of seventy years of history shows: four or perhaps more visible foreign interventions, thirty-seven revolutions, three mutinies, two international wars, two tyrannies and two dictatorships. In those seventy years there were eighteen presidents, four dictators, one Triumvirate, one Council of State and your half dozen small indefinable interregnums. Of those eighteen presidents only eight completed their mandate. The other ten either fell to revolution or rose through it or through insurrection. E. Rodríguez Fabregat, *Batlle y Ordóñez:*

el reformador (Buenos Aires: Editorial Claridad, 1942), p. 292. My translation.

2. Blanca Paris de Oddone, Roque Faraone, and Juan Antonio Oddone *Cronología comparada de la historia del Uruguay (1830-1945)* (Montevideo: Universidad de la República, 1961), p. 23.
The 1908 Census indicated a population of 1,042,686. Although the figures are sketchy and recent evidence indicates a possible overestimation, it is obvious that Uruguay, like Argentina, experienced a tremendous population growth based on heavy Spanish and Italian immigration. The 1908 census indicated that 42 percent of the population of Montevideo was foreign born, while the total national figure was 17 percent (*Cronología*, p. 81). On this issue see J. A. Oddone, *La emigración Europea al Río de la Plata* (Montevideo: Ediciones de la Banda Oriental, 1966) and Juan José Percira and Raúl Trajtenberg, *Evolución de la población total y activa en el Uruguay: 1908-1957*, (Montevideo: Instituto de Economía, 1966).

3. *El Día*, January 2, 1896, cited by Carlos M. Rama, "Batlle y el Movimiento Obrera y Social," in Jorge Batlle (comp.), *Batlle: su vida y su obra* (Montevideo: Editorial Acción, 1956), p. 42. All translations from Spanish sources are by the author. At all times, I endeavored to capture the spirit and flavor of the original.

4. Luis C. Benvenuto, "La Quiebra del Modelo," *Encyclopedia Uruguaya* No. 42 (Montevideo: Editorial Reunidos and Editorial Arca, 1969), p. 142.

5. *El Día*, June 19, 1905, cited in "Batlle," *Cuadernos de Marcha*, no. 31 (Montevideo: 1969), p. 56.

6. *El Día*, January 3, 1896, cited by Efraín González Conzi and Roberto B. Giudice, *Batlle y el Batllismo* (Montevideo: Editorial Medina, 1959 [1928]), p. 307. This massive volume was put together by two young *Batllista* politicians shortly before Batlle's death. It is an extensive compilation and partisan commentary on the whole record of *Batllismo* until that date.

7. *El Día*, May 15, 1911, cited in "Batlle," *op. cit.*, p. 58.

8. *El Día*, June 3, 1917, cited in González Conzi and Giudice, *op. cit.*, p. 390.

9. *El Día*, June 16, 1917, cited in González Conzi and Giudice, *op. cit.*, p. 379.

10. Message to the General Assembly, April 23, 1913, cited in González Conzi and Giudice, *op. cit.*, p. 287.

11. Antonio M. Grompone, *La ideología de Batlle* (Montevideo: Editorial Arca, 1967 [193]), p. 79.

12. José L. Buzzetti, *La magnífica gestión de Batlle en obras públicas*

(Montevideo: Editorial Ceibo, 1946), p. 35.

13. Ronald C. Newton, among others, makes this observation in "On 'Functional Groups,' 'Fragmentation,' and 'Pluralism' in Spanish American Political Society," *Hispanic American Historical Review* L (February 1970).

14. Alberto Demicheli, *Los entes autónomos* (Montevideo: 1924), cited by Simon G. Hanson, *Utopia in Uruguay: Chapters in the Economic History of Uruguay* (New York: Oxford University Press, 1938), p. 108.

15. Article 100 of the 1917 Constitution. (My translation.) This constitution created a bicephalous executive: The president was responsible for the police, army, and the conduct of international affairs, and the National Administrative Council was responsible for the remaining administrative functions of the state.

16. Simon Hanson, *op. cit.,* p. 54.

17. González Conzi and Giudice, *op. cit.,* p. 293.

18. *El Día,* January 4, 1916, citied in "Batlle," *Cuadernos de Marcha,* no. 32 (Montevideo: 1969), p. 34.

19. *El Día,* April 13, 1916, cited in "Batlle," *ibid.,* p. 40.

20. *El Día,* June 3, 1917, cited by Conzi and Giudice, *op. cit.,* pp. 375-376.

21. Cámara de Representantes, *Diario de Sesiones,* vol. 204, p. 288. cited by Issac Ganón, "Batlle y la Organización de la familia," in *Batlle: su vida y su obra,* p. 106.

22. *El Día,* October 31, 1915, cited by González Conzi and Giudice, *op. cit.,* p. 313.

23. *El Día,* October 24, 1915, cited by González Conzi and Giudice, *op. cit.,* p. 314.

24. *El Día,* September 3, 1919, cited and translated by Simon Hanson, *op. cit.,* pp. 24-25.

25. The complete program may be found in González Conzi and Giudice, *op. cit.,* pp. 386-389 or in Justino Zavalo Muñiz, *Batlle-héroe civil* (Mexico: Fundación de Cultura Educativa, 1945), pp. 247-255

26. A much more ambitious salary and profit-share plan was submitted to the legislature by the *Batllistas* in 1923. Among its provisions was a call for the elevation of the salary of all workers in state industrial enterprises to twice the average salary in the immediate area of the country in which they lived. Once this was accomplished it was further suggested that 25 percent of the earned income of the enterprise be distributed annually among workers, employees and directors. For the complete text of the proposal see González Conzi and Giudice, *op. cit.,* p. 330.

27. Cited by Julio A. Louis, *Batlle y Ordóñez: apogeo y muerte de la democracia burguesa* (Montevideo: Nativo Libros, 1969), p. 98

28. *El Día,* June 20, 1925, cited by González Conzi and Giudice, *op. cit.,* p. 396.

29. Speech at Party Convention (June 1925), cited by González Conzi and Giudice, *ibid*.

30. *Ibid*.

31. Aldo Solari, "Pensamiento y Comportamiento Político del Ciudadano," in *Uruguay: Una política del desarrollo, Cuadernos*, No. 17 (Montevideo: Facultad de Derecho y Ciencias Sociales), pp. 117-118.

32. Roberto Ares Pons, *Uruguay: ¿provincia o nación?* (Montevideo: Ediciones del Nuevo Mundo, 1967), p. 78.

33. Julio A. Louis, *op. cit.*, p. 196.

34. Ricardo Martínez Ces, *El Uruguay batllista* (Montevideo: Ediciones de la Banda Oriental, 1962), pp. 196-197.

35. *Ibid.*, p. 61.

36. *Ibid.*, p. 64.

37. Carlos Real de Azúa, *El impulso y su freno: Tres décadas de Batllismo y las raíces de la crisis uruguaya* (Montevideo: Ediciones de la Banda Oriental, 1964). See especially Chapter VI, "Las Grietas en el Muro."

38. *Journal of Latin American Studies* III, 2 (November 1971), pp. 173-190.

39. Carlos Reyles, "La Muerte del Cisne" (1905), cited by Luis C. Benvenuto, *op. cit.*, p. 155.

40. *Discursos del Dr. José Irureta Goyena* (Montevideo: 1948), cited by Benvenuto, *op. cit.*, p. 156.

41. *Ibid*.

42. *El Día*, April 17, 1906, cited in "Batlle," *Cuadernos de Marcha*, no. 32 (Montevideo: Editorial, Marcha 1969), p. 27.

43. Diario del Plata, July 30, 1916, cited by Eduardo Victor Haedo, *La caída del régimen* (Montevideo: 1936), p. 303.

44. H. D., *Ensayo de historia patria*, vol. II: *La República*, 10th ed. (Montevideo: Barreiro y Ramos, 1955), p. 394.

45. *Ibid.*, p. 395.

46. *El Día*, August 12, 1916, cited in Batlle, *op. cit.*, p. 46.

47. *El Día*, May 9, 1919, *ibid.*, p. 72.

48. Eduardo Victor Haedo, *Herrera: caudillo oriental* (Montevideo: Editorial Arca, 1969), p. 72.

49. *Ibid.*, pp. 73-74.

50. *El Debate*, April 7, 1941, p. 5.

51. Haedo, *op. cit.*, p. 72.

52. Antonio M. De Freitas, *Herrera; hombre del estado* (Montevideo: 1950), pp. 100-101. This volume is a massive study of Herrera's political activity between 1925 and 1931 and is an excellent analysis of his general ideological stance. Another incisive interpretation of *Herrerismo* may be

found in Carlos Real de Azua, *Herrera: el nacionalismo agrario, Encyclopedia Uruguaya,* No. 50 (Montevideo: Editorial Reunidos and Editorial Arca, 1969), p. 192. A similar interpretation by the same author may be found in "Herrera: el colegiado en Uruguay," in *Historia de América en el siglo XX* (Buenos Aires: Centro Editor de America Latina, 1972), pp. 29-56.

53. *El Debate,* April 19, 1941, p. 5.

54. *Ibid.,* April 3, 1941, p. 5.

55. The first editorial in *Diario Rural* began as follows:

Our Editorial Policy

Pursuing a journalism entirely dedicated to the defense of agricultural interests, Diario Rural proposes to improve constantly with ever expanding news and opinion.

Since this enterprise is owned, directed and controlled by ranchers, it is bound in every sense to defend agricultural interests by becoming their journalistic paladin. (*Diario Rural,* August 24, 1940, p. 3).
[My translation.]

56. Luis Batlle Berres, nephew of José Batlle, served as president from 1947-1951 following the death of Tomás Berrèta. He was a charismatic politician who built his faction of the *Colorado* party (List 15) into the most powerful political group in the country. His rivalry with the more conservative Batlle heirs at *El Día* (List 14) helped contribute to the *Colorado* defeat in 1958. See Chapters 3 and 4 for a discussion of his policies and their impact.

57. Aldo E. Solari, "Sistema de Clases y Cambio Social," in *Estudios sobre la sociedad uruguaya* vol. II (Montevideo: Arca, 1964), p. 131.

58. Carlos M. Rama, *Las clases sociales en el Uruguay* (Montevideo: Ediciones Nuestro Tiempo, 1960), p. 127.

59. Néstor Campiglia, "La Ideologia del Movimiento Ruralista a través de la vida de Artigas escrita por 'Chico Tazo.'" *Revista de la Facultad de Derecho y Ciencias Sociales* XIII, no. 4 (October-December 1962). Chico Tazo was Benito Nardone's pseudonym.

60. Chico Tazo, *Procesa a El Día: Fracaso del estatismo* (Montevideo: Diario Rural, 1955), p. 131.

61. Benito Nardone, *Peligro rojo en America Latina* (Montevideo: Diario Rural, 1955).

62. *Mundo Americano* I (June-August 1962), p. 3.

63. Benito Nardone, "Manifiesto Americano," in *Mundo Americano,* p. 90.

64. Chico Tazo, *Procesa a El Día,* p. 162.

65. *Ibid.*, p. 146.
66. *Ibid.*, p. 170.
67. *Ibid.*, p. 38.
68. *Ibid.*, p. 174.
69. *Diario Rural,* March 7, 1953, p. 3.
70. Chico Tazo, *Processa a El Día,* p. 90.

Chapter 3: Coparticipation: The Development of Political Institutions in Uruguay

1. Charles W. Anderson, *Politics and Economic Change in Latin America* (Princeton: D. Van Nostrand, 1967. See especially Chapter IV, "The Latin American Political System." Irving Louis Horowitz, "The Norm of Illegitimacy: The Political Sociology of Latin America," in Horowitz, de Castro, and Gerassi, eds., *Latin American Radicalism* (New York: Vintage, 1969). K. H. Silvert, "The Costs of Anti-Nationalism: Argentina," in K. H. Silvert, ed., *Expectant Peoples* (New York: Random House 1967).

2. In a formal sense there are perhaps two well-known comparative examples of coparticipation. In Latin America, Colombia, with its experiment in alternating the presidency between the Liberal and Conservative parties, offers a comparative example: see the discussion in Robert Dix, *Colombia: The Political Dimensions of Change* (New Haven: Yale University Press). In the Middle East, Lebanon offers the example of the division of the presidential and vice-presidential offices along religious lines: see Michael C. Hudson, *The Precarious Republic: Political Modernization In Lebanon* (New York: Random House, 1968).

3. Alexander Dumas was one of the hundreds of French, Italian (including Garibaldi), and British citizens who lent support to Montevideo. Dumas wrote an account of the siege entitled *Montevideo, The New Troy.*

4. Juan E. Pivel Devoto and Alcira Ranieri de Pivel Devoto, *Historia de la República Oriental del Uruguay (1830-1930),* 3rd ed. (Montevideo: Editorial Medina, 1966), p. 327.

5. *Ibid.,* p. 365.

6. *El Nacional,* April 19, 1896, cited by Pivel Devoto and Ranieri de Pivel Devoto, *op. cit.,* p. 368.

7. Letter by Julio Herrera y Obes, published in January, 1901, cited by "H. D." in *Ensayo de historia patria,* vol. 2., 10th ed., (Montevideo: Barreiro y Ramos, 1955), p. 353. "H. D." was Hermano Damascenso, a friar whose given name was Eduardo Gilberto Perret.

8. Aldo Solari, *El desarrollo del Uruguay en la postguerra* (Montevideo: Editorial Alfa.), p. 138. Also discussed in Solari, "Pensamiento y Comportamiento Político del Ciudadano," in *Uruguay: una política de desarrollo*, Cuaderno no. 17 (Montevideo: Facultad de Derecho y Ciencias Sociales, 1966), p. 98.

9. Solari, "Pensamiento," *ibid.*

10. *El Día*, September 4, 1897, cited by Efraín González Conzi and Roberto B. Giudice, *Batlle y el Batllismo* (Montevideo: Editorial Medina, 1959 [1928]), p. 98.

11. *Ibid.*, p. 104.

12. Interview in *El Tiempo*, January 23, 1903, cited by Antonio M. Grompone, *La ideología de Batlle* (Montevideo: Editorial Arca, 1967 [1943]), p. 95.

13. The British had been actively involved in the construction of railroads in Uruguay since the 1870s. By 1880 cattle were being shipped to market by rail. Between 1890 and 1893 the rail network was doubled from slightly over 700 to more than 1500 kilometers. On this subject see Nelson Martínez Díaz, *Capitales Británicos v ferrocarriles en el Uruguay del siglo XIX* (Montevideo, 1966). For a general picture of the epoch see Juan Antonio Oddone, *Economía v sociedad en el Uruguay liberal* (Montevideo: Ediciones de la Banda Oriental, 1967).

14. Juan E. Pivel Devoto and Alcira Ranieri de Pivel Devoto, *op. cit.*, p. 473.

15. González Conzi and Giúdice, *op. cit.*, p. 156.

16. Secretaría-Corte Electoral, *Leyes Electorales* (Montevideo: 1946), pp. 93-153.

17. Washington Beltrán, *De actualidad política* (Montevideo: 1910), pp. 6-7.

18. Carlos Mannini Ríos, *Anoche Me Llamó Batlle* (Montevideo: 1970), p. 65. This volume, written by the son of Pedro Mannini Ríos, is, as might be expected, an anti-Batlle history of politics in Uruguay from 1911 to 1919.

19. For a compilation of the proposals and the speeches and editorials in their defense see C. B. Paredes, *Batlle y el colegiado* (Montevideo: Club Colorado Batllista "José Batlle y Ordóñez," 1939).

20. See Gonzalez Conzi and Giudice, *op. cit.*, pp. 260-268.

21. The vote gave 105 convention seats to the *Blancos*, 23 to anti-*colegiado Colorados*, and only 87 to the *Batllista Colorados*. Carlos Mannini Ríos, *op. cit.*, p. 89.

22. Carlos Mannini Ríos, *op. cit.*, p. 207 n.

23. *Diario de la Plata*, August 12, 1916, cited by Mannini Ríos, *op. cit.*, p. 92.

24. Speech by Juan M. Lago as reported in *Actas de la Comisión de Constitución de La Honorable Convención Nacional Constituyente 1917*, vol. I (Montevideo: La República Oriental del Uruguay, 1920), p. 176.

25. *Actas*, pp. 90-91.

26. An attack on the constitutional pact may be found in Luis Melián Lafinur, *La acción funesta de los partidos tradicionales en la reforma constitucional* (Montevideo, 1918).

27. Martín Martínez, *Ante la neuva constitución, Colección Clásicas Uruguayas* vol. 48 (Montevideo: Ministerio de Instrucción Pública y Previsión Social, 1964 [1919]), p. 85.

28. Speech to the convention, July 21, 1917, in *Diaria de sesiones de la Honorable Convención Nacional Constituyente 1917* vol. 3, p. 269.

29. Martínez, *Ante*, p. 81.

30. Blanca Paris de Oddone, Roque Faraone, and Juan Antonio Oddone *Cronología comparada de la historia del Uruguay* (1830-1945), 2nd ed., (Montevideo: Universidad de la Republica, 1969?), p. 71. Hereafter cited as *Cronología*.

31. Martín C. Martínez, *Ante la neuva constitución* (Montevideo: Ministerio de Instrucción Publica y Previsión Social, 1964), p. 65

32. July 30, 1917, in *Diario de sesiones de la Honorable Convención*, vol. 3, p. 394.

33. *Ibid.*, p. 396.

34. See González Conzi and Giudice, *op. cit.*, p. 203, for Viera's reaction.

35. Batlle, writing under the pseudonym Zapicán, *ibid.*, p. 207.

36. *Cronología, op. cit.*, p. 99.

37. *Ibid.*, p. 101.

38. Corte Electoral, *Leyes Electorales* (Montevideo: 1946), pp. 93-153.

39. These and most other electoral statistics covering 1929 to 1946 are taken from Julio T. Fabregat, *Elecciones Uruguayas* (Montevideo: Cámara de Representantes: XXXV Legislatura, 1950), *passim*.

40. *Cronología, passim*.

41. Luis C. Caviglia, *Estudios sobre la realidad nacional* vol. 3, (Montevideo: Urta and Curbelo, 1952), p. 28.

42. Goran Lindahl, *Uruguay's New Path: A Study of Politics during the First Colegiado, 1919-33* (Stockholm, Institute of Ibero-American Studies: Broderna Lagerstrom, 1962), p. 132, as reported in *El Día*, October 5, 1927.

43. *El Día* (de la tarde), January 25, 1928, cited by González Conzi and Giudice, *op. cit.*, p. 246.

44. Simon G. Hanson, "Utopia in Uruguay." Chapters in *The Economic History of Uruguay* (New York: Oxford University Press, 1938), p. 210.

45. Luis A. Faroppa, *El desarrollo económico del Uruguay: tentativa de explicación* (Montevideo: Centro de Estudiantes de Ciencias Económicas y de Administración, 1965), p. 30.

46. *Cronología, op. cit.*, p. 113.

47. This election saw an incredible agreement that says much about electoral politics in Uruguay. The *Riverista* faction of the *Colorado* party was induced to run under the party *lema*, and not as a separate party, by being offered the presidency should the faction poll at least 17-1/2 percent of the *Colorado* vote. This so-called handicap was never brought to a test and the constitutional crisis it may have engendered never developed when the *Riveristas* fell just 150 votes short of their required percentage. The vote is an indication of just how closely the various factions could measure their electoral strength.

48. *Mundo Americano* I (June-August 1962), p. 9.

49. *Diario de sesiones de la Cámara de Senadores,* XXX Legislatura (September 14, 1931), p. 308.

50. *Diario de sesiones de la Cámara de Diputados,* XXX Legislatura (October 10-11, 1931), p. 415.

51. Gustavo Gallinal, *El Uruguay hacia la dictadura* (Montevideo: Editorial Nueva America, 1938), p. 191. This volume by a patrician *Blanco* who broke with Herrera and became a founder of the "Independent *Blancos*" is a scathing (if biased) denouncement of the 1933 coup and its aftermath.

52. *Cronología, op. cit.*, pp. 13, 17.

53. Uruguay, *Diario de sesiones de la III Convención Nacional Constituyente* vol. II (Montevideo: Imprenta Nacional, 1935), p. 182.

54. Gallinal, *op. cit.*, p. 348.

55. Uruguay, *III Convención* vol. II, p. 120.

56. *Ibid.*, vol. I, p. 465.

57. *Ibid.*, 469.

58. Taylor, *op. cit.*, p. 20.

59. Uruguay, *1934 Constitution,* Art. 52.

60. See Charles F. Delzell, ed., *Mediterranean Fascism, 1919-1945,* (New York: Harper and Row, 1970), pp. 304-305 and p. 121. Both documents consider work a "social duty."

61. Uruguay, *1934 Constitution,* Art. 70.

62. Gabriel Terra (h.), *Gabriel Terra y la verdad histórica* (Montevideo: 1962); computed from figures on p. 183.

63. *Leyes Electorales,* pp. 162-164.

64. A fairly complete record of the *Blanco* position on amendments

and electoral legislation is found in Angel María Cusano, comp., *El Partido Nacional y la reforma de la constitución* (Montevideo: 1937).

65. *Cronología*, p. 127.

66. Cusano, *op. cit.*, pp. 183-185.

67. *Ibid.*, p. 192.

68. *Ibid.*, p. 194.

69. Women voted for president for the first time in 1938, but the total vote did not reflect a significant vote increase. The significant fact was that comparing the 1938 to the 1930 elections, the *Blancos* lost some 30,000 votes while the *Colorados* increased their total by some 45,000.

70. Uruguay, Secretaría de la Asamblea General, *La reforma constitucional de 1942: procesa de la reforma* (Montevideo: Imprenta Nacional, 1946), p. 99. This volume contains the entire record of projects and debates concerning the 1942 reform.

71. *Leyes Electorales, passim.* For a discussion of the byzantine history of the electoral laws and their effect on party politics, see Oscar Bruschera, *Los Partidos Tradicionales en el Uruguay* (Montevideo: Ediciones del Río de la Plata, 1966), pp. 46-51.

72. *La reforma constitucional de 1942*, p. 100.

73. *Ibid.*, p. 88.

74. Ricardo Martínez Ces, *El Uruguay Batllista* (Montevideo: Ediciones de la Banda Oriental, 1962), p. 56.

75. *Ibid.*

76. Instituto de Economía; Facultad de Ciencias Económicas y de Administración, *El proceso económico del Uruguay: contribución al estudio de su evolución y perspectivas* (Montevideo: Universidad de la República, 1969), p. 150.

77. *Ibid.*, p. 148.

78. Aldo Solari, *El desarrollo social del Uruguay en la postguerra* (Montevideo: Editorial Alfa, 1967), p. 82.

79. An interesting revisionist analysis of Brazil's twentieth century industrial growth with relevance to the entire import substitution argument in Latin America is found in a recent article by Werner Baer and Annibal V. Villela entitled "Industrial Growth and Industrialization: Revisions in the Stages of Brazil's Economic Development," *The Journal of the Developing Areas* vol. VII, no. 2 (January 1973), pp. 217-234.

80. Instituto de Economía, *Uruguay: estadísticas básicas* (Montevideo: Universidad de la República, 1969), p. 56.

81. The government stimulus of agriculture had some early beneficial effects on the export sector. Between 1947 and 1958, 28 percent of agricultural production found its way into the export market. However, in the 1959-61 period, agricultural exports dropped to 12 percent of production. *Uruguay en cifras*, p. 175.

82. George Pendle, *Uruguay: Portrait of a Democracy*, 2nd ed. (New York: Oxford University Press; Royal Institute of International Affairs, 1957), pp. 70-71.

83. Sergio Rompani, ed., *Luis Batlle: pensamiento y acción* vol. II, *Selección de discursos* (Montevideo: Editorial Alfa, 1965), p. 49, June 26, 1948.

84. *Ibid.*, p. 113, February 14, 1951.

85. Uruguay, Secretaria de la Cámara de Representantes, *Reforma constitucional de 1951* vol. II (Montevideo: Imprenta Nacional, 1953), p. 320.

86. *Ibid.*, p. 130.

87. *Ibid.*, Vol. I, pp. 674-675.

88. *Ibid.*, Vol. II, p. 424.

89. In the 1945-1955 period the cumulative annual rate of growth in agriculture was 9.5 percent; in manufacturing it was 8.5 percent, while livestock production increased at a rate of only 2 percent. Luis A. Faroppa, *El desarrollo económico del Uruguay*, p. 76.

90. *Uruguay: estadísticas básicas, op. cit.*, p. 94.

91. *Ibid.*, p. 110.

92. *El proceso económico del Uruguay, op. cit.*, p. 174.

Chapter 4: Class and Nation in Uruguay

1. Antonio M. Grompone, *Las clases medias en el Uruguay* (Montevideo: Ediciones del Río de la Plata, 1963), pp. 32, 42-45.

2. Carlos Real de Azúa, *El impulso y su freno* (Montevideo: Ediciones de la Banda Oriental, 1964), p. 21.

3. Aldo Solari, Néstor Campiglia, and German Wettstein, *Uruguay en cifras* (Montevideo: Universidad de la República, 1966), p. 161. Hereafter cited as *Cifras*.

4. *Ibid.*, p. 136.

5. Direccion General de Estadística y Censos, *Anuario estadístico* vol. LV, 1961-63, pp. c-1, c-5. *Anuario estadístico*, 1964-1966, pp. 32-33.

6. *Cifras*, Chart VII-25.

7. Carlos M. Rama, *Las clases sociales en el Uruguay* (Montevideo: Ediciones Nuestro Tiempo, 1960), p. 138.

8. *Cifras,* Chart V-10.

9. *Ibid.,* p. 22.

10. *Cifras,* pp. 159-161.

11. *Cifras,* p. 161.

12. *Ibid.*

13. Comisión de Inversiones y Desarrollo Económico (CIDE). *Plan Nacional de desarrollo económico y social: 1965-1974,* Compendio vol. 2 (Montevideo: Centro de Estudiantes de Ciencias Económicas y de Administración, 1966), p. 45. Hereafter cited as CIDE, *Plan.* The Alliance for Progress, with its emphasis on specific data and concrete development plans in order for participating nations to avail themselves of funds, stimulated such data collection activity in Uruguay. The 1963 population census (the first conducted in Uruguay since 1908), the CIDE *Plan,* and other important studies on education and the rural situation (cited below) were the results of this stimulus.

14. *Ibid.*

15. *Cifras,* p. 159.

16. Guillermo Bernhard, *Realidad agropecuaria del Uruguay* (Montevideo: Nativa Libros, 1965), p. 21.

17. Carlos M. Rama, *Sociología nacional* (Montevideo: Club Vincente Grucci, 1965), p. 107. Vivian Trías, *Economía y política en el Uruguay contemporáneo* (Montevideo: Ediciones de la Banda Oriental, 1968), p. 27.

18. Centro Latinoamericano de Economía Humana, *Situación económica y social del Uruguay rural* (Montevideo: Ministerio de Ganadería y Agricultura, 1963), p. 108. Hereafter cited as *Situación rural.*

19. *Ibid.,* p. 106.

20. Carlos M. Rama, *op. cit.,* p. 185. The figure is based on the 1951 agricultural census.

21. Russell H. Brannon, *Agricultural Development in Uruguay: Problems of Government Policy* (New York: Frederick A. Praeger, 1967), p. 285.

22. Néstor Campiglia, *Migración interna en el Uruguay* (Montevideo: Universidad de la República, 1968), p. 48.

23. *Ibid.,* p. 147.

24. Aldo Solari, "Sistema de Clases y Cambio Social en el Uruguay," in *Estudios sobre la sociedad uruguaya* vol. II (Montevideo: Editorial Arca, 1965), p. 127

25. Instituto de Economía, *El proceso económico del Uruguay* (Montevideo: Universidad de la República, 1969), p. 63.

26. *Ibid.,* p. 76.

27. Ministerio de Hacienda, Dirección General de Estadística y Censo,

IV Censo de Población y II de Vivienda: datos definitivos (Montevideo: 1969), p. 21. The census was conducted in 1963. Many of the statistics in *Uruguay en cifras and Uruguay: estadísticas básicas* were taken from the preliminary census data.

28. Ministerio de Instrucción Pública y Previsión Social, Comisión de Inversiones y Desarrollo Económico (CIDE) and Comisión Coordinada de los Entes de Enseñanza, *Informe sobre el estado de educación en el Uruguay*, Tomo Primero (Montevideo, 1966), p. 24. Hereafter cited as *Informe sobre educación*.

29. *Ibid.*, p. 6.

30. *Ibid.*, p. XIV.

31. Blanca Paris de Oddone, Roque Faraone, and Juan Antonio Oddone. *Cronología comparada de la historia del Uruguay: 1850-1930* (Montevideo: Universidad de la República, 1961), *passim.*

32. *Informe sobre educación*, p. 37.

33. *Ibid.*, p. 51.

34. Universidad de la República: Oficina de Planeamiento, *Censo de estudiantes ingresados en 1968: proceso de reclutamiento en la Universidad de la República* (Montevideo 1968?), p. 6. Hereafter cited as *1968 University Census*.

35. *Ibid.*, p. 16.

36. *Informe sobre educación*, p. 170.

37. Germán W. Rama, *Grupos sociales y enseñanza secundaria* (Montevideo: Arca, 1968), p. 16.

38. Maria A. Carbonnell de Grompone, "La influencia de los factores sociales en la inteligencia," *Anales del Instituto de Profesores Artigas*, no. 6 (Montevideo, 1961), pp. 3-17.

39. *Ibid.*, p. 8.

40. *Ibid.*, p. 14.

41. Aldo Solari, "Educación y desarrollo de las elites," in *Estudios sobre la sociedad uruguaya* vol. II (Montevideo: Arca, 1965), p. 108. From an unpublished study with Grompone, Elida and G. Rama entitled *Investigación sobre los alumnos de los liceos de Montevideo*.

42. Germán W. Rama, *Grupos sociales y enseñanza secundaria*, p. 28.

43. *Ibid.*, pp. 34-38.

44. *Ibid.*, p. 90.

45. *Informe sobre educación*, p. 170.

46. *Ibid.*

47. *Ibid.*, p. 306.

48. *Ibid.*, p. 285.

49. *Uruguay en cifras*, p. 103.

50. *1968 University Census*, p. 40.

51. *Ibid.*, p. 41.

52. *Ibid.*, p. 42.

53. *Ibid.*, p. 66.

54. *Ibid.*, p. 71.

55. *Ibid.*, p. 75.

56. *Ibid.*, p. 74.

57. *Ibid.*

58. *Ibid.*, p. 288.

59. *1968 University Census*, p. 24.

60. *Informe sobre educación*, p. 293.

61. *Uruguay en cifras*, p. 103.

62. Computed from census information found in *Informe sobre educación*, p. 12 and *Uruguay en cifras*, Chart IV-6, immediately following page 96.

63. *Ibid.*

64. Figures for Grompone, Ganón (1953), Solari (1957), and Rama (1958) from Carlos M. Rama, *Las clases sociales en el Uruguay*, p. 107. Ganón (1966) in Isaac Ganón, *Estructura social del Uruguay* (Montevideo: Editorial AS, 1966), pp. 200, 203, 206. Solari (1964) in Aldo Solari, "Sistema de clases y cambio social en el Uruguay," in *Estudios* p. 123.

65. The survey conducted under the directorship of Solari and Jean Labbens was entitled "Estratificación y movilidad social en Montevideo." Two major studies were published from the data. Aldo Solari, "Movilidad Social en Montevideo," in *Boletim del Centro Latinamericano de Pesquisas em Ciencias Socias* IV (1961), reprinted in Solari, *Estudios sobre la sociedad uruguaya*, Vol. I. pp. 85-112; and Isaac Ganón "Estratificación social de Montevideo," *Boletim*, p. 310.

66. Solari, "Movilidad Social en Montevideo," *Estudios*, pp. 88-89.

67. Institute for the Comparative Study of Political Systems, *Uruguay Election Fact Book* (Washington, D.C.: Operations and Policy Research, Inc., 1966), p. 3.

68. *Ibid.*, p. 4. CIDE, *Plan* vol. I., p. 17.

69. Carlos M. Rama, *op. cit.*, p. 202, citing estimates by Carlos Quijano as well as a survey by IUDOP (*Instituto Uruguayo de Opinión Publica*).

70. Solari, "Sistema de Clases," *op. cit.*, p. 156.

71. *Uruguay en cifras*, pp. 83-85.

72. Solari, "Partidos Políticos y Clases Sociales en el Uruguay," in *Estudios sobre la sociedad Uruguaya* vol. II, p. 132.

73. Solari, "Las Estructuras Sociales y Su Posible Evolución," in *Estudios* vol. I, p. 167.

74. Frieda and Kalman H. Silvert, *Education and the Meaning of Social Development*, unpublished manuscript, Chapter 2, p. 5.

Chapter 5: Uruguay in the 1960s and 1970s:
A Requiem for Democratic Nationalism

1. There is a strong parallel between this reversal in Uruguay's economic policy and similar changes in Argentina. For an excellent interpretation of Argentina's economic development with relevance to the Uruguayan situation see Aldo Ferrer, *The Argentine Economy: An Economic History of Argentina* (Berkeley: University of California Press, 1967), especially Part IV.

2. *Marcha,* January 12, 1973, p. 7.

3. Julio T. Fabregat, *Elecciones Uruguayas* (Montevideo: Cámara de Senadores, 1967), p. 13.

4. In 1963, the Commission on Investment and Economic Development (*Comisión de Inversiones y Desarrollo Económico–CIDE*) produced an exhaustive study of the Uruguayan economy entitled *Estudio economico del Uruguay y sus perspectivas.* On January 7, 1967, CIDE was empowered to draft a long-range development plan. The plan was presented in 1965 and was to cover the 1965 to 1974 period, but was virtually ignored by the government.

5. CIDE, *Plan nacional de desarrollo económico y social* (1965-1974) vol. I (Montevideo: Centro de Estudiantes de Ciencias Económicas y de Administración, 1966), p. 188.

6. Ronald H. McDonald calculates that Uruguay's gross national product declined by 12 percent between 1955 and 1974, while per capita income declined by some 15 percent. See his "Electoral Politics and Uruguayan Political Decay," in *Inter-American Economic Affairs* XXVI, 26 (Summer 1972), 34-35. For a perceptive analysis of Uruguay's economic development see Luis A. Faroppa, *El desarrollo económico del Uruguay: tentativa de explicación* (Montevideo: Centro de Estudiantes de Ciencias Economicas y de Administractión, 1965); also see Instituto de Economía, *El proceso económico del Uruguay* (Montevideo: Universidad de la República, 1969).

For discussions in English on Uruguay's deteriorating economic position see: M.D.C. Redding, "The Economic Decline of Uruguay," *Inter-American Economic Affairs* XX, 4 (Apring 1967), 55-72; Eric N. Baklanoff, "Notes on the Pathology of Uruguay's Welfare State," *Mississippi Valley Journal of Business and Economics* II (Spring 1967); S. Shapiro, "Uruguay: A Bankrupt Welfare State," *Current History* LVI, 329 (January 1969), 36-41, 51; James P. Bell, Jr., "Uruguay's Economic Evolution: 1900-1968," *SAIS Review* XV (Spring 1971), 27-35; M.H.J. Finch, "Three Perspectives on the Crisis in Uruguay," *Journal of Latin*

American Studies III, 2 (November 1971), 173-190; and S. Shapiro, "Uruguay's Lost Paradise," *Current History* LXLL, 366 (February 1972), 98-103.

7. *Instituto Uruguayo de Opinión Pública* (IUDOP), August 30, 1966. The Uruguayan Institute of Public Opinion is affiliated with the Gallup organization.

8. *Ibid.*

9. For a complete and critical analysis of the reform process see Héctor Gros Espiel, "El proceso de la reforma constitucional," in *Estudios sobre la reforma constitucional. Cuadernos* 19 (Montevideo: Facultad de Derecho y Ciencias Sociales, 1967), pp. 9-38.

10. A favorable and thorough analysis of the 1966 constitution is found in Julio María Sanguinetti and Alvaro Pacheco Sere, *La nueva constitución: ensayo* (Montevideo: Editorial Alfa, 1967). For an article by article comparison of the new constitution with previous ones see Dr. Pablo N. Belderrain Razquin, *Constitución de la República* (Montevideo: Cámara de Representantes, 1968).

11. The *Colorado* party received 607,633 votes to the National party's 496,910. Voter turnout was slightly over 74 percent.

12. Article 168, section 17.

13. *Marcha,* December 30, 1971, p. 23.

14. *Marcha,* June 5, 1970, pp. 12-15. The translation used here is by Raymond Rosenthal in *State of Siege* (New York: Ballantine Books, 1973), p. 195. (Italics in original.) This volume is the screenplay and documentary appendix of the Costa-Gavras movie.

15. For an excellent discussion on the problem of inflation in Uruguay see Instituto de Economía, *El proceso economico del Uruguay,* especially Part II.

16. Instituto de Economía, *Estudio y coyuntura,* no. 2 (Montevideo, 1971). Reprinted in "Una Economía Latin americana," in *Uruguay Hoy* (Buenos Aires: Siglo Veintiuno Argentina, 1972), p. 104.

17. Daniel Costabile and Alfredo Errondonea, *Sindicato y sociedad en el Uruguay* (Montevideo: Universidad de la República, 1969), p. 136.

18. The literature on the *Tupamaros* is now rather extensive. For the early period see Carlos Nuñez, "The Tupamaros: Armed Vanguard in Uruguay," *Tricontinental* (Havana), no. 10 (January-February 1969), 43-66, and M. Rosencof, *La rebelión de los caneros* (Montevideo: Aportes, 1969). For later activity and documents see: Antonio Mercader and Jorge de Vera, *Tupamaros: estrategia y acción—informe* (Mexico, D. F.: Ediciones Era, 1971); *Actas Tupamaros* (Buenos Aires: Shapire Editor, 1971); A. Labrousse, *Los Tupamaros: guerrilla urbana en el Uruguay* (Buenos Aires: Tiempo Contemporaneo, 1971); María Esther Gilio, *The Tupamaro Guerrillas: The Structure and Strategy of the Urban Guerrilla*

Movement (New York: Saturday Review Press, 1972); Donald C. Hodges, ed., *Philosophy of the Urban Guerrilla: The Revolutionary Writings of Abraham Guillén* (New York: William Morrow and Co., 1973); and José A. Moreno and Arturo C. Porzecanski, "The Ideology of Uruguay's Tupamaros," unpublished essay in the departments of Sociology and Economics, University of Pittsburgh, 1972. For articles in English see: S. Connolly and G. Druehl, "The Tupamaros: The New Focus in Latin America," *Journal of Contemporary Revolutions* III, 3 (Summer 1971), 59-68; F. M. Foland, "Uruguay's Urban Guerrillas," *New Leader* LIV, 19 (October 4, 1971), 8-11; R. Moss "Urban Guerrillas in Uruguay," *Problems of Communism* XX, 5 (September -October 1971), 14-23.

19. "Carta Abierta a la Policía," printed in *Epoca,* December 7, 1967. Reprinted in Costa, *op. cit.,* p. 102, and Mercader and de Vera, *op. cit.,* p. 131.

20. Many of these documents are found in the works cited above.

21. Moreno and Porzecanski, *op. cit.,* p. 35.

22. The following five paragraphs are taken, with minor revision, from my "The Uruguayan Constitution and the 1971 Elections," in Gisbert H. Flanz and Albert P. Blaustein, eds., *The Constitutions of the Countries of the World* (Dobbs Ferry, N.Y.: Oceana Press, 1972).

23. Uruguay's electoral laws are found in Corte Electoral, *Leyes Electorales* (Montevideo: 1946), especially pp. 93-153. For a discussion of the effects of these laws on party politics see Oscar Bruschera, *Los partidos tradicionales en el Uruguay* (Montevideo: Ediciones de la Plata, 1966), pp. 46-51. Another discussion of the *Ley de Lemas* is found in "Primera sesión en el Instituto de Derecho Pública: Representación de mayorías y minorías en los sistemas electorales de Uruguay y Chile," in *Revista de la Facultad de Derecho y Ciencias Sociales,* X, No. 1-2 (January and June, 1959).

24. A comparison of the 1966 vote of the *Frente's* components with the *Frente's* 1971 vote shows a total increase of 5 percent, from some 13 percent to 18 percent. The increase in Montevideo was more impressive, moving from 21 percent to 30 percent. These and other election figures are adopted from *Marcha,* February 25, 1972, pp. 6-11.

25. *Marcha,* December 30, 1972, p. 23.

26. *New York Times,* August 14, 1969.

27. *El Día,* July 6, 1972, p. 7.

28. *Marcha,* November 3, 1972, p. 7.

29. *Facts on File* (New York), 1973, p. 115.

30. An analysis of the communique is found in *Clarín* (Buenos Aires), February 11, 1973, pp. 3, 24-25.

31. *Facts on File,* 1973, p. 282. The proposal may be found in *El País,*
March 22, 1973, p. 2.

32. *Latin America* VII, 13 (March 30, 1973), p. 98.

33. *New York Times,* February 14, 1973, p. 2.

34. *Ibid.*

35. *El País,* March 22, 1973, p. 2.

36. *El País,* May 14, 1973, p. 1, 15.

37. *El País,* June 29, 1973, p. 4.

38. Jorge Batlle announced on May 22, 1973, that his *Colorado* faction
(List 15) would no longer participate in Bordaberry's government and
would therefore resign all its cabinet positions and would not vote another
extension of the suspension of constitutional civil liberties. Since the last
extension had barely passed by a vote of 65 to 63, the government could
not hope to find the votes necessary for any further suspension.

39. *El País,* June 29, 1973, p. 4.

40. *Ibid.,* p. 6.

41. *Clarín* (Buenos Aires), July 10, 1973, p. 10.

42. *El País,* July 2, 1973, p. 2.

43. *Ibid.*

44. *El País,* July 8, 1973, p. 1.

45. *Ibid.* The almost mystical use of the term *orientalidad* to express
"Uruguayanness" (or "things Uruguayan," if you will) derives from the
official name of the country, *La República Oriental del Uruguay* (The
Oriental [Eastern] Republic of Uruguay). The designation "oriental"
refers to Uruguay's location on the eastern shore of the Río Uruguay.
The area which Uruguay now occupies was originally known as "La Banda
Oriental" (The East Bank or Eastern Shore) and to this day its citizens
are colloquially referred to as "orientales" (easterners).

BIBLIOGRAPHY

Government Publications

República Oriental del Uruguay. Administración de Ferrocarriles del Estado. *Memoria y Balance, gestion correspondiente al período 23 de mayo 1957-28 de febrero 1959.* Montevideo: 1959.

——, Administración General de las Usinas Eléctricas y los Teléfonos del Estado. *Los 25 años del teléfono automático en el Uruguay.* Montevideo: UTE, 1959.

——, Administración General de las Usinas Eléctricas y los Teléfonos del Estado. *Producción de energía eléctrica.* Montevideo: UTE, 1955-1958.

——, Alonso Criado, Matias, ed. *Colección legislativa de la República Oriental del Uruguay.* 30 vols. Montevideo: 1876-1908.

——, Asamblea General. *Actas de la Comisión de Constitución de la Honorable Convención Nacional Constituyente, 1917.* Montevideo: Imprenta Nacional, 1920.

——, Asamblea General. *Diario de la Cámara de Representantes.* Montevideo.

——, Banco de Seguros del Estado. *El Banco de Seguros del Estado. Creación, funcionamiento, dessarrollo.*

——, Banco de Seguros del Estado. "Estatuto del funcionario." *Diario Oficial* (August 29, 1956), pp. 553A-559A.

——, Cámara de Representantes. *Reforma de la constitución. Enmiendas propuestas por los señores Representantes. Resolución de la Cámara, y Proyectos de la Comisión de Reforma Constitucional en mayoria.* Montevideo: Imprensa "El Siglo Ilustrado," 1909.

——, Cámara de Senadores. *Instituto Nacional de Colonización.* Montevideo: 1948.

——, Cámara de Senadores. *Reglamento de la Cámara de Senadores, marzo 30 de 1955,* Montevideo: Editorial Florensa y Lafon, 1955.

——, Comisión de Inversiones y Desarrollo Económico. *Estudio económico*

del Uruguay-Analisis general: evolución y perspectiva. Montevideo: 1963.
———, Comisión de Inversiones y Desarrollo Económico. *Plan Nacional de desarrollo económico y social, 1965-1974:* Compendio. 2 vols. Montevideo: Centro de Estudiantes de Ciencias Económicas y de Administración, 1966.
———, Corte Electoral. *Elecciones Uruguayas.* 5 vols. Montevideo: 1948-1959.
———, Corte Electoral. *Leyes Electorales.* Montevideo: 1946.
———, *Diario Oficial.* Montevideo.
———, Diario Oficial. *Registro Nacional de Leyes y Decretos de la República Oriental del Uruguay.* Montevideo.
———, *Diario de sesiones de la Honorable Convención Nacional Constituyente de la República Oriental del Uruguay.* 3 vols. Montevideo: 1917.
———, *Diario de sesiones de la III Convención Nacional Constituyente.* 3 vols. Montevideo: Imprenta Nacional, 1935.
———, Gobierno Municipal de Montevideo. *Digesto Municipal.* 2 vols. Montevideo: 1958.
———, Ministerio de Economía y Finanzas, Dirección General de Estadística y Censos. *Encuesta de hogares: ocupación y desocupación.* Vol. I., no. 3. Montevideo (July-December 1969).
———, Ministerio de Ganadería y Agricultura, Departamento de Economía Rural. *Censo general agropecuario,* 1956. Montevideo: 1956.
———, Ministerio de Ganadería y Agricultura. Dirección de Economía Agraria. Departamento de Estadística: División Censos y Encuestas. *Censo general agropecuario,* 1966. Montevideo: 1968.
———, Ministerio de Ganadería y Agricultura. Oficina de Programación y Política Agropecuaria. *Crédito agropecuario en el Uruguay.* Montevideo: 1966.
———, Ministerio de Ganadería y Agricultura. Oficina de Programación y Política Agropecuario. *Estudio Económico y Social de la Agricultura en el Uruguay,* I and II. Montevideo: Impresora Rex, S. A., 1967.
———, Ministerio de Hacienda, Dirección General de Estadística y Censos. *Anuario Estadístico.*
———, Ministerio de Hacienda, Dirección General de Estadística y Censos, Departamento de Estadística Económica. *Indice de los precios del consumo.* Montevideo.
———, Ministerio de Hacienda, Dirección General de Estadística y Censos. *IV Censo de Población y II de Vivienda: Datos definitivos.* Montevideo: 1969.

————, Ministerio de Hacienda, Dirección General de Estadística y Censos. *IV Censo de Población y II de Vivienda: Muestra de Anticipación.* Montevideo: 1963.

————, Ministerio de Hacienda, Dirección General de Estadística y Censos. *Distribución territorial de la población y la vivienda.* Montevideo: n.d. Data taken from the *IV Censo General de Población y II de Vivienda* (October 1963); presented in pamphlets for each department.

————, Ministerio de Industrias y Trabajo, Dirección de Industrias. *Censo Industrial del año 1958.* Montevideo: El Debate, 1960.

————, Ministerio de Instrucción Pública y Previsión Social, Comisión de Inversiones y Desarrollo Económico, Comisión Coodinada de los Entes de Enseñanza. *Informe sobre el estado de educación en el Uruguay.* 2 vols. Montevideo: 1966.

————, Ministerio de Relaciones Exteriores. *Antecedentes de la ruptura de relaciones diplomáticas y su reanudación entre la República Oriental del Uruguay y la República Argentina.* Montevideo: 1932.

————, Ministerio de Salud Pública. *Estudio de la reorganización administrativa del Ministerio de Salud Pública.* 13 vols. Montevideo: 1956.

————, Museo Histórico Nacional. *Exodo del pueblo oriental.* Montevideo: 1927.

————, Poder Ejecutivo. *Mensaje del poder ejecutivo a la asamblea deliberante: la situación financiera para el año 1934.* Montevideo: 1934.

————, Secretaría de la Cámara de Representantes. *Reforma constitucional 1942: proceso de la reforma.* Montevideo: Imprenta Nacional, 1946.

————. Secretaría de la Cámara de Representantes. *Reforma constitucional de 1951.* 3 vols. Montevideo: 1952-1953.

————, Secretaría del Senado, Dr. Manuel M. de la Bandera, Jefe de la Oficina Asesora. *La Constitución de 1952: reportorio sistemáticoalfabético.* Montevideo: Editorial Florensa & Lafor, 1957.

Books

Acevedo, Eduardo. *Anales históricos del Uruguay.* 7 vols. Montevideo: Barreiro y Ramos, 1933-1934.

————. *Historia económica y financiera del Uruguay.* 2 vols. Montevideo: El Siglo, 1903.

————. *José Artigas: su obra cívica.* 2nd ed. Montevideo: Monteverde, 1933.

————. *Manual de historia uruguaya: Artigas.* 3rd ed. Montevideo: Monteverde, 1942.

————. *Manual de historia uruguaya: desde el coloniaje hasta 1930.* Montevideo: Barreiro y Ramos, 1935.

———. *Manual de historia uruguaya: después de Artigas*. 3rd ed. Montevideo: Monteverde, 1943.

Acevedo Alvarez, Eduardo. *La economía y las finanzas públicas después del 31 de marzo*. Montevideo: 1937.

Aguiar, José. *Nuestra frontera con el Brasil*. Montevideo: Universidad Relaciones Exteriores, 1936.

Albístur, Víctor. *El problema presidencial de 1907 y el manifesto nacionalista*. Montevideo: 1907.

Alexander, Robert J. *Communism in Latin America*. New Brunswick, N.J.: Rutgers University Press, 1957.

———. *Organized Labor in Latin America*. New York: Free Press, 1965.

Alisky, Marvin. *Uruguay: A Contemporary Survey*. New York: Frederick A. Praeger Publishers, 1969.

———. "Uruguay." *Political Systems of Latin America*. Edited by Martin C. Needler. Rev. ed. New York: Van Nostrand, 1969.

American International Association. *La prensa del interior del Uruguay*. Montevideo: AIA, 1966.

Anderson, Charles W. *Politics and Economic Change in Latin America*. Princeton: D. Van Nostrand, 1967.

Antuña, José G. *La junta de gobierno y el partido colorado*. Montevideo: 1933.

———. *Un reclamo vital: el golpe de estado del 31 de marzo de 1933*. Montevideo: 1933.

Apter, David E., ed. *Ideology and Discontent*. New York: Free Press, 1964.

Araujo, Orestes. *Historia compendiada de la civilización uruguaya*. Montevideo: Barreiro y Ramos, 1906.

Arcas, José Antonio. *Historia del siglo XX uruguaya (1897-1943)*. Montevideo: Arcas, 1950.

Ardao, Arturo. *La filosofía en el Uruguay en el siglo XX*. Mexico, D. F.: Fondo de Cultura Económica, 1956.

———. *Racionalismo y liberalismo en el Uruguay*. Montevideo: Universidad de la República, 1962.

Areco, R. J. *Divorcio: proyecto de reformas*. Montevideo: El Siglo, 1918.

Arena, Domingo. *Batlle y los problemas sociales en el Uruguay*. Montevideo: Claudio García, 1939.

Ares Pons, Roberto. *Uruguay en el siglo XIX: acceso a la modernidad*. Montevideo: Ediciones del Río de la Plata, 1964.

———. *Uruguay: ¿provincia o nación?* Montevideo: Ediciones del Nuevo Mundo, 1967.

Arias, Alejandro. *Vaz Ferreira*. Mexico, D. F.: Fondo de Cultura

Económica, 1956.

Asociación de Industrias Textiles del Uruguay. *Industria textil uruguaya.* Montevideo: 1952.

Asociación Nacional de Contadores. *Las industrias del mar.* Montevideo: Instituto de Economía, 1943.

Aznares, Julio G. *La industria azucarera en el Uruguay.* Montevideo: 1946.

Banales, Carlos. *La rebelión estudiantil.* Montevideo: Arca, 1968.

Banco Comercial. *El Banco Comercial a través de un siglo, 1857-1957.* Montevideo: Colombino Hnos., 1957.

Barbalegata, Anibal Luis. *El Consejo de Ministros en la constitución.* Montevideo: Biblioteca de publicaciones oficiales de la Facultad de Derecho y Ciencias Sociales, 1950.

Bardo, Raúl. *Del divorcio.* Montevideo: Medina, 1941.

Barrán, J. P., and Nahum, B. *Historia rural del Uruguay moderno.* 2 vols. Montevideo: Ediciones de la Banda Oriental, 1969.

Batlle, Jorge, ed. *Batlle, su obra y su vida.* Montevideo: Editorial Acción, 1956.

Batlle Berres, Luis. *El Batllismo y el problema de los combustibles.* Montevideo: Imprenta Colorado Nacional, 1931.

Bauzá, Francisco. *Historia de la dominación española en el Uruguay.* 3rd ed. Montevideo: 1929.

Belderrain Razquin, Pablo N. *Constitución de la república.* Montevideo: Cámara de Representantes, 1968.

Bell, Daniel. *The End of Ideology.* New York: Free Press, 1962.

Beltrán, Washington. *De actualidad política.* Montevideo: 1910.

Benedetti, Mario. *El país de la cola de paja.* Montevideo: Ediciones Ciudad Vieja, 1961.

———. *Terremoto y después.* Montevideo: Arca, 1973.

Benvenuto, Luis Carlos. *Breve historia del Uruguay.* Montevideo: Arca, 1967.

———, et al. *Uruguay Hoy.* Buenos Aires: Siglo Veintiuno Argentina, 1971.

Berchesi, Nilo, *Contralor de los gastos públicos.* Montevideo: Universidad de la República, 1957.

Bernardez, Manuel. *Política y moneda.* Montevideo: Barreiro y Ramos, 1931.

Bernhard, Guillermo. *Comercio de carnes en el Uruguay.* Montevideo: Aguilar E. Irazabal, 1958.

———. *La crisis nacional.* Montevideo: 1966.

———. *Realidad agropecuaria del Uruguay.* Montevideo: Nativo Libros, 1965.

Berreta, Tomás, and Buzzetti, José I. *Esquema de un planeamiento económico y social.* Montevideo: 1946.

Beuro, Juan Antonio. *El Uruguay en la vida internacional.* Montevideo: Universidad de la República, 1919.

Blanco Acevedo, Pablo. *Centenario de la independencia.* 2nd ed. Montevideo: Barreiro y Ramos, 1940.

──────. *Estudios constitucionales.* Montevideo: 1939.

──────. *El federalismo de Artigas y la independencia nacional.* Montevideo: Uruguaya, 1939.

──────. *El gobierno colonial en el Uruguay y los orígenes de la nacionalidad.* Montevideo: Barreiro y Ramos, 1944.

Bollo, Santiago. *Manual de historia de la República Oriental del Uruguay.* Montevideo: 1897.

Bollo, Sarah. *Literatura Uruguaya, 1807-1965.* Vols. I and II. Montevideo: Ediciones Orfeo, 1965.

Bon Espassandin, Mario. *Cantegriles.* Montevideo: Editorial Tupac Amaru, 1963.

Bowen, Ralph. *German Theories of the Corporative State.* New York: McGraw-Hill, 1947.

Bray, Donald W. "Uruguay." *Political Forces in Latin America: Dimensions of the Quest for Stability.* Edited by Ben G. Burnett and Kenneth F. Johnson. Belmont: Wadsworth, 1968.

Brena, Tomás G. *Democracia Cristiana en el Uruguay.* Montevideo: Impresora Zorilla de San Martín, 1946.

Brum, Baltasar. *Los derechos de la mujer.* Montevideo: Pena, 1925.

Bruschera, Oscar H. *Los partidos políticos tradicionales.* Montevideo: Ediciones Río de la Plata, 1962.

Buzzetti, José L. *Historia económica y financiera del Uruguay.* Montevideo: 1969.

──────. *La magnífica gestión de Batlle en obras públicas.* Montevideo: Editorial Ceibo, 1946.

Camp, Richard L. *The Papal Ideology of Reform.* Leiden: E. J. Brill, 1969.

Campbell, A. B. *The Battle of the River Plate.* London: Jenkins, 1940.

Campiglia, Néstor. *Migración interna en el Uruguay.* Montevideo: Universidad de la República, 1968?

Cannon, Mary M. *Social and Labor Problems of Peru and Uruguay: A Study in Contrasts,* Washington: Department of Labor, 1945.

Capurro, Federico E. *Una memoria más, 1958-1963.* Montevideo: Industria Gráfica Uruguaya, 1963.

Carbajal, Carlos. *La penetración luso-brasileña en el Uruguay.* Montevideo: Estudios de Historia, 1948.

Carr, E. H. *Nationalism and After.* London: Macmillan, 1968.

Cassinelli Muñoz, Horacio, ed. *A Statement of the Laws of Uruguay in Matters Affecting Business.* 4th ed. Washington, D. C.: Pan American Union, 1963.

Cassinoni, Mario A. *Ordeñanza de elecciones universitarias.* Montevideo: Publicaciones de la Universidad, 1959.

——. *La Universidad de la República en 1959.* Montevideo: Publicaciones de la Universidad, 1959.

Cassirer, Ernst. *An Essay on Man.* New York: Bantam, 1970.

Castro, Julio. *La escuela rural.* Montevideo: Talleres Gráficos "33," 1947?

Caviglia, Luis C. *Estudios sobre la realidad nacional.* 3 vols. Montevideo: Urta and Curbelo, 1952.

Centro Latinoamericano de Economía Humana. *Situación económica y social del Uruguay rural.* Montevideo: Ministerio de Ganadería y Agricultura, 1965.

Cerda Catalán, Alfonso. *Contribución a la historia de la sátira política en el Uruguay, 1897-1904.* Montevideo: Instituto de Investigaciones Históricas, Universidad de la República, 1965.

Cestáu, Saul D. *Modos de adquirir el dominio.* Montevideo: Claudio García, 1937.

Chiarino, J. V., and Saralegui, Miguel. *Detrás de la ciudad.* Montevideo, 1936.

Clagett, Helen L. *A Guide to the Law and Legal Literature of Uruguay.* Washington, D. C.: Library of Congress, 1947.

Consejo Interamericano de Comercio y Producción. *Uruguay y el plan Marshall.* Montevideo: 1948.

Converse, Philip E. "The Nature of Belief Systems in Mass Publics." *Ideology and Discontent.* Edited by David E. Apter. New York: Free Press, 1964.

Cosco, Oscar. *El Uruguay: su democracia y su vida política.* Montevideo: Universidad de la República, 1926.

Costa, Omar. *Los Tupamaros.* Mexico, D. F.: Ediciones Era, 1971.

Couture, Eduardo J. *Código de organización de los Tribunales Civiles y de Hacienda.* Montevideo: Centro de Estudiantes de Derecho, 1957.

——, Barbagelata, Hugo H., González, L. Segui, and Maggi, Carlos. *Legislación vigente en el Uruguay.* Montevideo: Universidad de Montevideo, 1956.

Cusano, Angel María, comp. and ed. *El Partido Nacional y la reforma de la constitución.* Montevideo: 1937.

de Ferrari, Francisco. *¿Es el Batllismo una tendencia socialista?* Montevideo: 1932.

De Freitas, Antonio M. *Herrera: Hombre del estado.* Montevideo: 1950.

de Herrera, Luis Alberto. *Por la patria*. 2 vols. Montevideo: Barreiro
y Ramos, 1953.

———. *La tierra charrúa*. Montevideo: Arca Editorial, 1968 [1901].

De María, Isidoro. *Hombres notables del Uruguay*. Montevideo: Pivel
Devoto, 1939.

de Oddone, Blanco Paris; Faraone, Roque; and Oddone, Juan Antonio.
Cronología comparada de la historia del Uruguay, 1830-1945. Montevideo: Universidad de la República, 1961.

de Sherbinin, Betty. *The River Plate Republics*. New York: Coward-McCann,
1945.

de Torres Wilson, José A. *La conciencia histórica uruguaya*. Montevideo:
1964.

Delle Piane, Aristides A. *Ante la reforma*. Montevideo: 1933.

Delzell, Charles F., ed. *Mediterranean Fascism, 1910-1945*. New York:
Harper and Row, 1970.

Demicheli, Alberto. *Lo contencioso administrativo*. Montevideo: Universidad de la República, 1937.

———. *Los entes autónomos*. Montevideo: Imprenta Nacional, 1924.

Didizian, Kurken, ed. *Julio César Grauert: discípulo de Batlle*. Montevideo:
Editorial Avanzar, 1967.

Directorio del Partido Nacional. *El Partido Nacional y la política exterior
del Uruguay*. Montevideo: 1947.

Discursos del Dr. José Irureta Goyena. Montevideo: 1948.

Dix, Robert. *Colombia: The Political Dimensions of Change*. New Haven:
Yale University Press, 1967.

Duarte, Jacinto A. *Dos siglos de publicidad en la historia del Uruguay*.
Montevideo: Editorial Sur, 1952.

Dumas, Alexandre. *Montevideo, ou une nouvelle Troie*. Paris: 1850.

Eguiluz, Juan A. *Consideraciones sobre la política de economía*. Montevideo: Banco de la República Oriental del Uruguay, 1941.

Errondonea, Alfredo, and Costabile, Daniel. *Sindicato y sociedad en el
Uruguay*. Montevideo: Universidad de la República, 1969.

Espalter, José. *Discursos parlamentarios*. 8 vols. Montevideo: 1952.

Fabregat, Julio. *Elecciones Uruguayas*. Montevideo: Cámara de Senadores,
1968.

——— *Elecciones Uruguayas: elecciones del 25 de Noviembre de 1962*.
Montevideo: Cámara de Senadores, 1964.

———, comp. *Elecciones Uruguayas (Febrero de 1925 a noviembre de
1946)*. Montevideo: Cámara de Representantes; XXX Legislatura,
1950.

———. *Ensayo para una sociología del votante*. Montevideo: Universidad de la República, 1962.

———. *Los partidos políticos en la legislación uruguaya.* Montevideo: Medina, 1949.

Faraone, Roque. *La prensa de Montevideo.* Montevideo: Facultad de Derecho y Ciencias Sociales, 1960.

———. *El Uruguay en que vivimos, 1900-1965.* Montevideo: Arca, 1965.

Faroppa, Luis A. *El desarrollo económico del Uruguay: tentativa de explicación.* Montevideo: Centro de Estudiantes de Ciencias Económicas y de Administración, 1965.

———. *El nuevo régimen cambiaria del Uruguay.* Montevideo: 1956.

Fernández, Artucio Hugo. *The Nazi Underground in South America.* New York: Farrar and Rinehart, 1942.

Fernández Saldaña, José. *Diccionario uruguayo de biografías, 1810-1940.* Montevideo: Biblioteca Nacional, 1945.

Ferrer, Aldo. *The Argentine Economy: An Economic History of Argentina.* Berkeley: University of California Press, 1967.

Fitzgibbon, Russell H. "Uruguay: A Model for Freedom and Reform in Latin America." *Freedom and Reform in Latin America.* Edited by Frederick B. Pike. Notre Dame: University of Notre Dame Press, 1959.

———. *Uruguay: Portrait of a Democracy.* New Brunswick, New Jersey: Rutgers University Press, 1954.

Fonseca, Manuel. *La política de coparticipación.* Montevideo: 1951.

Freemantle, Anne, ed. *The Papal Encyclicals in their Historical Context.* New York: G. P. Putnam's Sons, 1956.

Freitas, Newton. *Garibaldi en América.* Buenos Aires: Editorial Nova, 1946.

Frick Davie, Carlos. *Cual reforma agraria: reformas progresistas y regresivas.* Montevideo: Barreiro y Ramos, 1964.

Gallinal, Gustavo. *El Uruguay hacia la dictadura.* Montevideo: Editorial Nuevo América, 1938.

Ganón, Isaac. "Batlle y la organización de la familia." *Batlle: su obra y su vida.* Compiled by Jorge Batlle. Montevideo: Editorial Acción, 1956.

———, comp. *Estratificación y mobilidad social en el Uruguay, fuentes bibliográficas (1880-1958).* Rio de Janeiro: Centro Latinoamericano de Pesquisas em Ciencias Sociales, 1959.

———. *Estructura social del Uruguay.* Montevideo: Editorial As, 1966.

Garvey, James A. *La administración de muebles y útiles del estado.* Montevideo: Institute of Inter-American Affairs, June 1955.

———. *Importancia de una división de organización y método en el gobierno.* Montevideo: December, 1953.

———, and Hall, John O. *Comentarios al proyecto de ley sobre licitaciones públicas en el Uruguay.* Montevideo: Instituto de Asuntos Americanos, February, 1954.

Geertz, Clifford, "Ideology as a Cultural System." *Ideology and Discontent.* Edited by David E. Apter. New York: Free Press, 1964.

Gerth, H. H., and Mills, C. Wright, eds. and trans. *From Max Weber: Essays in Sociology.* New York: Oxford University Press, 1958.

Gilio, María Esther. *The Tupamaro Guerrillas: The Structure and Strategy of the Urban Guerrilla Movement.* New York: Saturday Review Press, 1972.

Giudice, Roberto B. *Los fundamentos del Batllismo.* Montevideo: 1946.

Giudice, Roberto B., and González Conzi, Efraín. *Batlle y el Batllismo.* 2nd ed. Montevideo: Editorial Medina, 1959.

Gómez, Rosendo A. *Government and Politics in Latin America.* Rev. ed. New York: Random House, 1964.

Gómez Haedo, Juan. *Relaciones de Inglaterra con los países del Plata: su influencia en el Uruguay.* Montevideo: 1939.

González, Aristo D. *Artigas: homenaje en el centenario de su muerte.* Montevideo: Instituto Historico y Geográfico, 1952.

―――. *Jose Serrato, técnico del estado.* Montevideo: 1942.

González, Ramón P. *Aparicio Saravia en la revolución de 1904.* Montevideo: 1949.

González Penelas, Walter. *El Uruguay y su sombra.* 2nd ed. rev. Montevideo: Ediciones Ciudadela, 1968.

Graceras, Ulises. *Los intelectuales y la política en el Uruguay.* Montevideo: Cuadernos de El País, 1970.

Graillot, Hélène. "Uruguay." *Guide to the Political Parties of South America.* Translated by Michael Perl. Middlesex, England: Penguin, 1973.

Grompone, Antonio M. *La ideología de Batlle.* Montevideo: Editorial Arca 1967 (1943).

―――. *Las clases medias en el Uruguay.* Montevideo: Ediciones del Río de la Plata, 1963.

Gros Espiell, Héctor. *Las Constituciones del Uruguay.* Madrid: Ediciones Cultura Hispánica, 1956.

―――. *La Corte Electoral.* Montevideo: Facultad de Derecho y Ciencias Sociales, 1960.

―――. *Esquema de la evolución constitucional del Uruguay.* Montevideo: Facultad de Derecho y Ciencias Sociales, 1966.

Haedo, Eduardo Víctor. *La caída de un régimen.* Montevideo: 1936.

―――. *Herrera: caudillo oriental.* Montevideo: Editorial Arca, 1969.

Hall, John O. *La administración pública en el Uruguay. Sugerencias para una reforma de la organización administrativa.* Instituto de Asuntos

Interamericanos, 1954.

—— *Un estudio de las funciones de la Secretaría del Consejo Nacional de Gobierno del Uruguay.* Montevideo: 1955.

——. *Un proyecto de ley de adquisiciones.* Montevideo: 1953.

——. *Reformas del régimen impositivo.* Montevideo: 1955.

——, and Garvey, James A. *La intervención en compras gubernamentales.* Montevideo: 1953.

Hanson, Simon G. *Utopia in Uruguay: Chapters in the Economic History of Uruguay.* New York: Oxford University Press, 1938.

Hayes, Carlton. *Essay on Nationalism.* New York: 1926.

——. *The Historical Evolution of Modern Nationalism.* New York: 1931.

H. D. [Gilberto Eduardo Perret]. *Ensayo de historia patria.* 2 vols., 10th ed. Montevideo: Barreiro y Ramos, 1955.

——. *Curso de historia patria.* Libro primero, 14th ed. Montevideo: Barreiro y Ramos, 1962.

——. *Curso de historia patria.* Libro segundo, 18th ed. Montevideo: Barreiro y Ramos, 1962?

Herrera, Carlos A. *Pedro Figari.* Buenos Aires: Poseidon, 1943.

Hodges, Donald C., ed. *Philosophy of the Urban Guerrilla: The Revolutionary Writing of Abraham Guillén.* New York: William Morrow and Co., 1973.

Hudson, Michael C. *The Precarious Republic: Political Modernization in Lebanon.* New York: Random House, 1968.

Hudson, W. H. *The Purple Land.* London: J. M. Dent & Sons, 1950 [1885]. Reprint.

Iglesias, Enrique. *Uruguay: una propuesta de cambio.* Montevideo: Alfa, 1966.

Indice Gallup de Opinión Pública. Montevideo: Gallup Uruguay, S. A., 1965-1970. Published semi-monthly.

Informe Gallup, 1969. Montevideo: Gallup Uruguay, S. A. Editorial, 1969.

Instituto de Ciencias Sociales. *Uruguay: poder, ideología y clases sociales.* Montevideo: 1970.

Instituto de Derecho Público. "Primera sesión en el Instituto de Derecho Publico: Representacion de mayorias y minorías en los sistemas electorales de Uruguay y Chile." *Revista de la Facultad de Derecho y Ciencias Sociales* X, no. 1-2 (January and June 1959).

Instituto de Economía. *Uruguay: estadísticas básicas.* Montevideo: Universidad de la República, 1969.

Instituto de Economía, Facultad de Ciencias Económicas y de Administración. *El proceso económico del Uruguay: Contribución al estudio de su evolución y perspectivas.* Montevideo: Universidad de la República, 1969.

———. *Estudio y coyuntura.* Montevideo: Fundación de Cultura Universitaria, 1970.

——— *Estudio y coyuntura.* No. 2. Montevideo: Universidad de la República, 1971.

Instituto de Estudios Políticos para América Latina. *Uruguay: un país sin problemas en crisis.* 3rd ed. Montevideo: 1967.

Instituto Uruguayo de la Opinión Pública. *Aspectos políticos de la encuesta "Los Sucesos del Año."* Montevideo: 1956.

———. *La austeridad y los problemas económicos-familiares. Un estudio de opinión pública realizado especialmente para el diario "El País."* Montevideo: 1959.

———. *Elecciones de 1958 en Montevideo. Un estudio sobre las posibilidades de predicción electoral a través de los métodos de muestra representativa.* Montevideo: 1958.

———. *Encuesta de los sucesos del año preparada especialmente para el diario "El Plata."* Montevideo: 1956, 1957, 1958.

———. *Un estudio sobre las posibilidades de predicción electoral y de las características socioeconómicas de los grupos particulares. Efectuado en la ciudad de Montevideo por el método de muestras representativas.* Montevideo: 1959.

———. *Una incógnita nacional. El empleado público.* Montevideo: 1956.

———. *La salud en nuestro país. Encuesta preparada para el diario "El País."* Montevideo: 1957.

Jiménez de Aréchaga, Justino. *La constitución de 1952.* 4 vols. Montevideo: Medina, 1952.

———. *La constitución nacional.* 10 vols. Montevideo: Medina, 1945-1948.

Johnson, John J. *Political Change in Latin America.* Stanford: Stanford University Press, 1958.

Juega Farrula, Arturo. *Las tres constituciones de la República Oriental del Uruguay, 1830-1917-1934.* Montevideo: 1941.

Kohn, Hans. "A New Look at Nationalism." *Nationalism and International Progress.* Edited by Urban G. Whitaker, Jr., San Francisco: 1960.

La constitución de 1952. 4 vols. Montevideo: Centro de Estudiantes de Derecho, 1966.

Labrousse, A. *Los Tupamaros: guerrilla urbana en el Uruguay.* Buenos Aires: Tiempo Contemporáneo, 1971.

Lane, Robert. *Political Ideology.* New York: Free Press, 1962.

Langer, Suzanne K. *Philosophy in a New Key: A Study of the Symbolism of Reason, Rite and Art.* New York: Mentor, 1969.

Lasplaces, Alberto. *Vida admirable de José Pedro Varela.* 2nd ed. Montevideo: 1944.

Lerner, Daniel. *The Passing of Traditional Society.* New York: Free Press, 1966.

Lewis, Sydney L. *Informe cubriendo el período de Febrero 10, 1959 a Junio 10, 1969.* Montevideo: 1959.

Lindahl, Goran G. "Uruguay: Government by Institutions." *Political Systems of Latin America.* Edited by Martin C. Needler. Princeton: Van Nostrand, 1964.

———. *Uruguay's New Path: A Study of Politics During the First Colegiado, 1919-33.* Stockholm: Institute of Ibero-American Studies, 1962.

Littwin, Lawrence. *Latin America: Catholicism and Class Conflict.* Encino, California: Dickenson Publishing Company, Inc., 1974.

Llana Barrios, Mario. *El juicio político.* Montevideo: 1942.

Lockhart, Washington. *El Uruguay de veras.* Montevideo: Alfa, 1969.

Lorenzo y Losada, Héctor. *Ante la reforma MCMLI.* Montevideo: Ediciones M, 1951.

Louis, Julio A. *Batlle y Ordóñez: Apogeo y muerte de la democracia burguesa.* Montevideo: Nativo Libros, 1969.

Maggi, Carlos. *Gardel, Onetti y algo más.* Montevideo: Alfa, 1964.

———. *El Uruguay y su gente.* Montevideo: Alfa, 1965.

Manacorda, Telmo. *José Pedro Varela.* Montevideo: Consejo Nacional de Enseñanza Primaria y Normal, 1949.

Mannheim, Karl. *Ideology and Utopia.* New York: Harvest Books.

Mannini, Ríos, Carlos. *Anoche me llamó Batlle.* Montevideo: 1970.

Marshall, T. H. *Class, Citizenship and Social Development:* Essays by T. H. Marshall. Introduction by S. M. Lipset. New York: Doubleday, 1964.

Martínez, José Luciano. *Gabriel Terra: el hombre, el político, el gobernante.* 3 vols. Montevideo: 1937.

Martínez, Martin. *Ante la nueva constitucion.* Vol. 48 of *Coleccion clásicas uruguayas.* Montevideo: Ministerio de Instrucción Publica y Previsión Social, 1964 [1918].

Martínez Ces, Ricardo. *El Uruguay Batllista.* Montevideo: Ediciones de la Banda Oriental, 1962.

Martínez Diaz, Nelson. *Capitales británicos y ferrocarriles en el Uruguay del siglo XIX.* Montevideo: 1966.

Martínez Lamas, Julio. *¿A dónde vamos?* Montevideo: Impresora Uruguaya.

———. *Riqueza y pobreza del Uruguay. Estudio de las causas que retardan el progreso nacional.* 2nd ed. Montevideo: Tipografía Atlántida, 1946.

Martins, Daniel Hugo, and Gros Espiell, Héctor. *Constitución uruguaya anotada.* 2nd ed. Montevideo: Editorial Medina, 1958.

Massera, José Pedro. *Estudios filosóficos.* Montevideo: Ardao, 1954.

McDonald, Ronald H. "Legislative Politics in Uruguay: A Preliminary Statement." *Latin American Legislatures: Their Role and Influence.* Edited by Weston H. Agor. New York: Praeger, 1971.

McIlwain, Charles H. "Fundamental Law Behind the Constitution of the United States." *The Constitution Reconsidered.* Edited by Conyer Reed. New York: Columbia University Press, 1938.

Melian Lafinur, Luis. *La acción funesta de los partidos tradicionales en la reforma constitucional.* Montevideo: Claudio García, 1918.

Mercader, Antonio, and de Vera, Jorge. *Tupamaros: estrategia y acción.* Mexico, D. F.: Editorial Omega, 1971.

Methol Ferre, Alberto. *La crisis del Uruguay y el Imperio Británico.* Buenos Aires: Editorial A. Pena Lillo, 1959.

Miranda, Hector. *Las instrucciones del año XIII.* Montevideo: Barreiro y Ramos, 1935.

Monegal, José. *Esquema de la historia del partido nacional, defensor de las leyes.* Montevideo: Editorial Cisplatina, 1959.

Montanes, María Teresa. *Desarrollo de la agricultura en el Uruguay.* 2nd ed. Montevideo: 1950.

Moreno, Francisco José. *Legitimacy and Stability in Latin America: A Study of Chilean Political Culture.* New York: New York University Press, 1969.

Movimiento Coordinador de Docentes Universitarios. *Convocatoria de la mesa del movimiento coordinador de docentes universitarios a las gremiales de facultades y escuelas para el plenario de 2 de junio de 1960.* Montevideo: 1969.

Muñoz, Juan José. *Apuntos históricos.* Montevideo: 1952.

Nardone, Benito. "Manifesto Americano." *Mundo Americano* I (June-August 1962).

———*Peligro rojo en América Latina.* Montevideo: Impresiones Diario Rural, 1961.

[Nardone, Benito] Chico Tazo. *Los Batlle contra Rivera y Oribe.* Montevideo: 1951.

———. *José Artigas, 1764-1820.* Montevideo: Diario Rural, 1951.

———. *Procesa a El Dia: fracaso del estatismo.* Montevideo: Diario Rural, 1955.

Oddone, Juan Antonio. *Economía y sociedad en el Uruguay liberal.* Montevideo: Ediciones de la Banda Oriental, 1967.

———. *La emigración europea al Río de la Plata.* Montevideo: Ediciones de la Banda Oriental, 1966.

———— and Paris de Oddone, M. Blanca. *Historia de la Universidad de Montevideo: la universidad vieja, 1849-1885.* Montevideo: Universidad de la República, 1963.

Orozco, Dr. Justo José. *Proyecto de reorganización de los servicios de secretaria. Anteproyecto de creación de las oficinas asesoras del C.N.G.* Montevideo: Consejo Nacional de Gobierno, 1956.

Paredes, C. B., comp. *Batlle y el colegiado.* Montevideo: 1939.

Paris de Oddone, M. Blanca. *La Universidad de Montevideo en la formación de nuestra conciencia liberal, 1849-1885.* Montevideo: Universidad de la República, 1958.

Parsons, Talcott, and Shils, Edward A., eds. *Toward a General Theory of Action.* New York: Harper Torchbook, 1962.

Paysee González, Eduardo. *Editoriales de 'Extra': una lucha por la libertad de prensa.* Montevideo: 1967.

Pendle, George. *Uruguay.* 3rd ed. New York: Oxford Unversity Press, 1965.

Pereira, Juan José, and Trajtenberg, Raúl. *Evolución de la población total y activa en el Uruguay: 1908-1957.* Montevideo: Instituto de Economía, 1966.

Pérez Pérez, Alberto. *Constitución de la República Oriental del Uruguay.* 2 vols. Montevideo: Facultad de Derecho y Ciencias Sociales, 1970.

Pintos, Francisco R. *Batlle y el proceso histórico del Uruguay.* Montevideo: Claudio García, 1942.

Pivel Devoto, Juan E. *Historia de los partidos políticos en el Uruguay, 1865-1897.* 2 vols. Montevideo: Editorial Río de la Plata, 1943.

————. *Historia de los partidos y de las ideas políticas en el Uruguay: la definición de los bandos, 1829-1838.* 2 vols. Montevideo: Editorial Río de la Plata, 1956.

————. *Raíces coloniales de la revolución oriental de 1811.* Montevideo: Editorial Medina, 1957.

————, and Ranieri de Pivel Devoto, Alcira. *Historia de la República Oriental del Uruguay (1830-1930).* Montevideo: Editorial Medina, 1945.

Porzecanski, Arturo C. *Uruguay's Tupamaros: The Urban Guerrilla.* New York: Frederick A. Praeger, 1973.

Prunell, J. Antonio. *Responsabilidad civil del escribano.* Montevideo: Biblioteca de la Facultad de Derecho y Ciencias Sociales, 1947.

Rama, Carlos M. "Batlle y el movimiento obrera y social." *Batlle: su vida y su obra.* Compiled by Jorge Batlle. Montevideo: Editorial Acción, 1956.

————. *La religión en el Uruguay.* Montevideo: Ediciones Nuestro Tiempo, 1964.

———. *Las clases sociales en el Uruguay.* Montevideo: Ediciones Nuestro Tiempo, 1960.

———. "The Passing of the Afro-Uruguayans from Caste Society into Class Society." *Race and Class in Latin America.* Edited by Magnus Morner. New York: Columbia University Press, 1970.

———. *Sociología nacional.* Montevideo: Club Vicente Grucci, 1965.

Rama, Germán W. *Grupos sociales y enseñanza secundaria.* Montevideo: Arca, 1968.

Ramela de Castro, R. *Entes autónomos: organización administrativa del dominio industrial del estado, con una colección de leyes sobre la materia.* Montevideo: Librería de Maximino García, 1923.

Ramírez, Juan Andrés. *Sinopsis de la evolución institucional.* Montevideo: 1949.

——— et al. *Uruguay and the United Nations.* New York: Manhattan Publishing Co., 1958.

Ramón Real, Alberto. *Las estructuras políticas y administrativas en relación con el desarrollo.* Montevideo: 1965.

Ravignani, Emilio. *Un proyecto de constitución relativo a la autonomía de la provincia oriental del Uruguay, 1813-1815.* Buenos Aires: 1929.

Real de Azúa, Carlos, ed. *Antología del ensayo uruguayo contemporáneo.* 2 vols. Montevideo: Universidad de la República, 1964.

———. *El impulso y su freno: tres décadas del Batllismo y las raíces de la crisis uruguaya.* Montevideo: Ediciones de la Banda Oriental, 1962.

———. "Herrera: El colegiado en Uruguay." *Historia de América en el siglo XX.* Buenos Aires: Centro Editor de América Latina, 1972.

Reyes Abadie, Washington. *La economía del Uruguay en el siglo XIX.* Montevideo: Ediciones de Nuestro Tiempo, 1969.

Reyles, Carlos. *La muerte del cisne.* Montevideo: 1905.

Rippy, J. Fred. *British Investments in Latin America, 1829-1949.* Minneapolis: University of Minnesota Press, 1959.

Riva-Zucchelli, Pedro. *Historia de la independencia de la República Oriental.* Montevideo: 1934.

Roberts, C. Paul, ed. *Statistical Abstract of Latin America, 1969.* 12th ed. Los Angeles: UCLA, 1969.

Rodríguez Fabregat, E. *Batlle y Ordóñez: el reformador.* Buenos Aires: Editorial Claridad, 1942.

Rodríguez Larreta, Eduardo. *El aporte de Inglaterra a la civilización occidental.* Montevideo: Historia, 1940.

Rodríguez Lopez, Juan. *Socialismo en el Uruguay.* Montevideo: 1928.

Rodríguez Villamil, Silvia. *Las mentalidades dominantes en Montevideo (1850-1900). Vol. I. La mentalidad criolla tradicional.* Montevideo:

Ediciones de la Banda Oriental, 1968.

Rogowski, Ronald C., and Wasserspring, Lois. *Does Political Development Exist? Corporatism in Old and New Societies.* Sage Comparative Politics Series #01-024. Beverly Hills: Sage Publications, 1971.

Rompani, Sergio, ed. *Luis Batlle: pensamiento y acción.* 2 vols. Montevideo: Editorial Alfa, 1965.

Rosencof, M. *La rebelión de los cañeros.* Montevideo: Aportes, 1969.

Sampay, Arturo Enrique. *La declaración de inconstitucionalidad.* Montevideo: Editorial Medina, 1957.

Sanguinetti Freire, Alberto. *Legislación social del Uruguay.* 2 vols. 2nd ed. Montevideo: Barreiro y Ramos, 1949.

Sanguinetti, Julio María, and Pacheco Sere, Alvaro. *La nueva constitución.* Montevideo: Editorial Alfa, 1967.

Saravia García, Nepomuceno. *Memorias de Aparicio Saravia.* Montevideo: Editorial Medina, 1955.

Sayagues Laso, Enrique. *Tratado de derecho administrativo.* Montevideo: 1959.

Scarone, Arturo. *Uruguayos contemporáneos.* Montevideo: Barreiro y Ramos, 1937.

Schutter, C. H. *The Development of Education in Argentina, Chile and Uruguay.* Chicago: University of Chicago Press, 1943.

Silva Vila, Juan. *Ideario de Artigas.* Montevideo: Barreiro y Ramos, 1942.

Silvert, Kalman H. "The Costs of Anti-Nationalism: Argentina." *Expectant Peoples.* Edited by K. H. Silvert. New York: Vintage, 1967.

———. "The Strategy of the Study of Nationalism." *Expectant Peoples.* Edited by K. H. Silvert. New York: Vintage, 1967.

———. "Welcome to the fold, Mr. Nixon or, Ariel and the Dilemma of the Intellectuals." *American University Field Staff,* vol. V. no. 6 (May 1958).

Simon, Francisco. *El ejecutivo colegiado.* Montevideo: 1915.

Smith, Anthony D. *Theories of Nationalism.* New York: Harper Torchbooks, 1971.

Solari, Aldo E. *El desarrollo social del Uruguay en la postguerra.* Montevideo: Editorial Alfa, 1967.

———. *El tercerismo en el Uruguay.* Montevideo: Editorial Alfa, 1965.

———. *Estudios sobre la sociedad uruguaya.* 2 vols. Montevideo: Arca, 1964 and 1965.

———. *Las ciencias sociales en el Uruguay.* Rio de Janeiro: Centro Latinoamericano de Pesquisas em Ciencias Sociales, 1959.

———. *Sociología rural nacional.* 2nd ed. Montevideo: Universidad de la República, 1958.

———, Campiglia, Néstor, and Wettstein Germán. *Uruguay en cifras.* Montevideo: Universidad de la República, 1966.

Sosa, Jusualdo. *La enseñanza en el Uruguay.* Montevideo: Ministerio de Instrucción Pública y Previsión Social, 1947.

Street, John. *Artigas and the Emancipation of Uruguay.* London: Oxford University Press, 1959.

———. *Artigas y la emancipación del Uruguay.* Montevideo: Instituto de Investigaciones Históricas, Universidad de la República, 1967. Translation of 1959 book.

Taylor, Philip B., Jr. *Government and Politics of Uruguay.* New Orleans: Tulane University Studies in Political Science, 1962.

Terra, Gabriel, (h). *Gabriel Terra y la verdad histórica.* Montevideo: 1962.

Terra, Gabriel. *La revolución de marzo.* Buenos Aires: 1938.

Terra, Juan Pablo. *Mística, desarrollo y revolución.* Montevideo: Ediciones del Nuevo Mundo, 1969.

Traversoni, Alfredo. *Historia del Uruguay y de América.* 2 vols. Montevideo: Editorial Kapelusz, 1963.

Trías, Vivian. *Economía y política en el Uruguay contemporáneo.* Montevideo: Ediciones de la Banda Oriental, 1968.

———. *El imperialismo en el Río de la Plata.* Buenos Aires: 1960.

Trías, Walter. *Batlle, periodista.* Montevideo: Editorial Colorado, 1958.

Ubaldo, Edgardo. *Artigas.* Buenos Aires: 1945.

Union Nacional Católica de Acción Social. *Aspectos económicos de la familia en Montevideo.* Montevideo: 1956.

Universidad de la República, Facultad de Derecho y Ciencias Sociales, Instituto de Ciencias Sociales. *Nuestro estudiante contemporáneo.* Montevideo: 1964.

Universidad de la República, Oficina de Planeamiento. *Censo de estudiantes ingresados en 1968: proceso de reclutamiento en la Universidad de la República.* Montevideo: 1968?

Vanger, Milton I. *José Batlle y Ordóñez of Uruguay: The Creator of his Times, 1902-1907.* Cambridge: Harvard University Press, 1963.

Varela, José Pedro. *El banquete de la paz.* Montevideo: Editorial de la Paz, 1877.

Vasconcellos, Amílcar. *Febrero amargo.* Montevideo: 1973.

Viera, Carlos A. *Proceso de una dictadura dirigista.* Montevideo: Medina, 1958.

Wallas, Graham. *Human Nature in Politics.* New York: Knopf, 1921.

Weil, Thomas E. et al. *Area Handbook for Uruguay.* U. S. Government; Superintendent of Documents. Washington, D. C., 1971.

Welker, Juan Carlos. *Baltasar Brum: verbo y acción*. Montevideo: Letras, S. A., 1945.

――――. *José Serrato: un ejemplo*. Montevideo: 1944.

Whitaker, Arthur P. "Nationalism and Religion in Argentina and Uruguay." *Religion, Revolution and Reform: New Forces for Change in Latin America*. Edited by Frederick B. Pike and William V. D'Antonio. New York: Praeger, 1964.

Williams, Edward J. *Latin American Christian Democratic Parties*. Knoxville: University of Tennessee Press, 1967.

Williman, J. C. (h). *El Dr. Claudio Williman: su vida pública*. Montevideo: 1957.

――――. *El 31 de marzo*. Montevideo: 1933.

Wirth, Juan D. F. *Colonia Suiza hace ochenta años: la imigración al Uruguay en 1861*. Montevideo: 1944.

Wonsewer, Israel, and Iglesias, Enrique V., Buscheli, Mario, and Faroppa, Luis A. *Aspectos de la industrialización en el Uruguay*. Montevideo: Publicaciones de la Universidad, 1959.

Zavala Muniz, Justino. *Batlle: héroe civil*. Mexico, D. F.: Fondo de Cultura Económica, 1945

Zum Felde, Alberto. *Evolución histórica del Uruguay: esquema de su sociología*. 3rd ed. Montevideo: Maximo Garcia, 1945.

――――. *Proceso histórico del Uruguay*. 5th ed. Montevideo: Arca, 1967.

――――. *Proceso intelectual del Uruguay*. 3 vols. Montevideo: Ediciones del Nuevo Mundo, 1967.

Articles

Albes, Edward. "Montevideo, City of Roses." *Bulletin of the Pan American Union*. October 1917, pp. 435-463.

Ardao, Arturo. "José Pedro Varela y la Universidad." *Nuestro Tiempo* II, no. 4 (August 1955), pp. 63-67.

――――. "La Universidad de Montevideo." *Revista del Centro Estudiantes de Derecho XIX*, no. 81 (July 1950), pp. 7-111.

Baklanoff, Eric N. "Notes on the Pathology of Uruguay's Welfare State." *Mississippi Valley Journal of Business and Economics* II (Spring 1967).

Barager, Joseph R. "The Historiography of the Río de la Plata Area Since 1830." *Hispanic American Historical Review*, November 1960, pp. 588-629.

Bell, James P., Jr. "Uruguay's Economic Evolution: 1900-1968." *SAIS Review* XV (Spring 1971), pp. 27-35.

Benvenuto, Luis Carlos. "La quiebra del modelo." *Encyclopedia Uruguaya*
no. 42. Montevideo: Editorial Reunidos and Editorial Arca, 1969.

Bruschera, Oscar H. "Estructura de los partidos políticos en el Uruguay."
Revista del Centro Estudiantes De Derecho XIX, no. 86 (September
1958), pp. 873-884.

"Batlle," *Cuadernos de Marcha*, No. 31 and No. 32 (Montevideo, 1969).

Campiglia, Néstor. "La ideología del Movimiento Ruralista a través de
la vida de Artigas escrita por 'Chico-Tazo'." *Revista de la Facultad
de Derecho y Ciencias Sociales* XIII, 4 (October -December 1962),
pp. 993-1022.

Carbonnell de Grompone, María A. "La influencia de los factores sociales
en la intelegencia." *Anales del Instituto de Profesores Artigas,* no. 6
November 1956), pp. 70-73.

Carruti, Héctor. "La defensa de las Cajas de Jubilaciones y de sus Afiliados."
Estudios Políticos-Económicos-Filosóficos-Culturales vol. 12 (September 1959), pp. 17-19.

――――. "El problema de las Cajas de Jubilaciones." *Ibid.,* vol. 3 (August-
November 1956), pp. 70-73.

Charlone, César. "The Economic Situation in Uruguay." *International
Labor Review* (May 1936), pp. 607-618.

Connolly, S., and Druehl, G. "The Tupamaros: The New Focus in Latin
America." *Journal of Contemporary Revolutions* III, no. 3 (Summer
1971), pp. 59-68.

Dahl, Victor C. "Uruguay Under Juan Idiarte Borda: An American Diplo-
mat's Observations." *Hispanic American Historical Review* (February
1966), pp. 66-77.

Daly, Herman E. "The Uruguayan Economy: Its Basic Nature and Current
Problems." *Journal of Inter-American Relations* (July 1965), pp.
316-330.

de Carvalho Neto, Paulo. "The Candomble, a Dramatic Dance From
Afro-Uruguayan Folklore." *Ethnomusicology* VI, no. 3 (September
1962), pp. 164-174.

Dealy, Glen H. "Prolegomena on the Spanish American Political Tradition."
Hispanic American Historical Review XLVIII (February 1968).

Figueira, Gaston. "Interpretación del Uruguay." *Journal of Inter-American
Studies* IX, no. 4 (October 1967), pp. 483-487.

Finch, M. H. J. "Three Perspectives on the Crisis in Uruguay." *Journal of
Latin American Studies* III, no. 2 (November 1971), pp. 173-190.

Fitzgibbon, Russell H. "Adoption of a Collegiate Executive in Uruguay."
Journal of Politics, (November 1952), pp. 616-642.

――――. "Argentina and Uruguay: A Tale of Two Attitudes." *Pacific
Spectator* VII, no. 1 (Winter 1954), pp. 6-20.

———. "The Political Impact on Religious Development in Uruguay."
   Church History XXII, no. I (March 1953), pp. 21-32.
Foland, F. M. "Uruguay's Urban Guerrillas." *New Leader* LIV, no. 19
   (October 4, 1971), pp. 8-11.
Frugoni, Emilio. "Partidos de ideas y partidos tradicionales." *Revista
   del Centro Estudiantes de Derecho* XIX, no. 86 (September 1958),
   pp. 885-903.
Galeano, Eduardo. "Uruguay: Promise and Betrayal." *Latin America:
   Reform or Revolution?* Edited by James Petras and Maurice Zeitlin.
   Greenwich: Fawcett Publications, 1968.
Ganón, Isaac. "Estratificación social de Montevideo." *América Latina*
   IV, no. 4 (November 1961), pp. 303-330.
———. "Introducción a la Ciencia Política." *Revista del Centro Estudiantes
   de Derecho* XIX, no. 86 (September 1958), pp. 807-816.
Gros Espiel, Hector. "El proceso de la reforma constitucional." *Estudios
   sobre la reforma constitucional. Cuadernos,* no. 19. Montevideo:
   Facultad de Derecho y Ciencias Sociales, 1967.
Haddox, John H. "Carlos Vaz Ferreira: Uruguayan Philosopher." *Journal
   of Inter-American Studies* VII (October 1966), pp. 595-600.
Hutchinson, Bertram. "Social Mobility Rates in Buenos Aires, Monte-
   video, and Sao Paolo: A Preliminary Comparison." *América Latina*
   V, no. 4 (October-December 1962), pp. 3-20.
Instituto Uruguayo de la Opinión Pública. "Una incógnita nacional: el
   empleado público. *El Pais,* April and November 1966.
Iutaka, Sugiyama. "Estratificación social y oportunidades educacionales
   entre metropolis latinoamericanos: Buenos Aires, Montevideo y Sao
   Paolo." *América Latina* V, no. 4 (October-December 1962), pp. 53-77.
———. "Mobilidade social e oportunidades educacionales em Buenos
   Aires e Montevideo: uma analise comparativa I." *America Latina*
   VI, no. 2 (April-June 1963), pp. 21-39.
Kitchen, James D. "National Personnel Administration in Uruguay."
   Inter-American Economic Affairs Vol. I (Summer 1950), pp. 45-58.
Martin, Percy A. "Artigas, the Founder of Uruguayan Nationality."
   Hispanic American Historical Review, (February 1939), pp. 2-15.
———. "The Career of José Batlle y Ordóñez." *Hispanic American
   Historical Review* (November 1930) pp. 413-428.
McDonald, Ronald H. "Electoral Politics and Uruguayan Political Decay."
   Inter-American Economic Affairs XXVI, no. 2 (Summer 1972),
   pp. 25-45.
Morse, Richard B. "Recent Research on Latin American Urbanization: A
   Selective Survey and Commentary." *Latin American Research Review*
   I (Fall 1965).

——. "Toward A Theory of Spanish American Government." *Journal of the History of Ideas* XV (1954).

Moss, R. "Urban Guerrillas in Uruguay." *Problems of Communism* XX, no. 5 (September-October 1971), pp. 14-23.

Newton, Ronald C. "On 'Functional Groups,' 'Fragmentation' and 'Pluralism' in Spanish American Political Society." *Hispanic American Historical Review* L (February 1970).

Nuñez, Carlos. "The Tupamaros: Armed Vanguard in Uruguay." *Tricontinental* (Havana), no. 10 (January-February 1969), pp. 43-66.

Peirano Facio, Jorge. "Amézaga, civilista." *Revista del Centro Estudiantes de Derecho* XIX, no. 85 (September 1956), pp. 464-474.

Pereda Valdés, Ildefonso. "El campo Uruguayo a través de tres grandes novelistas: Acevedo Díaz, Javier de Viana y Carlos Reyles." *Journal of Inter-American Studies* VIII, no. 4 (October 1966), pp. 535-540.

Pike, Frederick B. (ed.). *The New Corporatism: Social and Political Structures in the Iberian World.* Special edition of *The Review of Politics* vol. 36, no. 1 (January 1974).

Quijano, Carlos. "Población activa y renta nacional del Uruguay." *Revista de Economía* VIII, nos. 42-43 (1956).

Ramirez, Manuel D. "Florencio Sanchez and His Social Consciousness of the River Plate Region." *Journal of Inter-American Studies* VII, no. 4 (October 1966), pp. 585-594.

Redding, David. "Uruguay: An Advanced Case of the English Sickness?" Washington, D. C.: Federal Reserve System, 1966.

Redding, M. D. C. "The Economic Decline of Uruguay." *Inter-American Economic Affairs* XX, no. 4 (Spring 1967), pp. 55-72.

Shapiro, S. "Uruguay: A Bankrupt Welfare State." *Current History* LVI, no. 329 (January 1969), pp. 36-41.

——. "Uruguay's Lost Paradise." *Current History* LXII, no. 366 (February 1972), pp. 98-103.

Solari, Aldo E. "Las clases sociales y su gravitación en la estructura política y social del Uruguay." *Revista Mexicana de Sociología* XVII, no. 2.

——. "Movilidad social en Montevideo." *Boletim del Centro Latinoamericano de Pesquisas em Ciencias Sociais* IV (1961).

Taylor, Philip B., Jr. "The Electoral System in Uruguay." *Journal of Politics* XVII, no. 1 (February 1955), pp. 19-42.

——. "Interests and Institutional Dysfunction in Uruguay." *American Political Science Review* LVIII (March 1963), pp. 62-74.

——. "Inter-party Cooperation and Uruguay's 1952 Constitution." *The Western Political Quarterly* VII, no. 3 (September 1954), pp. 391-400.

————. "Meat Export Needs Jolted in Uruguay." *Christian Science Monitor,* August 24, 1960.

————. "The Uruguayan Coup d'Etat of 1933." *The Hispanic American Historical Review* XXXII, no. 3 (August 1952), pp. 301-320.

"Uruguay, Farewell to a Welfare State?" *Latin American Report* III, no. 2 (January 1959), pp. 10-14.

Vanger, Milton I. "Uruguay Introduces Government by Committee." *The American Political Science Review* XLVIII, no. 2 (June 1954), pp. 500-513.

Weinstein, Martin. "The Uruguayan Constitution and the 1971 Elections." *The Constitutions of the Countries of the World.* Edited by Albert P. Blaustein and Gisbert H. Flanz. Dobbs Ferry, N.Y.: Oceana Press, 1972.

Wettstein, C., and Pi Hugarte, Renzo. "Puntualizaciones sobre la familia rural." *Revista Tribuna Universitaria* no. 5 (April 1958).

Wiarda, Howard J. "Toward a Framework for the Study of Political Change in the Iberic-Latin Tradition: The Corporative Model." *World Politics* XXV (January 1973), pp. 206-235.

Wood, James R., and Weinstein, Eugene A. "Industrialization Values and Occupational Evaluation in Uruguay." *American Journal of Sociology* LXXII no. 1 (July 1966), pp. 47-57.

Newspapers

Montevideo

Acción; Diario Rural; El Bien Público (B. P. Color); El Debate; El Día; La Mañana; Marcha (weekly)*; El País; El Popular.*

Others

Clarín (Buenos Aires); *La Nación* (Buenos Aires); *The New York Times.*

Unpublished Materials

Biles, Robert D. "Patronage Politics: Electoral Behavior in Uruguay." Ph.D. dissertation, Johns Hopkins University, 1972.

Burton IV, Robert Henderson. "Uruguay: A Study in Arrested Economic Development." Ph.D. disseration, Louisiana State University, 1967.

Daly, Herman Edward. "Trade Control and the Uruguayan Economy." Ph.D. dissertation, Vanderbilt University, 1967.

Moreno, José A., and Porzecanski, Arturo C. "The Ideology of Uruguay's
    Tupamaros." Unpublished manuscript in the Departments of Sociology
    and Economics, University of Pittsburgh, 1972.
Silvert, Frieda, and Silvert, Kalman H. "Education and the Meaning of
    Social Development." Unpublished manuscript.
Stewart, G. T. "The Economic Development of Uruguay: 1936-61."
    Ph.D. dissertation, University of Alabama, 1967.
Taylor, Philip B., Jr. "The Executive Power in Uruguay." Ph.D. disserta-
    tion, University of California at Berkeley, 1953.

INDEX